NOTHING IS SACROSANCT
by
David E Balaam

Other titles by the same author;

Columbus Day
The Letter
No One Is Sacrosanct

Copyright © 2016 David E Balaam

All rights reserved

Published by: davidbalaam-books.co.uk

1st print edition 2016 (r) (c)
U.S. dictionary format.

ISBN: 9780993586408

This book is a work of fiction. The names, characters, places, and incidents are products of the writer's imagination or have been used fictitiously and are not to be construed as real.

Any resemblance to persons, living or dead, actual events, locales or organizations is entirely coincidental.

All rights are reserved. No part of this book may be used or reproduced in any manner whatsoever without written permission from the author.

www.davidbalaam-books.co.uk

PART ONE
Chapter One --------- 5
Chapter Two --------- 7
Chapter Three -------- 11
Chapter Four --------- 25
Chapter Five --------- 27
Chapter Six ---------- 29
Chapter Seven -------- 35
Chapter Eight -------- 39
Chapter Nine --------- 43
Chapter Ten ---------- 47
Chapter Eleven ------- 55
Chapter Twelve ------- 59

PART TWO
Chapter One ---------- 75
Chapter Two ---------- 79
Chapter Three -------- 85
Chapter Four --------- 95
Chapter Five --------- 109
Chapter Six ---------- 117
Chapter Seven -------- 121
Chapter Eight -------- 129

PART THREE
Chapter One ---------- 131
Chapter Two ---------- 141
Chapter Three -------- 147
Chapter Four --------- 155
Chapter Five --------- 159
Chapter Six ---------- 163
Chapter Seven -------- 167
Chapter Eight -------- 169
Chapter Nine --------- 173
Chapter Ten ---------- 187
Chapter Eleven ------- 205

Some History --------- 223

Acknowledgments ------ 224

*To all the innocent victims . . .
may your voices be heard one day*

PART ONE

Chapter One

1969

Daniel Mace stirred from his induced sleep. His vision was blurred, his head was throbbing with pain and he could feel a burning sensation on the side of his neck. Somewhere in the distance, he thought he could hear the faint sound of laughter and clapping. His eyes, still blurred, picked out the lined red, green and brown flocked pattern wallpaper on the stairs, although, something within his numb cerebral cortex, combined with his blurred vision, couldn't remember the pattern having a brown stripe. He blinked several times to focus, and it took a few moments for the adrenaline to kick in - and it did, as soon as he realized his predicament. Daniel Mace was tied and gagged, sitting on the first-floor landing of his house looking directly at a brown rope hanging from the open loft door – unmistakably a hangman's noose.

He looked around in fear, trying to call out to no avail. The first glimpse of his abductor was when the bathroom door opened. "Hello, Daniel. Sorry to keep you waiting." Said a cold calculated voice.

Daniel Mace murmured uncontrollably, not knowing what-on-earth this intruder was talking about. The stranger, with an unusual accent and polite smile, stood in front of Mace for a few moments looking at the pathetic man; pleased with himself he had achieved this much. He was now sure the final act would go smoothly, and his undertaking would be complete. The stranger sat opposite Mace and leant back against the wooden landing uprights. He crossed his legs, looking relaxed as he re-stretched the Latex gloves on each hand whilst giving Mace a disturbing smile. "Daniel," he finally said, in a measured tone, "let me tell you why I am here." The stranger's face tightened and his smile dissolved. "You've been naughty, haven't you, Daniel. *Very naughty.*"

Chapter Two

1979 December

Marcus was lying on his bed, naked, allowing Rosa to give him a massage. "I was thinking of Isabel and Charlie," he said casually. Rosa stopped massaging his unique hairless chest. She was also naked, straddling his lower abdomen, his penis partially erect due to the massaging. Rosa looked at Marcus suspiciously. "You said it was a one-off, no more. You promised," she said, with a concerned that touched Marcus. He leant forward and cupped her face with his right hand. "I thought you liked them. You said they were willing and responsive . . . your words, my angel." Rosa sighed and took hold of Marcus's semi-erect penis and started to massage it. She worked her hand up and down expertly, as she had been taught, and he remembered how he had found her, and how much fun it had been teaching her many things, just those five short years ago.

His thoughts drifted back to his youth and his family, and those black times during the war. He placed his hand over Rosa's hand. "Not there. Not just now, my love," he said, somberly. Rosa nodded and returned to work on his chest, pouring warm scented oil on his stomach, then working her hands rhythmically over his glistening torso. He let Rosa continue her expert manipulation as he closed his eyes, remembering, as he did from time to time, how lucky he had been, escaping from occupied Austria.

The allies'; Russia, France, America and Britain had divided his country into four zones. Marcus's family had lived in the south-east province of Styria, in the small village of Mariahof, which was in the British sector. Although remote, the allies quickly spread over the newly liberated state and found the young Marcus alone in his parent's large country Schloss. The commanding officer who came upon the isolated house that day in June 1945 found a woman hanging from the kitchen rafters. Further inspection of the rooms found a young boy aged about ten years old, shivering and hiding in one of the bedrooms' dressing rooms, huddled behind a row of women's dresses. The officer who found him asked him his name. The boy had said nothing, preferring to stare into space, squatting on the floor with arms folded, shivering and afraid.

The boy was taken to an internment camp where he was cleaned and fed and then interrogated by British military officers, in particular, a Major Ferris. However, at all the interviews, even with German-speaking personnel, the boy refused to answer any questions. A few weeks later Marcus was informed his father had been captured by the Russians and executed as an SS officer. Marcus showed no emotion on receiving this news, but inwardly was joyous and relieved that he was now also free of his father, but wondered why there was no word from his brother. Surely, now the war was over, Marius would come and take him home where they would be safe, and play together like they did when he was younger.

They questioned Marcus for days, wanting to know how his mother hanged herself, especially as her hands had been cut off at the wrists. Marcus acted the dumb orphan and just stared at his accusers with his bright steel blue eyes until they realized the interrogation was going nowhere.

As a minor, his captors were undecided what to do with him. Several translators were unable to get anything out of him and stopped short of beating him. Later, Marcus thanked God he had not been in the Russian or American sectors – he was not sure how he would have fared with their interrogation methods.

After four weeks of intensive questioning, an army doctor intervened. He had been supervising Marcus's condition since his arrival and insisted on being present during the questioning. He also spoke some German so was able to communicate with Marcus on a different level, as a friend, rather than an inquisitor. He would bring chocolate bars and treats to Marcus in his dormitory and talk to him quietly, gaining his trust. Marcus distrusted any close associations after his enslavement by his parents. He assumed all adults were child molesters, no matter how caring they seemed to be.

But Dr Nathan Star was kind and compassionate to Marcus, and slowly gained his trust. He gave him errands to run and tried to keep him busy, until he gradually succumbed to a more normal way of life, if that was even possible, in what was nothing less than a detention camp for displaced people.

After a while, Dr Star gave him a job as an orderly in the medical unit. There he had access to fresh clothes, regular hot meals and even started to interact with other normal decent people. By now he had learnt some English and was able to converse a little - with those he chose to. The population of the displacement camp dwindled over time when relatives had been found or they were allowed to leave having been cleared of any atrocities. One day Dr Star took Marcus to one side. "Marcus, they want to hand you over to the police, in Vienna." Dr Star spoke slowly so Marcus could understand what he was being told. "The death of your mother is still unexplained, but Major Ferris says it is now a civil matter."

"I will not go," is all Marcus would say, looking Dr Star defiantly in the eyes.

Rosa was still massaging him, and he sighed with pleasure at her gentle touch.

Dr Nathan Star had argued on behalf of Marcus as to why the boy was to be handed over, but he was stone-walled every time. "Don't interfere, doctor. See to the sick." Was the retort from the commanding officer.

Dr Star's tour of duty was coming to an end and he was looking forward to going home – back to his wife and five-year-old daughter, Barbara, whom he had not seen for over a year.

The day came. Several of his colleagues were travelling with him and they were to depart by bus to Graz, then a plane to Berne, and finally a flight back to London. Accompanying them were two gravely wounded men; one a soldier and one a civilian, who needed urgent treatment at the Queen Victoria Hospital, East Grinstead in England, where new and successful techniques were being carried out on burns victims. However, the day before departure the young civilian patient died in the middle of the night from trauma. Dr Star was called but nothing could be done for the young man, but there was something he could do for someone else.

With the help of a trusted nurse, they swapped the identities of the dead patient with Marcus's and bandaged Marcus's face and arms so he could not be recognized. Six medical staff and two patients left the camp the following day as planned, and arrived back in England four days later. As Marcus's stretcher was carried out to the waiting truck, an orderly was overheard to say, "Blimey, this guy weighs a tonne."

Marcus stayed with Dr Star and his family in Surrey as their adopted son, although nothing was officially recorded. He went to the local school and sung in the church choir, and was very quick to learn. By the time he was eighteen he was fluent in five languages and had a good head for maths. In 1953 an old friend of Dr Star, who worked at the London Stock Exchange, took Marcus on as an apprentice *'Trader'*.

A few days after Dr Star's departure, Major Ferris requested his sergeant to bring Marcus to him for transfer to Vienna but was informed he could not be found.

"What do you mean, sergeant? He has to be here somewhere. Bring me Doctor Star." He bellowed. The Sergeant seemed unmoved by his superiors' outburst. "Sir, Dr Star left four days ago to return to the UK. His replacement has not arrived yet."

Ferris stared momentarily, analyzing this information. "Who left with him, sergeant?"

"Doctor Freeman, nurse Anne Cowell, Nurse Sally Peters, anesthetist Raymond Smith and two patients on stretchers, being transferred to a burns hospital in England, sir."

"What were their names?" Ferris asked.

"Private Banner and an Austrian civilian, Herr Rosenberg. He was badly burnt in a fire two weeks ago if you remember, sir." Ferris sat thoughtfully tapping his fingers on the desk. "Sergeant, do a thorough search for Marcus von Hartstein. He has to be somewhere in this camp."

Nathan Star and his wife were the only ones who knew Marcus's true story, and they took it with them to their graves when they died in a car crash in 1956. Marcus knew he would tell Rosa, as he had Barbara, the same story one day – when the time was right.

It seemed longer than five years ago since Marcus had rescued Rosa from her own nightmare in Armenia, and wondered what would have happened to her if he had left her there to fend for herself.

He felt the warmth of Rosa as she maneuvered herself into him. "You were asleep I think," she said playfully. "What were you dreaming about? You started to mumble something."

"I was . . . remembering. I was remembering how lucky I have been. I do want to help those two young people, Isabel and Charlie, and I want you to help me. Will you do that for me, my dear Rosa?"

Rosa cocked her head to one side and smiled. "You know I cannot refuse you anything, Marcus. When do we start?"

Chapter Three

When the sun sets over the River Thames it is one of the most beautiful sights I have had the pleasure to witness, especially in the 'Golden Hour', as the sun dips low, bouncing off the glistening water at low tide; something I have photographed many times. The ice in my Martini has melted, but it still tastes good as I drain the residue and nibble on the sliver of lemon. I always remember him when I drink a Martini Vermouth; Marcus Hartmann, friend, lover, benefactor and . . . and . . . someone I really didn't know that well. Whatever life he lived, I only know him as a kind and gentle man. If he had secrets, which I am sure he did, then they have disappeared with him, wherever he is. From where I am sitting on the small patio of our Victorian terrace house in Barnes, contemplating reaching fifty in a few months, I can see the two large paintings he left Charlie and me, and, although I can't quite see it, I know the Chair is to my left, against the wall. The Chair that captivated me and seduced me. The Chair that taught me Free Will . . . The Chair that brought me into the world of Marcus Hartmann, back in 1979.

1979 Midsummer's Day

Charlie, my boyfriend, and I had been impressed with Marcus Hartmann, a soft-spoken man of uncertain age, (a moustache always throws me, but I'm guessing around forty) with a guarded smile and an unplaceable accent. We had met him one evening at the pub where we were staying, The Fox & Hounds, and he had invited us back to his house, only a mile away, for a nightcap after closing time. In those days pubs closed at ten-thirty. It was midsummer and the air was humid, and my thin cotton mini dress was sticking to me like wet tissue. It was one of those evenings when the light seemed to go on forever – not knowing when to give up and let everyone sleep. The full moon was making the star-filled sky even more unnatural by ten-thirty – not night, not day – I felt I was in another world, or maybe that was the pint and half of cider talking?

Marcus's large cottage looked impressive. Typical English rose garden with an arbor and wooden bench seats in the front porch. He opened the heavy wooden front door without unlocking it, which I thought strange; but that was just my city thinking kicking in – it's not something we do back home. "Come on in," he said with a smile, guiding me over the threshold with his hand on my clammy lower back.

Chas stood staring, mouth open in awe at the spacious interior. He and I had met at a party the previous New Year's Eve, and he was all over me the entire evening – very persistent I remember, not taking no for an answer. I knew he only wanted to sleep with me, and like most men of that age, twenty-two, going on twelve, and full of alcohol, sleeping is exactly what they do. He did make up for it the following day, or I should say evening, as we had to sleep off the previous night's excesses first.

Neither of us had had a lot of lovemaking experience even though I was twenty-three. My first was five years earlier when I was eighteen, and like most first times it was a disaster. Necking, ear-nibbling, breast fondling, thigh touching, and then a hand down the knickers. Hardly seductive. It was also his first time so he was on a learning curve as well. However, after he saw blood on his fingers he ran a mile. There had been one or two others since then, with intercourse, but not knowing what it was supposed to feel like I was never sure of myself, and relationships soon ended.

None of the boys seemed to have had much experience, and they always seemed so young. What they thought they knew was mostly gained from porn films or men's magazines. Chas had been different, once he was sober. He was still a little naive, but had more concern than others, although still inexperienced at the end of the day. The 'missionary' position was the limit of our foray, but I did like the cuddles and quiet moments afterwards, if not the cigarette smoke.

"So," Marcus asked, "what do you think of my humble abode?"

"Fantastic!" Chas uttered, transfixed by the décor but especially two paintings that adorned one of the walls in the large open-plan lounge that greeted us. Chas gasped in delight. "Bloody hell, man, is that a Picasso? It can't be, can it?" he asked, staring at the large painting, almost in a trance.

"Very good. Unfortunately, it is a reproduction. The original is at the Museum of Modern Art in New York. They refuse to sell it. I have asked them enough times." Marcus laughed, remembering something. "It's called Girl with Mandolin, from his cubism period. So you like art?" He asked, seeing Chas was in seventh heaven.

"Yes, love it," Chas answered, still mesmerized, but now looking at the other imposing image - the suppressed artist in him begging to surface.

"OK then, can you tell me what this is?" Marcus challenged.

It was not, in fact, a painting – it looked to me like photographs. "Not sure," Chas said, hands on hips, transfixed, and looking puzzled.

"It's a David Hockney. It's made up of hundreds of photographs of Theresa Russell, the film actress. I think the two subjects, this and the Picasso, work well together – the Hockney is mirrored by the cubism of Picasso, don't you think, Chas?"

"Yes, err . . . totally. Christ man, you must be rich."

"Chas," I said rather too abruptly, "don't be rude." Hoping Marcus was not offended. On the contrary, he just smiled and shrugged. "Everyone should have a hobby. Mine is collecting beautiful objects," he said, looking at me with a captivating smile, making me blush ever so slightly. "Now, what about that drink I promised." He offered, trying to put me at ease.

Marcus poured me a Martini with lemonade, and Chas a whisky. "If you like these, Chas," Marcus said, nodding at the two paintings, "come and see what I have in the other room."

And the two of them left me alone with my drink. Looking around the white-walled oak-panelled lounge I had the chance to observe more closely the furniture and other objects and artefacts. There were several unusual bronze sculptures; some on shelves, and one, four foot tall standing on the floor. The subject matter for most of them was a naked or near-naked woman squatting, sitting, standing, or in one case, bending over.

A large button backed burgundy sofa faced an old inglenook fireplace, but what took my attention was a very unusual chair against the wall, opposite the paintings. I was about to inspect it closer when Chas called me.

"Bell, come and see these," he called from somewhere close by. I followed the sound of voices along a narrow hallway to another room. This looked like an office or study with a large writing desk against one wall, and rows of bookshelves on the two adjacent walls. Chas and Marcus however, were occupied with the other wall adorned with framed photographs.

"Look, Bell, aren't these fantastic. So atmospheric . . . so . . ."

"Erotic?" I offered.

"Bell, don't be a prude. This is exceptional art." Chas beamed, hoping I had not offended Marcus.

"Isabel, these are recent works from a very talented English photographer, Michael Payne. He captures the human form perfectly, don't you think. Yes, erotic if that's what you see, but the human form should be seen as having many other qualities, not just eroticism." Marcus said, looking at me for a response. I was holding my drink with both hands – shivering slightly.

"Are you cold?" he asked.

"No, just the ice in the drink." I lied. Not cold but slightly aroused by the images I was looking at. I knew they were beautiful but I was not going to encourage Chas about something we could not afford. Marcus seemed convinced I disapproved of the photos, but in fact, I did admire them. Photography was one of my secret ambitions, but all I could afford back then was a compact Kodak digital, with hardly any features.

"Ah, you didn't think someone like me would consider having such . . . sensual, contemporary images adorning the walls of this old cottage." And smiled reassuringly at me.

"I think they are bloody marvelous. Can we have some in our pad when we get one, Bell?" Chas asked excitedly. His Welsh accent accentuated by the recent alcohol.

At any other time, I would have shouted back. "Don't call me Bell!" but I just smiled and sighed.

"I think you prefer Isabel, and quite right too," Marcus said, sensing the distaste of my shortened name, and so Chas could hear. "How do you spell it?" he asked with interest.

"I.s.a.b.e.l"

"Ah, the French way, then you are not Jewish, that would be Isobel."

I looked at him, but his words seemed distant and I felt light-headed. My legs gave way and I found I was falling backwards before I could resist. Instead of hitting the floor I was swept up into Marcus's arms and carried back along the hall to the lounge where he laid me on the sofa.

"Hey, what's happened? Is she Ok?" I could hear Chas's voice somewhere, but not sure where he was. "Bell, are you OK? Look at me. What happened?" I felt Charlie's hand on my cheek, and then forehead.

"She will be fine. It's probably just the heat, and a little too much of our local cider. Let's leave her to rest a while – let her sleep a little. Come, let me show you the rest of the house. I think you will enjoy some of the other artistic offerings I have, and let me get you another drink, same again?" Marcus took Chas's arm and guided him away from me. I laid there on the sofa, drifting into unconsciousness. My dress askew, showing a sliver of exposed white knicker.

I don't know how long I had been asleep but suddenly Marcus appeared, kneeling at my side, smiling. "Are you feeling better? Here, drink this." I managed to sit upright and took the drink willingly. My throat was dry.

"What is it?"

"It's just a refreshing drink. I thought you may need one. Are you feeling better?"

I was feeling better. No nausea. No dizziness. I felt warm and comfortable, and not shivering anymore. He took the glass from me and took my hand. I looked around for Chas, not in a panic mode, more out of curiosity. "Where did Chas get to?" I asked.

"He had another whisky and promptly fell asleep in the other room. I am beginning to think I am a bad effect on you two." He smiled as he stood up, and walked over to the chair I had been admiring earlier, before my fainting spell. It was a strange shape, like nothing I had seen before. It was tall, at least six feet and covered in studded deep burgundy leather, with a canopy which made it all the more mysterious.

"Do you like it? It's called a Porter's Chair. I found it in Europe. It came from a very old hotel in Vienna which was having a refurbish. It is very comfortable, come, try it."

He held out his hand, and without hesitating, I rose and walked over to this man, this man who was at least twenty years my senior, and of whom I knew nothing about whatsoever.

The light had well and truly vanished and I had no idea of time. I noticed the room was dimmer, and flickering candles cast shadows that danced on the walls and ceiling, and sandalwood incense filled the air. Chas, or Marcus, must have removed my sandals after the fainting spell, as I felt my toes tingle against the soft pile as I walked the few paces to stand in front of Marcus, who was now sitting in the chair.

I hadn't noticed earlier when I awoke, but Marcus had changed into a long satin dressing gown, decorated with fine embroidery of oriental characters and dragons. He took hold of my hands and leant forward to kiss each one. I shivered, not out of coldness but something else.

"Are you going to kill us?" I whispered. I don't know what made me say it, but something in me felt a need to know. Marcus looked more hurt than anything. "Good heavens, woman. What made you ask that?"

Goosebumps tingled my arms and ran down my spine. I could have left, should have left maybe, but fear and curiosity are strange bedfellows, and curiosity will usually win over in the end. "I don't know . . . I'm sorry, Marcus, I . . ." but I was lost for words, feeling foolish and embarrassed.

He patted his left knee. "Come, sit here," he said gently, never losing eye contact with me. I flattened my dress down as far as possible and gingerly sat on his left leg, feeling his hand on the small of my back, as if to support me. "How long have you and Chas been together?" His voice was soft and his tone was measured with that still unplaceable accent. Our heads were close, and I could smell the sweet fragrance of Southern Comfort on his breath.

"Since the New Year. We met at a party." I whispered, holding down the hem of my dress.

"Put your arm around my neck, you will feel more comfortable." I obeyed without question. I didn't want to give the impression I was scared or mistrusting again. I met his gaze and felt somehow reassured by his clear steel-blue eyes gently smiling at me. His pale moustache was trimmed neatly and seemed in contrast to his thick dark blond hair, loosely combed back on both sides. Many men his age would have killed for such a head of hair.

I felt his right hand touch the top of my leg, gently caressing it with his fingers in a circular motion. "It's OK, Isabel. Do you know what '*Free Will*' is?" His soft voice must have had a calming effect on me because I nodded in the positive, but not really knowing for sure.

"I will take you to another world if you want me to. One of pleasure and passion. A safe world where no harm will come to you, I promise."

He sounded sincere in what he was saying and I was feeling more relaxed now; absorbed by his words, but saying nothing – not even NO or STOP, as you think I should have.

Sensing I was OK with the situation he moved his hand to my face and gently caressed my cheek with the back of his hand. His middle finger moved over my lips and I voluntary kissed it. My mouth opened, and I sucked in the tips of his fingers. I closed my eyes and my heart pounded faster, and the Goosebumps surfaced again. He leant closer to kiss my lips, teasing them open, his tongue parting them further to touch mine and explore my ready mouth. The back of his hand caressed my inner thigh, and I pulled back from his embrace. He smiled, again, reassuringly.

I bit my lower lip and he continued stroking my thighs. I closed my eyes again, enjoying the experience although something in me knew this should not be happening. "Chas. Where is Chas?" I whispered, letting this man, this stranger, continue to do whatever he wanted to me.

How was this happening? Chas and I are happy, and we have a good relationship which seems to be going somewhere. Sex has been good . . . it's been OK . . . but nothing like this.

This is another world where it is impossible to tell right from wrong or good from bad, although nothing really bad has happened, so far, has it? I am in control, I told myself and murmured with pleasure to what was happening to me. I voluntarily parted my legs a little wider, now gripping Marcus's shoulder for support as I was about to explode. Just when I thought this was happening, he stopped and kissed my neck.

"Do you remember Rosa, from the pub?" I opened my eyes and blinked several times, and promptly closed my legs, trying to hide my embarrassment at seeing this beautiful woman appear from nowhere.

"Hello, Isabel. I see Marcus has been taking good care of you." She spoke softly, and she too, with an accent I didn't recognize. I looked around the room wondering where Chas was. "Don't worry," she said, "Charlie is fine", and positioned herself on Marcus's other leg, opposite me, and kissed him lovingly. "Can you take us both?" she said, smiling. Marcus grinned. "You are not that heavy my dear if that's what you mean." But I knew she didn't mean that.

Rosa was indeed slim, around five foot seven with thick shoulder-length black hair and a wonderful natural Mediterranean complexion. Her deep-set brown eyes were bright and alert. Her lips were full and moist and her tongue was pierced with a silver stud. She wore black satin pajama trousers with a white embroidered oriental style top, fastened by red braided loops from the neck down. She looked gorgeous. She turned and smiled at me, then taking my left hand kissed it on each side. That overwhelming feeling of uncertainty returned. I shuddered again, but with inquisitive desire rather than trepidation.

"I want you to copy me. Do what I do." And she kissed my hand again. I looked at Marcus for confirmation I suppose, but he just nodded a surreptitious smile. I took Rosa's right hand and slowly raised it to my lips, kissing it once. She nodded, smiling. She took my hand again and turned it over, working her tongue between my fingers. I copied her, liking how she tasted of sweet coconut milk and almonds. She lowered my hand onto her upper leg, and leant forward, placing her hands on my thin clammy legs.

Our faces were almost touching. I could smell her perfume and her soft breath on my face. Our lips touched, and again, I did not resist as she parted them with her tongue and kissed me as I had never been kissed before. As we kissed she moved her hands slowly up and down my thighs, pushing my dress higher and higher until my knickers were in full view. I moved my hands to her shoulders to stop myself falling backwards, even though Marcus's arm was holding my back.

"You are lovely," she said, touching my face and kissing me again. I closed my eyes and let her hands find my thighs while Marcus caressed the back of my neck, and I felt a surge of ecstasy as he cupped my breasts – I felt I was being touched by a thousand angels as my body reacted to all the pleasure points; thighs, neck, lips, breasts . . . but how was this possible, all at once, it would take . . . I opened my eyes and looked down at the hands holding my breasts - it was Chas. I took hold of his hands, which he did not remove, and squeezed them harder, feeling the pleasure surge through me again. "Where have you been?" I asked, lifting my head to see his upside-down face smiling back at me.

"I see you are in good hands," he laughed back, looking at Rosa. He moved and knelt in front of me, leaning in to kiss me – long, and more tenderly than I can remember. I touched his face.

"I don't know what happened . . . it just did. . . I . . ." He put a finger to my lips. "Hush, my darling. Do you want to enjoy more . . . there is more," and looked at Rosa with a knowing grin.

"If you are OK, then I suppose," but before I could finish, Chas and Rosa stood. She kissed him, which took me by surprise and a twinge of jealousy pricked me on seeing my man with another woman.

Why was I having these feelings? I know nothing of lovemaking. We are just an ordinary couple living our ordinary lives. What is this world we have found ourselves in? It feels safe and warm. I feel . . . wonderful, I feel . . . enlightened. I watched as Chas touched her arm as they kissed, and she ran her hand down his front to his now obvious erection. "I think you need to be taken in hand young man," Rosa said, looking at me, and winked. I realized what was about to happen. I had read about orgies and group sex in men's magazines, and I had even masturbated once on seeing Jason Donavan nearly naked in a full-page spread (I was very young after all). But now it was about to happen, for real.

Marcus eased me off his knee and swept me up in his arms. I instinctively put my arms around him to steady myself as he moved, with purpose, across the floor to the open staircase leading to the first floor. Rosa was following, but I saw Chas still standing in the lounge rubbing his crotch.

From the first floor, Marcus took a shorter flight of stairs leading straight into a large sparsely furnished room. It was lit with candles, and again, sweet incense perfumed the air. Instead of a bed, the floor was covered with four large mattresses adorned with rugs and cushions.

Each mattress was covered in a different colored satin sheet; burgundy, matt black, cadmium yellow and Prussian green.

Marcus laid me down gently on the black bed, my head against a silk crimson pillow. "I will see you soon." And he kissed my forehead and backed away, touching Rosa on the cheek as he left us alone.

"I thought . . . that is . . . he and . . . Chas . . . and you."

Rosa knelt by my side, un-phased by my nervous stammering. "There are times when we don't need men around us," she said gleefully, unbuttoning her satin top, adding, "Have you ever had a massage?"

"No, never," I replied, now feeling more anticipation than apprehension.

*

Downstairs, Marcus poured Chas another whisky. "So, how was Rosa?"

"Need you ask?" Charlie replied, smirking.

Marcus grinned at the answer. "She is always a pleasure. Cheers." And the two men sipped the warm liquor. "You were getting hard again just now. Are you still aroused?"

Chas looked at Marcus not knowing how to answer truthfully. "Charlie, can I call you Charlie?" Marcus asked, seeing Charlie's apprehension.

"Yes, of course."

"Charlie, you did not know what experiences you would encounter this evening when you accepted my invitation back here, did you."

Chas shook his head ruefully. "No, of course not."

"I realized you and Isabel were special. I saw something in you both that could be nurtured . . . could be cultivated perhaps. Notice I said both of you, not just Isabel. I also want you to appreciate new sensations and acquire experiences perhaps not yet known to you. Making love should always be special, but you do not need to be 'in love' to make love. Do you follow?" Marcus asked, seeing Chas was finding it hard to concentrate.

"Yes, I think so," Charlie answered cautiously. "You want to have sex with both of us?"

Marcus shook his head. "No. Make love. Sex is just a word - it means nothing. Making love means so much more. It says you want to be intimate, caring, loving. Allowing both of you to give and take - not just take."

Chas nodded as if he understood, but in truth, he really was not sure what Marcus was talking about.

*

Rosa stepped out of her satin pajama trousers, leaving her in a pair of white laced pearl thongs. I stared at her sculptured pubic hair and the two strings of pearls connected to the front of her lace thong. As she turned I saw she had a most colorful and intricate tattoo of a unicorn adorning her back, which started at the shoulder blades and finished just above the base of her spine.

Rosa touched the pearls between her legs. "They are very . . . sensual," she said, gently rubbing the two strands of pearls with her first and second finger. She knelt next to me. Her skin was warm and soft, and her breasts a perfect size and shape with dark brown nipples standing proud.

A small jewel decorated her belly-button. She ran a finger along my right leg, up across my wet knicker crease onto my navel, and came to rest on my lips.

"I can't massage you with your clothes on," she smiled and took hold of both my hands and pulled me up to a kneeling position in front of her. She reached behind me, her warm breath teasing the skin of my neck, and unzipped my dress. She skillfully lifted the dress from the hem and took it over my head, revealing my pallid breasts. On instinct, I cupped them – not knowing why. I was feeling both intrigued and uncertain at the same time. I knew what was happening, and I could still have left, but I stayed, and experienced something wonderful - something I could never have imagined would be so beautiful and fulfilling – with another woman.

"I've never had a massage," I said, naively.

Rosa smiled. "Well, I could give you one - I am a trained masseur after all," she said with some pride in her voice, "but tonight we will, how you say, cut to the chase."

She knelt with one leg between my legs and gently eased me back onto the soft satin, placing my arms at my side. Her right knee pushed home into my pubic area, before lifting it onto my lower groin, swaying up and down, then left and right. I clutched the mattress with both hands, and arched my back, riding the passion that was washing through me.

Just when I thought I was about to come, she stopped, and leant over and kissed me. "Not yet," she whispered, and took hold of either side of my knickers and pulled them off in one stroke. She parted my thighs. I did not resist.

Her manicured fingers moved deeper, gently caressing the inside of me in a rotating motion. The more I moaned the deeper she went. She then replaced her finger with her tongue, and I moaned even louder with the pleasure of this new experience – by a woman that is. Chas gave me oral once, but never like this – this was different – this was an artist's brush-stroke, a poet's sonnet, a woman's touch.

Of course, I came prematurely, but that was only the first of three times over the course of the next hour, and I gradually learnt to control them with Rosa's tuition. I, too, practised on her what I had learnt, and we kissed, cuddled and fucked - and it was bliss.

We lay, holding each other, drifting into a sublime dream world when Marcus and Chas appeared in the doorway, totally naked. "Are you ready for us yet?" Marcus asked, with a smile. Rosa untangled herself from our embrace, kissing me warmly on the lips. She stood and kissed Marcus, then, taking his hand, they walked to the other side of the room and knelt in front of each other on the dark green mattress. Chas sat next to me, and I leant over to kiss him. "What have you two been up to? I whispered.

"I'll tell you later, but you must tell me what you two have been doing," he smiled. I touched his thigh, then still looking into his eyes, took hold of his erect penis and massaged it, up and down. I half expected we were going to change partners again, and Marcus would have . . . well . . . had me, but he and Rosa made love before falling asleep in each other's arms. I could not help looking in their direction when I was on top of Chas, seeing how good they were together in the shadows, how gentle they were with each other. I knew that night was going to change my perception of lovemaking and relationships forever and prayed it would be for the better.

We woke not knowing the time. The only daylight crept through the doorway from the landing window. All was quiet, and Marcus and Rosa were nowhere to be seen. "I smell coffee," Chas muttered, face down on the mattress.

"Chas, look at me," I said, shaking him. He half-turned. One eye open. "What?"

"What happened here . . . are you OK with it? I mean, now, after the event and all that, are we still OK?" I asked seriously.

Chas steadied himself on one elbow and cupped my face in this hand. "It was an unusual nightcap, I'll give him that," he said, trying to make light of it, and kissed me. "Are you asking if we are still OK, Bell? I am if you are. I think we put it down to a most unusual and memorable evening. I certainly learnt a lot about myself."

"Me, too." I agreed, a little more casually, taking his hand. "It didn't seem . . . bad . . . it always felt good, as if it was planned in some way. Did you get that feeling, Chas?"

"Do you think they make a habit of picking up strangers and seducing them," he said, rolling on top of me and pretending to bite my neck, vampire style. I had that Sunday morning feeling and was prepared for a quickie now Chas was on top of me, but we heard a tap on the door and Rosa came in carrying two mugs of coffee.

"Don't stop on my account," she smiled. Chas rolled off of me and I instinctively pulled the sheet over my breasts. Rosa smiled but said nothing, except, "there's toast and cereal downstairs if you are hungry," and placed the mugs of coffee on the floor. "After breakfast, I'll drive you back to the pub to collect your things."

"Oh, hell!" I had completely forgotten we had paid to stay at the pub. "The landlord will have wondered what happened to us . . ."

Rosa shook her head. "It's fine. Cathy and George . . ." and she hesitated to find the right words, ". . . are good friends of ours, and saw you leave with Marcus, and assumed you would be late, or possibly stay over."

She tilted her head and raised one eyebrow, checking we understood. We nodded silently. "Good, then come down soon." And she was gone.

"You see," I said, as soon as she had left, "they have done this before. The landlord and his wife are in on it." Chas rolled over and sighed. "Bell, you are sounding paranoid. It happened, and it turned out OK. We are OK, aren't we? No one strangled us in the night," he said, head dipped, eyes piercing me for my approval.

"Yes, of course, we are. It was good . . . in a strange, weird way. . . but good. I think we have both learnt something. I never knew how good sex could be with another woman. Are you OK with that?" I asked thoughtfully. Chas sat up and cupped his hands to my face and kissed me gently on the lips. "Marcus told me it was about 'making love', not sex. He wanted us to experience something new and different, which I think we just did."

Chas sounded different for sure. Could last night have changed him, made him more of a thoughtful lover? Then a thought crossed my mind . . . is that what they do . . . choose young naive couples and guided them in the art of sex, or love-making.

It was a wild thought but it seemed plausible. Marcus and Rosa are a couple, yes, but there was a good age difference, so he could well have 'chosen' her in the beginning. I decided to keep these thoughts to myself for now and see how the day and the following weeks panned out for us. If it was a once-in-a-lifetime experience then no harm has been done, and we could even consider ourselves fortunate. After the eventual quickie, we got dressed and found our way to the kitchen, following the smell of fresh coffee and grilled bacon. "Sit down and have breakfast," Rosa said cheerfully. "What do you have planned for the day?"

"Actually, we must be going soon. We have a long drive back to London." I said, realising I didn't really want to leave so soon.

"We could stay another day," Chas said, and saw my surprised look. "It's possible. You could take a sickie; say we were held up on the way back . . . which we were, kind of," he said, laughing and smiling at Rosa.

"No . . ." I said, giving the idea some credence. "I promised Sally I would be back tomorrow to take over her shift. I work at a checkout in a local Supermarket." I said, turning to Rosa with the explanation.

Rosa raised her eyebrows and shrugged. "Pity, we thought you may like to go for a picnic near the lake and then . . . well, that doesn't matter now if you are going."

"And then what?" Chas asked eagerly, sounding like a little boy wanting another treat.

"And then nothing . . ." I said, resolutely. "We must go back, I promised. I do not like letting my friends down."

We sat in silence for a while, losing our appetites which were so apparent only a short time ago.

"Where is Marcus by the way?" Chas asked.

Rosa indicated with a nod of her head. "He is not an early riser, but I will make sure he comes down to say goodbye."

I finished my coffee and automatically went to go upstairs to pack, then suddenly remembered we were staying at the pub. "Oh, God, what will the landlord think of us staying out all night. I hope our things are OK . . . Chas will you . . ." My mind was racing and Rosa and Chas could see I was in the early stages of a panic attack.

"Bell, it's fine . . . I promise you." Rosa said, giving me a gentle cuddle. It was the first time we had touched that day, and the smell of her bath oil brought back the memory of last night, and the first time we touched. She kissed me on the cheek and smiled as if subduing a distraught child. "I'll call the pub and explain we will bring you back soon. Is that OK?"

"Fine, Rosa. That would be good." Chas appeared at my side, and took over from Rosa with the hugging, and giving me a kiss. We went back into the kitchen and I started to clear away the cups and plates. "Hey, that's not your job, Bell. Come and sit down and let's talk about today."

"There is nothing to talk about, Chas. We are going home."

"OK . . . OK . . . Bell. I just thought you would want to stay around Marcus and Rosa a little longer to find out more about them," he said, looking at me as if he had just made a remarkable discovery.

"Yes, well, no." I stammered. Not thinking straight. "Don't do that, Chas. Don't try and make me out to be the bad one here. We have to go back and I am going, even if I have to get a train." Chas was about to sweet-talk me again when Rosa come back in the kitchen saying she could drive us back if ready.

"What about Marcus?" I asked, genuinely wanting to say goodbye, and thank him . . . I think.

"He sends his regrets but thanks you for your company last night, and to have a safe journey home."

"That's it?" I said. "After everything, he can't come down even to say goodbye." My disappointment was obvious but Rosa just shrugged in silence.

She drove us back to the pub to collect our things. The landlord greeted us with a 'good morning' and said the accommodation had been settled. I assumed it was Marcus, or Rosa, but he would not say.

Chas and I drove back to London in silence, except when I had to navigate from the AA map. The next morning, however, he seemed different . . . happier. "So, what shift are you on today?" he asked cheerfully over breakfast.

"One to eight," I answered, tentatively, surprised by his sudden change of attitude. "I'll bring something in from work for dinner."

"Good girl. Fancy some steak tonight," he said enthusiastically.

"I'll see what's going. I can only get what's not sold on the day." And forced a smile. He kissed my head and went to work.

I sat there staring at the table. At the unfinished toast and cold coffee and the pile of unopened post from the week's holiday.

The five days leading up to Saturday were a distant blur. We visited old towns, cathedrals, museums, art galleries and of course pubs. We had stayed in several pubs for B&B during the week, and found them cheap and convenient, not having to go far for food and drink, but I couldn't tell you any of the places we visited or stayed during that week, except the last one.

The Fox and Hounds in Little Upton. That stay has changed our lives. We have not talked about the other night, but we will have to soon. I need to know if what happened has changed our relationship. On the outside, Chas seems much the same. I can't say I am. I keep replaying what happened over and over trying to find something wrong in it . . . something evil maybe, but I only find pleasure and fulfilment. The phone rings and I shake as it brings me back to reality. It's mum, wanting to know how the holiday went and was I still with that *'hanger-on'* as she calls him.

Chapter Four

1955 Cranleigh Village, England.

The streets were lightly covered in frost, and smoke from the chimneys filled the air with memories of an earlier life for Rupert Ferris. A life before the war. One of peace and harmony. Of love and passion. Of deceit and adultery. All that seemed a long time ago now. Twenty years in the army changes any man. It rips them inside out. Cleanses them of love and passion. Only purpose and truth are left. Truth. In this case, what happened to the young Marcus von Hartstein back in Austria? A week after Dr Star's leaving it was discovered the young man known as Marcus von Hartstein had died and been cremated the same day.

Ferris was furious he had not been informed, but the medical unit was not obliged to report every death in the camp unless they were army personnel, which Marcus was not. Ferris contacted East Grinstead in England to confirm if two people had arrived recently from Austria as expected. The next day he received a reply;

From: Queen Victoria Burns Unit, East Grinstead
Attention: Major Ferris

Re your recent communiqué - we have received one patient, Private Banner who is in a serious, but stable condition. The second patient, Herr Rosenberg did not arrive - assumed died.

Signed
S Marshall
Chief Medical Officer

Major Ferris then realised who had been cremated - not the young Marcus von Hartstein, but Herr Rosenberg - the good doctor had spirited Marcus out of Austria. However, before Major Ferris could launch a full-scale enquiry and report his findings, fate intervened when he contracted T.B, and was sent to Switzerland to recover and convalesce for nine months. After serving another two years in Austria on his return to duty he finally retired and promised himself he would seek out those unanswered questions back in England, no matter how long it took.

Early evening. Car in the drive. Good chance everyone was at home. Ferris rang the bell. Mrs Star answered the door seemingly flustered at the interruption. "Sorry, my husband is not here just now. In fact, I am meeting him at the station and we are going to see our daughter perform in the school Nativity play. What did you say your name was?"

"Major Ferris. I served with your husband in Austria, after the war. He may have mentioned me." Ferris said, turning on the charm. Rosemary Star looked thoughtful in-between checking the contents of her handbag and looking in the hall mirror. "Sorry, no, I don't think so." She answered convincingly. "I really must go, Mr Ferris. I am late as it is."

"Of course. I am sorry to have disturbed you. I was just in the area looking at property and remembered Nathan mention he lived around here. I am sure we can meet again." He said, tipping his trilby. "By the way, are both of your children performing in the school play, Mrs Star?"

Rosemary did not hesitate and looked surprised at the question. "Two children? We only have a daughter, Barbara."

"So sorry, my mistake. I must have got you mixed up with another surgeon. We met so many people during that time. Do forgive me." Rosemary Star smiled and nodded her agreement as she got into her car and drove away, leaving the ex. Major pondering his next move. One that will flush out any close friends and relatives for certain.

Chapter Five

When Rosemary and Nathan Star were killed in the car accident, Barbara was in the back seat of the car. She was just ten years old.

Her parents died instantly but she was in a coma for nearly five months in East Surrey Hospital. Rosemary had adored Marcus, as had Barbara, whom she looked up to as the brother she never had. It had been such a pointless death, as are all deaths, but Marcus could not understand how it had happened. The police reports said they swerved to avoid another car, but the road was wide and dry that Sunday afternoon, with little traffic around. He read every report on the accident including the coroner's report, who returned a verdict of accidental death. Barbara was still in a coma when the funeral was held. The small village church in Cranleigh was filled with close relatives, friends and neighbors, and Nathan's colleagues from the hospital, but one important 'friend' was missing.

"Are you sure you want to be in the choir today, of all days, Marcus," the vicar asked with genuine concern, on hearing his request to sing at the funeral.

"Please, vicar, it would mean so much to me to sing the hymns they loved," Marcus replied with sincere remorse.

So Marcus sat in the choir stalls giving him a vantage point to oversee the faces of the congregation. He knew the locals and a few of the relatives, but one mourner stood out from the crowd whom he recognized immediately, seated at the back of the church. Some people cannot blend-in, or they are so arrogant they just don't consider the consequences. Major Rupert Ferris sat staring at every member of the congregation, looking for a young blond man. His face was long and grave, and fellow mourners genuinely thought he was mourning for the Star's, but he was just depressed as he could not find his quarry. Marcus followed Ferris out of the church and into a waiting car, which Marcus noted the number plate of. He now had the advantage. His time would come.

Barbara woke from her coma five months after that fateful day and called out for her parents. Marcus was there, holding her hand. "Hi, precious. Where have you been all this time?" He had persuaded the doctors to allow him to break the news to his sister, which he did as gently as possible. She closed her eyes, but that had not stopped the tears and Marcus patted her face with his handkerchief, and kissed her forehead. "We will be OK, you and me. I promise," he said, hoping it was a promise he could fulfil one day.

As Barbara was only ten years old she was placed with her grandparents until she was eighteen. She had inherited her parents' house which had been sold, but most of the money was spent on her education at a ridiculously expensive private boarding school for girls, so her grandparents did not have the responsibility of looking after her. After sixth form, she won a place at St Andrews University where she studied, Politics, Sociology, Art and History. At her graduation, which Marcus attended, he promised again to take care of her, and she could be as free as she wanted. It would be a wonderful co-existence.

*

Marcus had to deal with the one problem in his life that could ruin everything, Major Rupert Ferris. Marcus's research showed he was living in rented accommodation in Hampstead. He had no help and was not married. Marcus surveyed his coming and goings for a month until he knew exactly where he would be on any given day. The day in question was a Thursday and the place was Walthamstow dog track. Ferris also liked the horses, in fact, anything he could put a wager on. Marcus remembered seeing him playing cards on several occasions back in the camp, and the word was he was really very good at it. The dog track, however, was a gift to Marcus. The crowds and the noise made it a perfect place for revenge. Ferris was in his mid-fifties but still fit and agile. Marcus spotted him standing at the rails. "Can I buy you a drink for old time sake, Major?" Ferris turned expecting to see one of his old regiment or an old acquaintance from the Home Office, but his face turned to stone on seeing Marcus. "You . . ." He was lost for words momentarily. "What are you doing here?" Marcus had a firm grip on Ferris's arm, and the hard pointed object at the small of his back told Ferris it was a gun. Nathan Star's old service pistol.

"It was good of you to go to the Star's funeral by the way," Marcus stated unemotionally. "Do you want me to tell you what you were wearing?" Ferris froze, working out his options, but they were not looking good.

"You are an illegal, and a murderer. You hanged your mother didn't you?" Ferris tried to look around for help but Marcus's grip was tight.

"She deserved it. The Star's didn't. You do." Ferris just caught a glimpse of Marcus's grin as he slumped onto the steps behind him. Marcus propped him up against a hand-rail. "Stay there old man, and I'll get you some water." He said loudly enough for his words to be heard by other punters, but none were paying attention. Marcus walked away hoping the small bullet hole would not be noticed too soon.

Chapter Six

1956 London

The day Marcus killed Major Ferris he set in motion a chain of events that even he could not escape from. After Ferris's execution, Marcus had carried on with life as normally as possible, but something kept eating away at him- his conscience. He sat alone in his rented flat in Wimbledon, draining half a bottle of brandy within one hour. He so wanted to tell Barbara that she was safe. That he had taken revenge for her parent's murder. "Yes, Barbara, murdered." Murdered, all because of him. "All because your father helped me escape to England. If I had stayed, he and your mother would be alive."

Marcus sank another shot of whisky and closed his eyes. Would he ever have the opportunity to tell her the truth? Could he confess to her that he was responsible for her parent's death?

Six months after the shooting Marcus was consuming more liquor than ever each evening, eventually falling into a restless sleep. His work was suffering and his many days off work were being noticed. In these evening stupors, dark dreams with haunting faces appeared. His mother hanging from the kitchen airing rig, eyes closed one moment, then opened wide. Her handless arms waving uncontrollably, blood flying everywhere. Then he saw himself cowered in his mother's dressing room - faint voices coming from somewhere in the distance. "What have you done, Marcus, Marcus . . . we must go . . . no, stay there . . ." Then his father standing, looking straight ahead at a firing squad, suddenly turning to look at him and smiling. "Come here boy, come to your Father . . . stand with me." Then he heard the shots being fired, but his father was still looking at him, smiling. They fired again, and again, but still, he would not die. The noise was louder, someone was calling his name, louder and louder. He woke, shivering, and finished the leftover glass of liquor in front of him.

Focusing slowly, he heard his name again. "Mr Hartmann, please open up." Followed by more persistent rapping on the door. Marcus staggered from the table to the door and unlatched the bolt. He had hardly turned the Yale lock before a man dressed in a suit and black raincoat entered, pushing Marcus aside. "All clear, sir," he said, without looking at Marcus, or even to whom he was addressing.

A man in his mid-thirties walked slowing into Marcus's flat. He removed his trilby and gloves and handed them to the other man. Still without introducing himself, he walked over to the small table by the window and took a seat. The other man closed the door and stood there, guarding Marcus's exit, or protecting his employer - Marcus wasn't sure at first.

"Please, Mr Hartmann, have a seat." The man said politely, indicating Marcus should sit opposite him. Marcus was trying to sum-up the situation quickly, but after nearly a bottle of whisky, he was not getting any results. "Please, Marcus, have a seat before you fall down." This time the tone was non-negotiable.

Realizing this man knew his name, Marcus walked as casually as possible and sat at his own table. "Perhaps you could make us both a coffee, please Smith." The man asked the guard. "How do you take it, Marcus? White, two sugars I believe." Marcus nodded. "Hell," Marcus thought, did he guess that or what? Marcus blinked and took a deep breath. "Who are you?" he asked pointedly.

"Your friend, Marcus, for now at least." The man opposite replied, stony-faced. "My name is Dyke. And yours is Marcus von Hartstein. Age twenty-one." Dyke opened a leather attaché case and placed a buff colored folder on the table, and opened it. Marcus was tense, his blurred eyes trying to scan the contents of the folder. He remained silent. It was something he had learnt back in the camp after the War. "Keep quiet. Say nothing, they think you are stupid or something, and leave you alone," another inmate had told him. It had worked for a while, but Major Ferris was persistent, and he had wanted answers.

"Mr Hartstein." Dyke snapped. "Drink your coffee. I need you to concentrate. Do you understand me?"

Marcus looked around to see the other man had resumed his guarding duties at the door. The coffee smelt good but he really wanted another whisky. Marcus stood unexpectedly, and the guard went to take a pistol from his inside jacket pocket, but Dyke raised his hand. Marcus retrieved the near-empty liquor bottle and poured a measure into his coffee cup. Dyke smiled, and slid the bottle over to his side, and replaced the cap. "Enough I think, Marcus. I want you sober, so I don't need to have my man here wake you up."

Dyke flipped over the document in front of him. "From now on I will only refer to you as Marcus von Hartstein, as that is your name. If our meeting goes well, then I shall leave you as Marcus Hartmann, the name you elected to use when Dr Starr brought you to England. Do you understand me?" Dyke said firmly, pressing the point home.

Marcus understood alright. His file has landed up in the hands of the police and Ferris had won. Marcus dropped his head and took a deep breath. "Since there is no point in denying anything, let's get this over with," Marcus said, accepting his fate. He had done his best, and he hoped Barbara would forgive him one day when she was older and understood.

Dyke smiled. "Good. You are paying attention," he said. "Major Rupert Ferris, deceased, seemed to have had a personal goal in verifying who you are. After you're . . . disappearance, from Austria, he searched for months trying to work out how you had been spirited away. Ferris assumed, correctly, the body Dr Star had cremated was, in fact, an Austrian civilian, who should have been recovering in a burns hospital in England, but they reported he never arrived." Marcus said nothing. He sat staring at Dyke knowing his friend had died in vain.

"It seems Major Ferris sat on this information. Only his Staff Sergeant, a Harold Kershaw, knew the full story. As Doctor Star had covered his tracks well, Ferris kept quiet, taking stock of the situation, as he would have questions to answer if his superiors found out. Ferris was to have retired but contracted tuberculosis over there, so he was sent to Switzerland for treatment and to convalesce. He eventually returned to England in the summer of 1950."

Dyke sipped the lukewarm coffee and looked at Marcus. Seeing Marcus did not want to contribute anything to the history lesson, he continued. "It took a while for him to trace Kershaw as he had been thrown out by his wife, and was now a petty criminal, living with a prostitute in Bick Lane, East London. Ferris persuaded him to locate Doctor Star." Dyke paused and turned over another document from the folder. "I am truly sorry for what happened to Mr & Mrs Star, but you see, Marcus von Hartstein, you killed the wrong man."

Marcus exploded, suddenly sober and full of adrenaline. He thumped the table. "Liar, liar. Ferris killed them. I know he did." Marcus stood up pushing the chair away. "SIT DOWN." Dyke shouted back, "we are not finished." The silent guard relaxed his pose and Marcus reluctantly sat back at the table.

"Having located Nathan Star, Ferris told Kershaw to arrange an accident. The idea was that you would come and visit them, and Ferris would then arrest you. Unfortunately, Kershaw's arranged accident went horribly wrong, and they both died." Dyke paused again, in thought. "Thank God the child survived." He said solemnly. "I hear she is doing well at boarding school," he added, perhaps offering Marcus some small token of optimism.

"Where is Kershaw now?" Marcus asked, unemotionally, hoping for a second chance at revenge.

Dyke smiled briefly. "He was arrested trying to leave the country. He will go to prison for a long time, if not hanged, which would probably suit you better given the circumstances."

The thought of killing the wrong man was taking its toll on Marcus. He leant back on the wooden chair, rocking on its two fragile back legs, and closed his eyes, praying he could put the clock back and do things right. With Kershaw now in custody he was never going to get his rightful revenge. It all depended on what Dyke's motive is. "What does he want from me?" he asked himself. Marcus realized he was in a tight spot, but the thought of Barbara kept him focused. She was the only reason he had to keep going, to keep alive, at least until she was old enough to know the truth. She deserved to know it, warts and all. "So," Marcus finally asked, feeling depressed, "what happens to me now?"

Richard Dyke, although looking solemn, inwardly was congratulating himself on reaching this far. He had no idea how Marcus would react. His gut instinct told him Marcus was worth saving. Given the circumstances, it was not impossible to feel some empathy with his actions towards his mother. However, any court would condemn him and he would be locked away, not for a fixed term in an offender's prison, but indefinitely, in an alyssum, here or in Austria.

"I am not the police, Marcus, well, not as you know them. I work for the Home Office."

Marcus blinked and looked up once again at his interrogator. As interrogators go Dyke was very good. Just the right amount of charm when needed, but his tone always delivering a feint suggestion of coercion. Marcus realized his future was in jeopardy, but then a feeling of quiet relief came over him as if he had seen the road to salvation.

All these years he believed he would face retribution for his transgression - a transgression only a Priest could give absolution for if he believed in a Devine power, but now, here in London this man has seen his value and, just maybe, offer him the mercy and understanding he so desperately needed.

"The same question applies - what happens to me now?"

Dyke opened the buff folder again and turned a page. "I am in charge of a section at MI5. Have you heard of MI5, Marcus?"

"Not by name, but I assume England has a Secret Service like all countries."

"Indeed, and for a very good reason, especially now. I assume you have heard of The Cold War."

Marcus tilted his head slightly. "Are you asking me to be a spy?"

"Not exactly. We need people with special skills. Skills like yours' and languages particularly." Dyke looked at the page in front of him, "Russian, for instance, and German. What else do you have?"

Marcus smiled briefly, wondering if he should lean over and rescue the bottle of confiscated whisky. "French, Spanish, Italian and some Croatian." He confirmed casually. "And what are these skills needed for. I don't kill spies."

"You have scruples. That's not always a trait we encourage, but tell me why." Dyke asked with genuine interest.

"Your spies, their spies, whoever they are, are just people doing a job. They are not criminals. To me they are civilians, and I do not go around killing innocent people if that's what you are asking." Marcus finished defiantly; realizing only then he had made a fist with his right hand and was inwardly shaking with emotion. "I am not a killer. I did what I did to survive . . . and for . . . yes, for revenge."

Dyke closed the folder and tapped his right index finger on the table. "Europe, and the rest of the World, has changed dramatically since the end of the War, and although the War is over, battles not literally fought, we are still at War. Britain has enemies, more than you can imagine. Russia, once our ally just ten years ago, is now a world threat to the peace millions of men, women and children died for. There is tension all over the World; the new India, Israel and Korea for example, and nearer to home, Northern Ireland. There are many fractions that want, for many reasons, conflict to continue. It could be a coup d'état by the military, it could be a revolution sponsored by communist minorities - whatever the reasons if we consider our interests are being jeopardised, we will act accordingly, we will do what we have to, to survive."

Marcus slowly pushed the chair back and stood, stretching his arms above his head and yawned. "Nice speech. Another coffee?" he asked, wanting to keep awake a little longer. It was nearly midnight and he hadn't had a drink for over an hour. "I assume I can't go back to Austria, even if I wanted to?"

Dyke shook his head but paused before replying. *"Nihil est sacrosanctum."* Marcus looked at him curiously. "Sorry, my Latin is a little rusty."

"Nothing is sacrosanct." Dyke translated, smiling at a memory. "My old Latin teacher used to say that. Do you know what it means, Marcus?"

Marcus frowned and shrugged. He didn't want a lesson in Latin, or any other language. He wanted it to all go away and start over again, with Rosemary and Nathan Star still alive and he, living happily ever after with them. "Marcus!" Dyke's voice shocked him out of his daydream. "Do you know what it means?" Marcus shook his head in submission.

"Nothing is sacred - Nothing is forever, take your choice, but the sentiment is the same. Anything set in stone by law or human dictate can be changed if the *will* is there. Now, do you understand, Marcus? I am saying anything is possible . . . if I decide it." Marcus blinked and focused on Dyke's last sentence. "Ah, you do understand. I can see it in your eyes, Marcus. Good, we are getting somewhere." Dyke was feeling more confident than he had thirty minutes ago. He was convinced he would have to signal Smith to eliminate the young Marcus, but he was glad the tide was turning. He was beginning to like his new protégé.

Marcus cupped his hands around his coffee mug. His eyes willing the bottle of cheap liquor to move back across the table. Dyke sensed Marcus's yearning and voluntary slid the bottle across to Marcus. "Thank you," Marcus said, pouring the dregs of the bottle into the murky coffee. Dyke gave him time to digest the now drinkable beverage before bringing down the hammer. "We will train you in fire-arms, self-defense and other skills you will need. You will be what we call a 'sleeper'. We will call on you whenever we need your skills. You will come anytime, day or night, from wherever you are, without question, and carry out the orders we assign to you." Dyke paused, but Marcus just listened, waiting for the punch-line, and it came.

"In return, Marcus von Hartstein will disappear, forever cremated in Austria where Dr Star left him. You can continue with your new persona, and carry on with your life at the Stock Exchange."

"And if I decline?"

Although Dyke was looking directly at Marcus, he could see his man at the door reaching slowly into his inside jacket pocket. Dyke didn't blink or move his head to indicate any instructions to his man, not then.

"Let's just say Barbara will grow up without a brother. Do you want that?"

Marcus knew that he had no choice. Using Barbara as a bargaining chip was a clever move on Dyke's part, and Marcus was reluctantly impressed with this man, although life had warned him never to trust anyone, no matter how charming and sincere they appear.

Marcus nodded in the affirmative. "OK, but I have one condition."

"If it is in my power to approve," Dyke answered, intrigued.

"I don't want any payment for anything I do for you. I am not an employee. Do you understand?"

The man at the door frowned. It didn't make sense to him that someone would work for free.

"If that's what you want to keep your conscience clear, then yes, I can arrange that. Anything else?"

"No," Marcus answered, wearily, hanging his head. Wanting just to lie down and sleep for a week.

Dyke smiled gently. "Thank you, Mr Hartmann."

Marcus looked up and sighed. He stared momentarily at his new boss and nodded his appreciation. At the same time Dyke shook his head indicating his man to 'stand-down'. "Good. One last thing. You will need a code-name." Dyke looked as if was thinking. "A mythological beast. Strong in stamina. Loyal to his friends. Defender of his territory. Unicorn," Dyke smiled, "after all, you do have something in common - you don't exist either, do you, Marcus?"

Marcus shook his head, bemused at the analogy. "Very amusing. What else?"

Dyke opened his attaché case once more and took out a Manila A4 envelope. "This contains some documents you haven't had up to now; birth certificate, passport etc. plus instructions of when and where to report to for training."

"You were very sure of yourself," Marcus said, fingering the envelope,

Dyke said nothing. He picked up his case and retrieved his hat and gloves from Smith.

"We will meet again after your training, Mr Hartmann. Good luck."

The two men left without any further dialogue, leaving Marcus sitting at the table, head on folded arms, weeping uncontrollably.

Chapter Seven
1968

Marcus's new six-bedroom house in Shirley Heights, an up-market area near Croydon, was a sign of his early success in the City. The house was sparsely decorated, to begin with: scattered bean-bags for chairs, and a Habitat glass dining table with aluminium bar stools plus the latest in 1960's modern technology - a Hi-Fi Unit. The house, however, was lacking a woman's touch until Barbara arrived, although Marcus was not interested in material things, at least not back then. They lived in peaceful bliss, each living their own life and respecting each other's privacy - well, that was the plan.

Although each had their own bedroom, Barbara was restless and continually drawn to Marcus. One night, around six months after moving in she slipped into Marcus's bed, naked, and cuddled up behind him. He turned to face her. "What are you doing, Barbara?" he asked, startled by her presence.

"Seducing you," she whispered, unbuttoning his pajama top. She then pulled on the pajama trouser cord and searched for his cock. Pushing the bedspread back, she removed the pajama bottoms and sat astride her prize. "Barbara, please . . . don't . . . this is not right," he said, his face showing signs of fear.

Barbara replied by gently rocking on his soft cock. "Take off your top. I always sleep naked. You should know that by now," she teased. Marcus held her by the shoulders and looked at her forlornly. "Barbara, I am sorry. I can't do this." And he pushed her off onto the other side of the king-size bed. They laid side by side, silent for a while. Barbara was not sure what was wrong; she had never thought of Marcus as being queer, and she felt bad at having embarrassed him. To Marcus it was the moment he knew could come, would come one day, but for now he knew he was not strong enough to handle it.

"Tell me, Marcus, what happened to you? I deserve to know. You need to talk it out." She said with concern and kindness, caressing his arm, seeing he was being tortured by his homosexuality. Marcus rolled over to face her and cupped his hand to her cheek. "You are right, of course, as always," and smiled at her gorgeous face. He told her everything that night, including her father's part in spiriting him out of Austria. She listened with tears flowing down her cheeks, and when he had finished she hugged him so tightly she never wanted to let him go. They fell asleep entwined in a lover's knot, each wanting what should not be possible, as she now knew her earlier assumption was further from the truth than even she could have imagined.

In the morning they stirred slowly, Barbara caressing his face, kissing him gently. Marcus responded with firmer kisses, his hands searching out her warm flesh.

She eased herself on top of him and continued to rock rhythmically as she had done earlier that night. Marcus responded more than he had ever done, and swayed in time to her rhythm, but was failing to become completely erect again.

Noticing his awkwardness she took hold of Marcus and slowly rubbed up and down the foreskin with one hand whilst teasing one of his nipples with her free hand. "How come you know so much about sex, young lady?" Marcus asked with interest - enjoying her warm flesh on his.

"Have you forgotten I spent my formative years at Chaucer's boarding school for girls, and it's *'love-making*,' not sex," she said, with some smugness in her voice. The foreplay had the desired effect and she carefully took his full and underused cock and slipped it into herself. "Have you never been with a woman since . . . well, back then," she asked sympathetically. He shook his head, although curiously not unashamed to be a virgin at twenty-six. Perhaps he was waiting for the right woman after all, and now she was here to lead him into the Garden of Eden.

"Then allow me." Barbara took his hands and placed one on each of her breasts, and squeezed them so he knew what to do. "Circle my nipples with your thumbs, like this," she said, sucking on her forefinger, leaning into his smooth hairless body and touching his left nipple in a circular motion. Marcus stiffened and looked as if he was about to suffer a cardiac arrest, but the resulting stimulation was, in fact, his first and true experience in ejaculation.

During a brief respite, Marcus asked Barbara a leading question which was bothering him. "If you were at an all-girls school how come you learnt so much about . . . sex . . . sorry, lovemaking?" he asked in all innocence.

Barbara could not suppress her laugh. "Sorry, Marcus. You really are an innocent, aren't you?" And kissed him on the lips. "Well, to answer your question, I had a very good teacher, not just in Music and French, but in lovemaking . . . Ms Simone was . . . is . . . thirty-something, five foot six with short auburn bobbed hair, slim waist, and perfect breasts, and oh, yes, and a wonderful tattoo of a butterfly on her right buttock." And she smiled broadly at the memory.

Marcus was intrigued and slightly aroused by Barbara's description of her teacher. "Well," Marcus said, "don't stop there."

"I can see you are interested," Barbara said, reaching down between his legs. "OK, well, Ms Simone asked me back to her rooms one winter's evening, I was sixteen and seven months, and yes, a virgin. She was dressed in a beautiful full-length orange satin robe. We sat on the floor in front of a small log fire and drank Martini's, which I had never had before but thought they were so exotic. Then, casually, she asked, "Have you ever made love, Barbara?" I don't know why, but I was not shocked at all. I shook my head and said "No." She smiled, and then asked, "to a man or woman?" Then I did laugh. "No . . . not even a woman," but added, "why, have you?"

She smiled and indicated for me to sit next to her, with our backs against the sofa. "Yes," she whispered, "and it is the most beautiful single thing you can ever imagine. I am sure you will sleep with a man eventually, and perhaps marry, but I want you . . . and maybe some others . . . to experience the alternative. I can show you something that is both beautiful and touching as well as erotic and fulfilling. Do you know what *free will* is, Barbara?"

Barbara smiled, remembering that evening as if it were yesterday. Ms Simone gently caressed Barbara's arm, then reaching across her, took her hand and placed it on her own arm. "Copy me," she instructed. Barbara stroked and caressed as instructed, and when Ms Simone did, cupped her breasts gently at first, but then firmer, feeling her nipples harden under the soft fabric. Ms Simone unfastened her robe to reveal her totally naked body, and perfectly shaved pubic area.

Then, cupping her face she kissed Barbara, at first playing with her lips, teasing them open, then licking her mouth and finding her tongue. Barbara responded without hesitation, and Ms Simone knew she had chosen well.

Barbara's body tensed and her back arched. Although warm and damp all over, she trembled at her teacher's touch. "That's the feeling you want, my dear. Let it wash over you, from head to toe; that's the new experience you have found today, one that you will never forget."

"I not only learnt how to make love to a woman, in later meetings she introduced me to different *'play toys'*, and how to massage, which is very erotic."

Marcus was intrigued and slightly taken-aback by these revelations. Barbara may have been agreeable, but he could not help comparing the similarity of an adult taking advantage of a young child, and what her teacher did to her.

"Marcus . . . did you hear me . . . do you want a massage?"

Chapter Eight

The log fire gave out a pleasurable sense of warmth and security while a Mozart serenade drifted across the room from the Hi-Fi. Marcus sensed Barbara's Chanel No.5 as she entered the lounge and stood behind the sofa where he was sitting, eyes closed, absorbing the atmosphere of the room and feeling an overwhelming sense of contentment.

He reached for Barbara's hand and guided her around to sit beside him. She rested her head on his shoulder, and he kissed her damp hair. "I love the smell of wet hair," he said, lazily, kissing her again. He stroked her cheek with his right hand and let it fall onto her lap where he slowly untied her dressing gown. She touched his hand. "Not yet," she whispered, "let's just cuddle."

Barbara cuddled up, still holding his hand, but now firmly. "Will we be together forever, Marcus?" she whispered. Marcus opened his eyes and stared ahead contemplating the question. "Why are you asking now, my love, we've only just begun?" He said, lifting her hand and kissing it.

"I'm afraid you will leave me one day, and I will be alone," she said, feeling a lump in her throat, and then crying into Marcus's chest. "I am sorry. I just want it to last forever. You and me forever."

Marcus lifted her head and smiled gently. "I love you like no other, and if and when our paths take a different direction, I will still be there for you. We are tied not just by our love, but by our deeds. I promised I would care for you and look after you, and I shall, my love."

Barbara closed her eyes and felt the warmth of his body wrap around her. For now, she was safe. For now, she could dream of how she would one day marry her lover, her protector, her brother.

They held each other in silence for a while, each contemplating the future. Barbara wanted to start an art collection, although Marcus was not sure how much she knew about art. "You are a philistine when it comes to modern art, Marcus!" She yelled at him not so long ago when she brought home a painting by Patrick Hughes, purchased with the money Marcus had given her on leaving University. Marcus stared at it for five minutes and just shrugged. "Sorry, Barbara I don't get it." She was furious but vowed to educate him in time. 'He will believe in me when I am a success,' she promised herself.

It was true, Marcus's taste in art, music and literature were more conservative than Barbara's. While he favored Mozart, Hayden and Tchaikovsky, she preferred Fleetwood Mac, Nina Simone and The Byrds. But when it came to art he realized he knew very little. He made a promise to himself to encourage her in this new venture if that is what she wanted, and maybe see if this 'contemporary art' phenomenon rubs off on him.

He was well aware they made an odd couple. He, quiet and reserved, conservative by nature; mostly a by-product of his past, he reflected. His past had taught him to be guarded and mistrusting. Keeping a low profile was the way to survive his past, and it had served him well for the most part.

The last few months, however, had been a revelation and a change of pace was what he now needed. Being around Barbara had given him a new perceptive on life. He was doing well at the Stock Exchange and his other 'activities' for MI5 were not over-taxing him. Time, he thought, to indulge himself in some more earthly pleasures now he had shaken off the guilt of his mother's unhealthy influences. After the initial shock of being 'taught' how to make love, he felt fulfilled for the first time in his life. His past anxieties were becoming a distant memory, and he was convinced he could lead a new and more gratifying life if he took the lead.

She, on the other hand, was young and twelve years his junior - but a woman of the age. A sixty's girl for sure. Clever, opinionated, irrational, fun-loving and not a care in the world. Old beyond her years in many ways - Rosemary and Nathan would be proud of her, he reminisced silently, his eyes smarting at the thought of his adopted parents. He quickly wiped away the embarrassment and kissed his lover on the cheek.

"What was that for?" she asked lazily.

"Do I need a reason?" Barbara returned his kiss, working her way across his face to his neck and shoulders.

"So," he asked, "have we finished cuddling?" Barbara's hand reached under his bathrobe. "Does that answer your question, my love?" she said, smiling.

Hoping for a long and pleasurable love-making session, Barbara, now fully aroused, pulled on Marcus's robe, but he suddenly held her hand over the tie. "What?" she asked confused.

Marcus still had some unresolved concerns about how Barbara was instructed in love-making by her former teacher, Ms Simone, at her boarding school. "Did Ms Simone have a last name?" He asked casually. "Of course. Why do you ask?" she sighed, looking even more perplexed, and with more than a hint of frustration.

"You told me you were one of three girls she educated. I was wondering if a reunion was possible - would you like that?"

"Marcus!" Barbara was shocked. "What have I unleashed? A 'Love Machine'. I am jealous already . . . but it is a marvelous idea. I'll give one of my old girlfriends a call to see if they have any idea where she is now, assuming she is not still at Chaucer's." Marcus smiled to himself and decided that love-making instruction with consenting adults could be a very pleasurable pastime.

*

Later that night Marcus woke suddenly, startled by a noise he thought he heard downstairs. Barbara was sound asleep and he did not attempt to wake her. Reaching into the bedside drawer he felt for Nathan Star's old service revolver and crept out of the bedroom into the semi-darkness of the hall landing. Was he being paranoid?

His nightmares did not usually involve the present - just the opposite, so what did wake him? Downstairs he stealthy made his way through the lounge to the kitchen.

The backdoor was secure and there were no signs of a break-in. He checked the latches on the two front bay-windows, but all looked in order.

Feeling annoyed with himself he started to return to bed when he heard a car pull away sharply. Three thirty-five was an unusual time for any of his neighbors to take a drive, even for the golf-crazy insomniac next door. Paranoia or simple caution? Either way, he felt uncomfortable with the prospect of an intruder, especially with Barbara in the house. He made a mental note to see what kind of burglar alarm he could get installed - after all, Barbara was starting to bring home some valuable pieces of art, albeit overnight, before taking them to the gallery. Satisfied he had covered all his options he crept back to bed, but sleep eluded him for the rest of the night.

Chapter Nine
1969

Barbara was excited at the prospect of seeing her old teacher again, and two of her old school friends. Now aged twenty-two she was a mature confident young woman, in control of her destiny, except, she hid the doubts she had . . . how long could this wonderful, exceptional relationship with Marcus last? The age difference was not the issue - they were a perfect match. Both highly intelligent. Fluent in several languages, and . . . well, there the interests finished really, although she was pleased when he agreed to join her on a trip to America over Christmas to seek out some new 'art'. And, they enjoyed making love . . . what was there to worry about?

Barbara had contacted an old friend, Naomi, a fellow student at Chaucer's boarding school for girls. Naomi came up trumps and gave Barbara Ms Simone's details. Soon a date had been arranged in late January for them to meet and have a reunion.

Barbara and Marcus arrived at Ms Simone's modern top floor flat at 7.30pm as arranged. "Barbara, how lovely to see you, my dear, do come in." The two women hugged and kissed. "And who is this charming gentleman?" Ms Simone asked, smiling at Marcus.

"Bonjour, Mademoiselle. Mon nom est Marcus. Comment allez-vous?" Marcus said, handing over a very expensive bottle of Champagne, whilst trying to sum up this enigma of a woman. Ms Simone was very attractive, Marcus thought. She had a quality of reserved beauty. Not stunningly striking, but a clean simple face that radiated warmth and friendliness. Her now blonde hair was shoulder length and bounced on her shoulders, and her slightly turned-up nose gave her a 'cuteness' that was very appealing.

"Ahh. You speak French. How nice." Ms Simone said, impressed with Marcus's grammar and fluency. "And Champagne. How lovely, merci."

"He speaks many languages, Miss, more than you and I put together," Barbara explained, taking off her coat and shoes.

"So, Marcus, come and meet our other guest." Simone led them into the lounge and Barbara let out a shriek of delight on seeing Naomi. They embrace and kissed, and both started talking at once. "Marcus, this is the beautiful Naomi, from Morocco. Her father is a Sheik," she added to impress.

"Bonsoir, Naomi. C'est un plaisir de vous rencontrer." Marcus said, kissing her on both cheeks.

"Are we speaking French all evening?" Barbara asked looking deflated at the prospect.

"Sorry, my dear. I was just being polite to our hostess. But I can go with whatever the language is this evening," he said, smiling seductively at his all-female audience.

"In that case let us keep it English, in case we have any misunderstandings," Simone suggested, offering Marcus a smile. "Now, let's get comfortable."

"Where's Claire?" Barbara enquired; hoping her other school friend would be there. "She called earlier to say she could not make it. There had been some family crisis, but she would not go into detail. Perhaps you can call her tomorrow to see how she is. She did sound a little distraught, but she said nothing more."

The two old school friends sat together on a sofa, while Marcus and his hostess sat together on another sofa, opposite. Barbara and Naomi talked incessantly, each admiring the other's attire, and both being exceptionally tactile to one another. Barbara caressed Naomi's arm, and within a short time, they were kissing and petting.

"How do you find that, Marcus? What are you feeling, do tell me." Ms Simone whispered, seeing the two women embracing intimately.

Marcus was surprised he was not feeling jealous. Maybe it was because Barbara was being intimate with a woman, and not a man, but he was sure he would have been OK with either sex, as long as he knew them. "I am . . . feeling aroused, Ms Simone," he answered, truthfully.

"That is good," she said, stroking his thigh and leaning into him until their mouths touched. "Let's take this to the bedroom where we will all be more comfortable."

The bedroom was larger than Marcus had imagined, and the only piece of furniture was an enormous bed with a beautiful intricate wrought iron headboard. Above it, a large gilt-framed mirror. The walls were painted dark mauve, and a luxurious white shaggy carpet adorned the floor, while ceiling lights provided intimate shadows which completed the atmosphere that would be essential for what was to come.

"Marcus, come and lay next to me," Simone said, patting the bed. Marcus removed his shoes and took his position next to teacher, who was wearing lime green fitted flared slacks and a white satin blouse. The two girls knew the routine and stood facing each other at the end of the bed. "The art of lovemaking is passion, seductiveness and tenderness. There are no time limits, no set routines. Every occasion should be different, but one rule is paramount . . . always undress your partner, tenderly."

On cue, Naomi caressed Barbara's face and kissed her. She unbuttoned the front of her smock dress, sliding the material off her shoulders, letting it fall. Barbara wasn't wearing a bra, and stood petite and beautiful in pink panties, her nipples erect, ready in expectation. Naomi kissed her friend's neck and mouth, then her breasts, one by one.

Barbara lifted Naomi's angora top over her head and unzipped her jeans. By now the two girls were giggling so much they collapsed onto the bed in hysterics. "We've never done this to a male audience." Barbara laughed out loud, and Naomi slapped her friend in jest on the bottom. "Right, get those Jeans off, woman," Barbara demanded, and pulled at the legs, relieving Naomi of them in an instant. Simone and Marcus took their cue from the girls, as Barbara crept up the bed towards her teacher and proceed to lick her feet, while the ebony-skinned Naomi removed her bra and straddled Marcus.

Simone was right, Marcus thought - time is of no consequence when making love. It should be as long as it takes, and in this instance, it took two hours before they surfaced for refreshments.

The two girls took a shower together while Marcus and Simone sipped Champagne in bed. "So, Marcus, how is Barbara? Is she happy now after the sad episode with her parents?"

"Yes, she . . . we . . . are very happy. She has been good for me, and I for her. I think we have saved each other to tell you the truth."

Simone touched Marcus's arm tenderly. "Thank you. I can see you are good for her." And she kissed him on the cheek sincerely and appreciatively. "Don't be a stranger, Marcus. You are welcome anytime." Marcus smiled at the invitation wondering if she meant just him or did the invitation include Barbara? After a moment of silent reflection, Simone rolled over on her side and fingered Marcus's chest. "So, you like the idea of making love to strangers, yes?" Marcus smiled and sank the last of the Champagne. "It is becoming more appealing by the day."

Marcus and Barbara arrived home the next day just after lunchtime, exhausted. Over pizza and coffee, Marcus told Barbara of his idea. She listened with interest, nodding in all the right places, but always looking on with mild amusement. "So, if I understand it, you . . . we, that is . . . seduce complete strangers and teach them how to make love, then give them loads of money."

Marcus sighed at her potted synopsis. "No, well, yes, but not quite the way you put it. It may be only once a year, or once every several years. It will depend on how the situation presents itself." He took Barbara by the hand and sat her on the sofa. "Imagine we are on a tropical island; swimming, snorkeling, sunbathing - having a wonderful time, and we meet a young couple, say in their twenties or thirties, who we make friends with. You are very good at making friends, so it would not be a problem."

"So are you, I see, after last night," Barbara replied, mockingly. "Simone was in awe of you, by the way."

"Really? The feeling is mutual, but to answer your question . . . yes, OK . . . so we make friends with them and invite them to . . ."

"Make love, Not War" Barbara interrupted, holding her fingers up in a 'Peace' sign. "The world is full of hippies wanting to Make Love, Not War, Marcus. It's going on all around us. Why would we be so different?"

Marcus didn't have an immediate answer to what he assumed was, in part, a rhetorical question, but he knew they would be different, and make a difference.

Chapter Ten

1970

Marcus's only public self-indulgence, outside of home, was his passion for fast cars. With the money he was making he could buy almost anything - and he did. A shiny new Triumph Stag convertible in British racing green. Barbara loved it, and they drove, with hood down, to Brighton every weekend. They explored The Lanes, famous for antiques and art shops, as well as bohemian bric-a-brac, sex emporiums and back street tattoo parlors, where Barbara acquired a very small, but intricate, oriental design on her lower back, plus some very intimate piercings.

The A23 London to Brighton road is narrow and very busy on weekends and Bank holidays, but Marcus still liked to test his driving skills by pushing the Stag to its limits. Barbara would raise her arms in the air, feeling the jet stream of warm air rush past her as the Stag reached top gear, and Marcus's adrenaline rush kicked in. Keeping up with a car of the Stag's performance would be difficult if being driven on a fast open road, but the driver of the black Humber Snipe was able to play catch-up with the Stag easily on the A23. On one particularly long stretch of road near Handcross the Humber made its move and indicated to overtake the Stag. Marcus had pulled back to a steady 50mph as he was looking for a turn-off to visit a charming old pub for an evening meal. The Humber pulled alongside the Stag, and Marcus caught sight of the driver's silhouette and did a double-take. Can't be, he said to himself, but in those few seconds of hesitation, the Humber swerved and clipped the Stag's offside bumper forcing Marcus to swerve. Barbara screamed as Marcus slammed on the breaks but skidded off the road into a side ditch. Barbara was flung out of the car and Marcus could be seen slumped over the steering wheel. The Humber continued its journey, pleased with the outcome that had killed two birds with one stone.

The plain white walls and frosted glass windows, coupled with that distinctive aroma only a hospital has told Marcus he was not only alive but tucked up in a private room. He gingerly moved his left arm, then right arm. Both seemed to be working. It was only when he attempted to sit up he felt the bolt of pain piercing his skull. "Mr Hartmann, what are you doing?" Asked a concerned nurse on entering the room. "You must keep still."

"Where am I? How is Ms Star?" Marcus wanted to know that first and foremost. "Is she OK . . . alive I mean?"

The nurse smiled politely, and gently pushed him back to a horizontal position. "The doctor will be with you shortly, but you have a visitor. It's not normally allowed but he had clearance." Marcus was wondering who this important person could be when Dyke stepped into the room. "Thank you, nurse. I shan't keep him long," he said, closing the door behind her.

"Dyke." Marcus uttered in surprise, "What the hell are you doing here?"

"Good to see you . . . especially after what happened. How are you feeling?"

"Fine. Apart from a headache."

"That will be the concussion. Apart from that, they say you are fine. You had a lucky escape, Marcus." Dyke said, settling into a bedside chair. Marcus turned to face him although his neck was painful.

"Barbara . . . is she . . ."

"She is fine. She was thrown out of the car into the ditch. She has a twisted ankle, some cracked ribs and concussion. It could have been a lot worse." Marcus sighed relief, although he was angry that she had been hurt at all. "It is not a coincidence you being here, is it, Dyke?" Richard Dyke frowned at the question. "No. And I am sorry you have both ended up in hospital. The truth is Kershaw escaped from Durham prison three weeks ago." Marcus could feel an overwhelming sense of anger building, coupled with disbelieve.

"I knew it!" he almost shouted, trying to sit upright. "I caught a glimpse of the driver and could have sworn it was Kershaw. Why the hell didn't you tell me he was out?" he insisted fervently. Dyke nodded in submission.

"He was on unsupervised outside work when he escaped. Probably wasn't planned, just spur of the moment. Being in the Borders, we thought he would head either West to Ireland, or East to Scandinavia. However, yesterday morning we got a call from his ex-girlfriend in Brick Lane. Said he had called in wanting money and a car, neither of which she had to give him, and was left severely beaten for her trouble." Dyke paused. Marcus was still listening. "We tried to call you but there was no answer. No one knew where you were. We have a policeman outside your house now."

"You think he will try again when he finds out he failed this time?"

"It's likely, considering he seems to have a vendetta against you - for killing Ferris for example." Marcus dropped back onto the pillow. His body was aching and his head was spinning with questions.

"The doctor said you can leave tomorrow, but Barbara will need to stay a few more days. I will make sure a plainclothes policeman keeps guard, just in case he comes here." Dyke said, offering some cold comfort. Marcus nodded, indicating he understood.

"I'll send a car for you around two p.m., yours is a write-off by the way. Hope the insurance was up-to-date." Marcus frowned. "I don't care about the car. I just want Barbara safe, and Dyke, make it before lunch tomorrow."

Later that evening Marcus attempted to stand. He hobbled to the door and checked the coast was clear. Following the signs to the women's wing, he checked side rooms searching for Barbara. Three doors down on the left he found her. She was sleeping and looked so peaceful. The thought of her experiencing a second car crash was too much to bear, and he prayed he would have the chance to come face to face with Kershaw sometime soon.

The next morning his doctor came and signed him fit to leave. After dressing he found Barbara's room again. This time a plain-clothes policeman was sitting outside. "I just want a minute with her." The policeman nodded and let him into the room. "How are you, my love?" Marcus asked tenderly, leaning over her to kiss her forehead.

"Bloody painful," she said, trying to sound amusing. "When can we leave?"

"I'm leaving this morning, but you have to stay here a little longer . . . plus . . . it's safer for you. It was not an accident, Barbara. I think it was the same man that killed your parents, and now he wants to get to me for what happened to Ferris." Marcus let Barbara feed on this information. Her facial expression changed from amusing to one of fear and confusion. "But I thought he was in prison."

"He was, until three weeks ago. The police will be watching you while you are here, and I promise to come and get you as soon as I can." Marcus held her hand and kissed her forehead, then her mouth, tenderly. "Do you want some books or magazines?" She shook her head in silence. A tear ran the length of her cheek. "It's happening all over again, Marcus. I can't lose anyone else . . . I can't." Barbara sobbed into Marcus's shoulder and he hugged her as tight as he could. "You won't, my love. I promise."

* * *

Kershaw read in the papers of a car accident on the A23 near Handcross which described the two occupants' as having a lucky escape. Very lucky, thought Kershaw. There will always be a next time. Now would be too soon - he will be on his guard. Best wait until he thinks he is safe.

1971

After the car incident, Marcus was always on edge - alert every time he went out for fear of being attacked. Although he possessed an outwardly calm persona, his state of mind was shaken by that event, resulting in him avoiding people as much as possible outside of business, and their pleasurable activities were put on hold.

*

A newspaper report caught Marcus's attention one day. It was not headline news, but nonetheless an interesting, although disturbing story. It caught his attention because it involved the same subject matter that got him involved with Daniel Mace, two years previously - child abuse. The report stated that Christopher Searle, residing near Wolverhampton was known to the police, and had previously been arrested on several charges relating to young boys. Searle was a swimming instructor, at the council baths, but was dismissed over some allegations of fondling young boys. On each occasion, not enough evidence was gained to ensure a conviction. The last charge for which he also escaped justice, involved the abduction and rape of a ten-year-old boy who died of his ordeal. The article stated it could not be proved that Searle murdered the boy, or if he died of his ordeal, resulting in manslaughter. As he had been charged with murder he was acquitted, and sentenced to three years, suspended, as he had already spent nearly that time on remand.

Marcus was shaking by the time he had finished reading. He knew then what he must do, again.

*

Since the *'accident'* a couple of years ago, Marcus vowed to keep a closer eye on Barbara. He would accompany her whenever she needed to look at a prospective purchase for the gallery, or even to the theatre or cinema, which Marcus rarely frequented.

Barbara was pleased with the attention of course but thought it rather excessive at times. She did, however, put his chivalry to the test one day. "Marcus, darling," she said, coyly, wrapping her arms around his waist. "Naomi and I are going to a music festival for a weekend. You will love it. We camp out, and hardly wash for two days." Unable to keep a straight face she turned to Marcus and saw his face full of horror, contemplating the scene.

"You are joking . . . tell me you are joking, Barbara." Marcus said in a stunned voice.

Barbara raised her head and looked Marcus in the eyes. "Of course, darling. We are staying with our friends, Mark and Christina, in Shepton Mallet."

"Not funny, my love." Marcus grinned and kissed her forehead. "What type of music festival is it? Anything I would like?" he asked, giving the idea some credence if Mark and Christina were to be involved.

"It's at a place called Glastonbury, and Mark told me over a thousand people turned up to hear all sorts of great music last year; rock, folk, blues - everything . . . and this year it's going to be even bigger, with David Bowie and Joan Baez . . . please come, Marcus, it will be fun . . . you do do fun sometimes." Barbara teased. Marcus's apparent enthusiasm suddenly became deflated. "I have never heard of the place, let alone any of the names you mentioned . . . I don't think it would be for me, but of course, you and Naomi go and have a good time." Barbara cocked her head, thinking. "You could always stay with Christina at the cottage while we girls have fun," she suggested, hoping the idea would appeal to his more licentious way of thinking.

"No," Marcus said, "you're a big girl now, I am sure a music festival will be safe. So go and have fun."

"And what will you do all weekend?" Barbara asked, out of curiosity.

"I am sure I can find a good book and curl up on the sofa," he replied, but really only thinking of one alternative option.

*

There was always a problem standing around, waiting and watching someone in the middle of the night, no matter the month; it was damn cold. How much longer was he going to be in there, and what the hell was he up to? Occasionally he would take one hand out of his coat and feel under his waistband for the old Colt M1911 he had bought from the back of a car and prayed it worked.

Now numb with cold, he retraced his steps back to his rental car and decided to wait for Mr Hartstein back at his hotel in the Dunstall Hill area of Wolverhampton.

He knew his chances of a clean shot were more promising when his hands were warmer.

Kershaw had been keeping a close watch on Marcus ever since his aborted attempt to drive him off the road. Not satisfied with just scaring him, Kershaw was prepared to wait until he was sure of a successful kill. He had spent the past couple of months renting a small bedsit in Thornton Heath, north of Croydon, but in easy reach of central London or south, to Shirley Heights. His ex. girlfriend had been less than helpful when he called on her for a loan, threatening him with the police. Bitch! He would deal with her again, after Hartstein. Ten years in a prison cell does wonders for sharpening the brain. Planning revenge. Revenge for the killing of his superior, and friend, Major Ferris. He would make Hartstein pay for his mistake, and remind him that it was he, Kershaw, who killed the Star's, not Ferris. Honor must be restored - the guilty destroyed.

Kershaw sat in his hotel room in the dark looking out over the car park, waiting for his target to return. What the hell was he doing? Kershaw had no idea that Marcus was handing out retribution of his own - how could he? There was some irony in the scenario that no one could appreciate. Each was dispensing their own punishment. One by a bullet - quick and satisfying - the other more measured and meaningful - more suited to the crime in hand.

Kershaw's patience was rewarded when a car pulled into the car park at 3.20am, and Marcus slipped into the hotel, eager for sleep. He had used a medium-size hotel where guests are just numbers and not remembered, hopefully. Kershaw's problem was finding Marcus's room number. He knew Marcus would recognize him on sight, so stalking was not an option. Plan B always worked - bribery. He had fed the receptionist a line that his brother had left his wife, and as a concerned relative wanted to help him through his problems.

Twenty Pounds usually does the trick, but this time it cost him fifty. Somehow the guy behind the desk was not one-hundred per cent convinced with Kershaw's story, but fifty pounds was a week's wages. "Room 305 on the third floor," he said, pocketing the cash.

Marcus dropped his bag on a chair and threw his overcoat on top of it. He felt thoroughly fatigued, as well as thankful that all had gone to plan, again. He had learnt from the Daniel Mace case first times can always be improved upon. On reflection, the removal of Christopher Searle went like clockwork. The cattle prod worked better when deployed at the side of the neck, Marcus noted, not sure if he would need it again, but worth remembering.

Searle had been a tall, skinny specimen of a man. Marcus had noticed how dry and thin his hair was as he hauled him up the stairs to the first-floor landing. Searle also looked undernourished, and Marcus, for a fleeting second, felt sorry for the wretched man, but quickly re-focused on the task at hand. Like Mace before him, Searle naturally begged for his life, although when Marcus looked into his watery eyes just before the fateful push, he sensed that Searle was resigned to his fate.

Marcus undressed down to his underpants, and was about to collapse onto the bed, exhausted when he heard a light tapping on the room door. Marcus put his ear to the door just in case he was mistaken. "Mr Star. Urgent message came while you were out this evening."

Marcus was suddenly awake. Adrenaline pounded through his veins - survival instincts kicking in, just as he had been trained by MI5. "Slip it under the door," he whispered. Marcus knew that Barbara was the only person in the world who knew where he was, and the name he used. "I need a signature, sir." Came the whispered reply. Marcus silently reached for his bag and grasped the cattle-prod, hoping the batteries had not run-out. "OK, just a second," Marcus replied, as casually as he could in a life-threatening situation. Marcus turned the key in the latch with his right hand, then the door handle. Kershaw burst in with all his strength as soon as he saw the door move an inch, pinning his prey behind the door.

Marcus's left arm was aloft with the cattle-prod and came down swiftly onto Kershaw's right hand causing him to drop the gun he was holding. Kershaw squealed in agony as Marcus grabbed his arm and dragged him into the bedroom, closing the door as quickly as possible, before kicking the weapon across the room.

Kershaw's next mistake was to turn towards Marcus, clutching his arm which was throbbing with an electrifying pain. With one direct fist to the chin, Kershaw collapsed onto the floor. He woke to find he was gagged, and tied to the bed, with no sign of Marcus. Kershaw struggled with his bindings to no avail and eventually collapsed back on the pillow wondering his fate. As soon as Marcus had secured Kershaw he had wiped the room of fingerprints and packed his overnight case. Satisfied everything had been removed and cleaned, he switched off the lights and closed the door behind him, leaving a *Do Not Disturb* sign hanging on the door handle.

On the M1 motorway, Marcus stopped at the Watford Gap service station and made a quick telephone call. "Dyke, there is a package for you in room 305 Best Western Hotel, Dunstall, Wolverhampton." He had considered killing Kershaw but preferred him now to serve his sentence, probably now without remission which gave Marcus some satisfaction. He realized too they had not exchanged one word. Perhaps that was for the good, he thought. A conversation could have led to raised voices and the outcome would have been a lot different. He sat in his car pondering the night's events, wondering if Kershaw's intervention would have any long-term consequences on his dealings with Searle. He was sure Dyke would not document his name regarding the tip-off, and the hotel did not have his real name - he drove south earlier than intended, but happy in the knowledge that he had not left any incriminating evidence.

*

From the Watford Gap service area, Marcus headed south on the A5, working his way eastwards and then south. It took him just over four hours to reach Tunbridge Wells, stopping once more for petrol and coffee.

He parked two streets away from his destination and finally knocked on the front door of the secluded terrace house at eight-fifteen. Simone opened the door gingerly. "You look awful," she said truthfully, and pulled him into her arms, closing the door before the neighbors spotted her visitor.

Marcus slept until early afternoon. "Hello," Simone said, as he entered the cozy kitchen/diner area. "Hungry?"

"Starving, actually," he said, kissing Simone on the cheek as if they were in a domestic husband and wife scenario. Simone knew better than to ask probing questions. She sat and watched him eat, reading the newspaper as he did. "Anything in here I should be looking for?" she asked, hesitantly, looking over the top of the tabloid. Marcus looked at her and frowned. "Why should there be?" he asked, finishing his brunch. Simone had no idea why Marcus had visited her at short notice, although his visit was a welcome diversion from her mundane life. Since leaving Chaucer's Boarding School for Girls, Simone had survived teaching French privately, and some translation work for a London publisher. Truth was, however, her life was a contradiction. She had embraced free love and sensual pleasures with both men and women, but she had never had a long-lasting meaningful relationship, with either sex. She was, if she had to admit it, jealous of Barbara, her one-time student, now living with a man more her age; a man whom she could commit to and devote her life to.

"Sorry, Marcus, just joking with you." Simone folded the paper and sipped her coffee. "That's the problem, is it not, with us, Marcus, being European?" Marcus looked confused. "What problem?" he asked with interest.

"Us . . . me . . . you . . . being foreigners here in England. I have been here for nearly twenty years, Marcus, and I still yearn to return to France. I have never felt at home here. Don't you feel the same, coming from Austria?" Simone asked, hoping she could get closer to this mysterious man.

Marcus thought of Simone as intelligent, charming and sensual, and without inhabitations. So what was worrying her? "I don't understand, Simone. I thought you were happy here. Why all this talk of returning to France." Simone shook her head and forced a smile. "You and Barbara have a wonderful relationship, and I suppose I am looking for *my Marcus*, but I have left it too late."

She stood to turn, not wanting Marcus to see her cry, but the sobbing could not be hidden. Marcus stood behind her holding her shoulders. "You could always come and live with us if you wanted to," he said, sincerely. Simone turned to face him but looked down, blinking away a tear. *"Je suis juste être stupide."*

Marcus tipped her chin upwards to look into her watery eyes. "No, you are not. I mean what I said. At least think about it, please. Besides, Barbara needs taking in hand, sometimes." Simone choked a laugh. "She does not," she said, playfully slapping his arm, then hugging him tightly. "Thank you, Marcus. I will think about it," she said sounding brighter, moving her arms around his neck, pulling him down to her moist and needy mouth, knowing she could never share him, with anyone.

Chapter Eleven

Detective Chief Inspector Eric Waldron read the post-mortem report of one Christopher Searle for the third time and sighed deeply. "What kind of monster goes around doing this?" he asked rhetorically.

"A madman, Gov." Was all the young DC Hicks offered.

"Mad or not, we have to catch this bastard, Hicks. From this report, he knew what he was doing. Having hung Searle, he apparently let the blood coagulate before removing the penis." Waldron stubbed out his fourth cigarette of the day, and it was only 11.00am. "Your average murderer would not know that. If anyone else had tried it, it would have resulted in a bloodbath. The hall and stairs would be covered in blood, but because he waited three to four hours hardly any blood was spilt. Bloody clever. I've never seen anything like it in my career, Hicks."

Waldron lit another cigarette. "We've got to keep the penis part out of the press, Hicks. As far as everyone else is concerned, Searle committed suicide - unbalanced by the guilt of his recent court appearance." Secretly most policemen were glad when a murderer or rapist is found dead, but the circumstances, in this case, gave DCI Waldron grave concern. "Hopefully, that will stop any copycats out there."

The weary detective looked old beyond his fifty-seven years, and the past week had added a further few unkind years to him. Seeing the crime scene and the expression on Searle's face was something he will never forget.

He had come up against all kinds of sick-minded criminals in his thirty-five years as a detective but never had he witnessed such a calculated murderous attack on another human being. "What else do we know about the victim, Christopher Searle?" he asked, focusing again, looking at Hicks for answers.

DC Hicks rubbed his forehead. "Guv, we know he was into young boys. Six acquittals over ten years for luring boys into his car or home and having sex with them, but in every case the defense tore the witnesses to pieces and the cases were dismissed. His last court appearance was for the murder of a ten-year-old boy. He was got three years, suspended for manslaughter." Hicks shook his head.

"So," Waldron said, "someone thinks he got off the murder charge and wanted revenge. Another grieved victim or a relative maybe, or a vigilante – God I hope not. Let's see what this new so-called National Computer System can throw up. See if any other forces have had a similar incident in the past ten years – that is, if all the information has been put into this new contraption."

"Gov, how do you want to play this? Priority or what? We are short-staffed as it is."

DCI Eric Waldron looked his young colleague in the eyes. "Whoever did this needs to be caught, Hicks. It's not a case of someone being stabbed or shot, for God's sake. The man was castrated and hung-up. That is revenge in any book. He's sending a message, whoever did this." The chief inspector leant back in his chair, stony-faced, and lit another cigarette. "And I want him before I retire, Hicks, and before he does it again."

* * *

DCI Waldron was to be denied his wish. Two years later another convicted pedophile was tried and released due to lack of evidence. Jamie Atkins, thirty-four, from Exeter was found strangled and mutilated on 6th March 1973 in his flat, where he lived alone. As with the other reported case, the police kept back vital information and reported the death as a suicide.

*

Marcus drove to Simone's house hoping she would be as welcoming as she had been a couple of years previously. He had not expected to carry out another killing but the news of Jamie Atkins crime left him with no choice. Again the courts had set free a man convicted of rape and murder of a nine-year-old boy who he had lured from a fairground to his flat, with promises of food and fun. Atkins and four others raped the boy all weekend. Atkins and his friends could not have known the boy had a weak heart. He argued it was not murder, the boy had just collapsed. Instead of calling an ambulance Atkins calmly dumped the boy's body three miles away back near the Fairground, where it was found the next day. DI Phil McKenzie, from Exeter, had traced the boy's disappearance from a witness at the fairground, and with some local knowledge of pedophiles tracked down one of the gang members who eventually confessed. Atkins was tried for murder but the jury was split, and he was acquitted. Atkins was the only one of Marcus's victims that caused him a problem - he lived in a flat with no loft access.

Atkins was a weak-looking character with bad teeth and callous eyes. The cattle-prod worked for Marcus as it had done previously, but once inside the flat Marcus had to think fast. There were no convenient wall fittings strong enough to hang a rope. Marcus looked around weighing up his options, which were virtually zero. The time was approaching midnight, and there was still a lot of activity in and around the flats on the rundown Moss Side area of Exeter which worried Marcus.

Atkins was stirring from the eclectic shock to his neck. With blurred vision he saw a shadow pass him and walk around the back of the chair he was tied to. Ten seconds later he was dead.

Marcus took the only action he could see fitting and broke the man's neck from behind. Now, Marcus had to calculate how long he had before anyone came looking for Atkins. After ninety minutes Marcus felt he could not wait the full three hours needed for rigor mortis to be at the level he needed to perform the cutting, so reluctantly, and as carefully as possible, took the new garden pruners and removed Atkins penis. More blood than usual escaped, but not as much as he had expected. He left Atkins tied to the chair and placed the noose around his neck, symbolizing the event he was denied, but leaving the message he wanted the police to see. After clearing all signs of him being there he left the pathetic creatures' flat at two-fifteen and drove eastwards.

Splinters of morning light found their way through the Venetian blinds into the bedroom. Marcus was naked, lying on his side facing Simone's back. He gently ran his fingers down her spine until she purred. He parted her legs and teased the Goosebumps on her inner thigh with his fingers. Parting her legs further he slid into her effortlessly, adopting the comfortable Curled Angel position where the two lovers could rock gently for as long as they wanted. Simone, however, had other ideas and needs. She rhythmically pushed back onto Marcus's groin, faster and faster, until they both explode at once. "That's what I am missing in my life, Marcus, waking up to that," she said laughing, but Marcus could not see the tears in her eyes as she bit her lip to stop herself from choking with emotion.

Six months after that visit Simone returned to France. She sent him a short note.

'My dear Marcus, forgive me. It seems, after all, I will be close to you, and have something to remember you by. Simone xx'

The postmark was Lyon, France. Marcus sat, eyes closed for hours contemplating the possible scenarios, but he knew that there was only one; the status quo would continue. He would help her if she asked for help. Marcus burnt her letter and the contents were never discussed, with anyone.

Chapter Twelve

1973

Marcus had prospered at the Stock Exchange, especially over the past six years working in foreign exchange investments, during which time major changes were introduced in the buying and selling of currency, and those in the forefront of this new free trade benefited rapidly.

His other work with MI5 had been slow to materialize, and Marcus even thought, hoped, he had been forgotten. The security services had been thrown into chaos in the early sixties with several of their spies being found working for the Russians, and other protocols had been put on hold.

It was two years after his meeting with Dyke he received a note: *'Unicorn, your owner wants you'*. His first assignment had been to silence an arms dealer in America. He had arranged to meet with the seller on behalf of the Provisional IRA. Security had been tight and Marcus had to wait two weeks for the right opportunity to present itself. In his report to Dyke, Marcus was critical of the assignment, saying his target was *'a very small cog in a big wheel'*, and named others higher up in the organization. Dyke had got what he had wanted all along - confirmation of the important names, although Marcus was never aware of his true role in obtaining this information.

Over the years Marcus had been given seven assignments in total, covering every continent in the World, and without exception, all had been executed successfully. Now Marcus wanted to live a normal life. He and Barbara were a good team, and they had built a lifestyle he did not want to jeopardize.

He had sent a note to Dyke but it had taken three weeks for a reply to reach him. Dyke's office had not changed much over the years in Great Marlborough Street, London, although this was only the third time Marcus had been invited to the *inner sanctum*. "Good of you to see me," Marcus said, accepting a cup of tea from Dyke. "I was wondering if you had received my letter."

Richard Dyke was looking his age. He had just turned sixty-four but looked older. Marcus had no idea of his age but thought he was looking tired. "Is everything OK?" Marcus asked, with more respect than he ever thought he would have for his surreptitious employer. Dyke smiled. "Yes . . . and no . . . but you're not here to talk about me, are you." He added, dismissing Marcus's concern.

"I want to retire. You've had use of me for nearly twenty years and I have done everything you have asked. My slate should now be well and truly clean." Marcus said, dipping a Garibaldi in his tea. Dyke sat, pondering this man in front of him, wishing he was him, so he could start over again, and maybe have a second chance at the top job. The Director General's post in 1972 went to Michael Hanley, and Dyke knew he would not be around when the position represented itself.

"Well, Marcus, that makes two of us. I'm leaving the service at the end of the year." Dyke said, soberly.

"Well, what will they do without you?" Marcus said, trying to lighten the tone of the meeting. Dyke smiled shaking his head. "I am sure they will survive. Too many changes going on anyway. Gadgets and machines everywhere now. I feel I am in a different world with all these young people coming in," he said, with more than a hint of bitterness in his tone, but then remembered his *alma mater* - *Nihil est sacrosanctum*. Marcus saw Dyke's lips form the faintest of smiles, before returning to the familiar sober facade Marcus was used to seeing.

"So," Dyke finally asked, after composing himself, "what will you do?"

"I have made a good living in the City, and I have other interests," was all Marcus was prepared to divulge. No matter how he felt about Dyke, he had to have some secrets.

The evenings were drawing in since the clocks had been put back at the end of last month. The single fifty-watt banker's lamp on Dyke's desk cast a shadow over the walls and ceiling, making the stark interior more depressing than usual. Rain started to trickle down the Victorian sash windows causing Marcus to shiver involuntarily. Dyke, seeming oblivious to Marcus's discomfort, opened a folder on his desk, and then looked back at Marcus.

"In answer to your request . . . yes, I think you can retire . . . but," and he looked back at the documents on the desk, "I need you for one last assignment, then you can go and live your life as you want to." Looking directly at Marcus again he closed the folder and leant back in his chair, hoping he had made the right decision.

1973

Marcus's destination was Armenia. His cover was that he was in the capital, Yerevan on business, and, finding he had some time spare, hired a Toyota Land Cruiser, and drove the three-hour journey to Gyumri, where he had heard there were some fine antiquities to be found, or sold, for the right price.

His target was a Russian arms dealer, Ernest Movsesian, fifty-four years old and leader of a vicious mob dealing in prostitution, drugs, guns, antiques and human trafficking, especially young girls to be sold too rich Middle Eastern countries. Getting close would be difficult, so Marcus had to have a water-tight, full-proof plan. As he knew something of Eastern European antiquities he used this as an excuse to visit Gyumri. He parked in the old historic quarter, behind a church, and near where he had been told Movsesian had a warehouse.

Rosa, with her mother and young brother, Sergei, had fled across the border from Turkey to Armenia, and hoped to eventually make their way to Georgia , and to a better life, if that were ever possible.

The Kurdish community in Georgia was stronger, with far less persecution than in Turkey. Rosa's mother felt it was safer to travel from Kars in Eastern Turkey across the Armenian border and eventually enter Georgia from northern Armenia, rather than the more challenging direct route over the perilous border mountains. Now in Gyumri, they were planning the final stage of their journey.

Rosa was twenty-eight, although she looked a sullen teenager to the casual observer. Her jet black shoulder-length hair was a tangled mess most of the time. Her clothes were in tatters and her only surviving warm garment was her heavy long-sleeved jacket, once brightly colored, but now faded and threadbare, and looking two sizes too large for her, due to her lack of nourishment. The full-length white skirt she hadn't removed in four weeks was nearly black, and her only pair of boots were beginning to show serious signs of wear. Her one prized possession she kept well-hidden was her Lira belt. Made entirely of gold coins, it was a wedding present five years ago, but the wedding had never taken place.

It was approaching mid-day and Rosa had only a few coins in her begging bowl. Not enough for a loaf, let alone enough food for three people for a week. Rosa was worried about her mother. She hadn't said anything but she was looking tired, and the thought of another week walking was not something she expected her mother to complete. The thought of being robbed, or worse, was also now a real possibility, so Rosa made the painful decision to try and sell the gold belt. Finding someone to give her a fair price would be difficult unless she could locate a Kurdish trader.

Rosa saw the tall blond stranger before he saw her. She kept her head down as he walked past her, only hearing the few coins hit the wooden dish after he had passed by. She looked up, bewildered, and watched him walk down the narrow street towards the main square without turning around, or even give her a second thought. When she looked back to the small space she occupied on the square rug, she saw lying near the coin dish a folded piece of paper.

Marcus reached for the address once more to ensure he was in the right area. He didn't want to ask directions too many times and arouse suspicion. The fact he was a tall blond European was beside the point, asking for Movsesian's warehouse too often may have someone alert him and send him into hiding. He felt in his pocket once more. Gone. He felt in the other trouser pocket. Not there. Jacket pockets. Back pockets. All empty. "дерьмо", he cursed and turned to retrace his footsteps. A few minutes later he recalled seeing a girl begging, and he had thrown her some loose coins.

She seemed so fragile and desperate, it was the least he could do, but she was not there when he turned the corner.

"Shit," he cursed again. He looked around trying to see which way she may have gone. Two streets were leading off the one he was in and she could have gone either way.

He looked down each in turn, scratching his head. He asked passers-by, "Have you seen a beggar girl just now . . . walking this way?" Each and every one shook their heads, and most were surprised to hear this blond stranger speaking Russian to them. Marcus walked several hundred yards in each direction, ending back where he started, where he last saw the girl.

Rosa stood staring at the grand entrance to the Alexandrapol Hotel. It's sweeping marble steps, inviting her in. Its gleaming tall windows open to the late summer sun, allowing the cool breeze to caress its occupants. Rosa fingered the coins again. With the money the stranger had given her added to the rest she had collected, there was enough for at least a bowl of soup and some bread. She had only taken two steps leading to the hotel entrance when a very large man in a black suit and sunglasses, blocked her path. "Get lost, Kurd. You cannot come in here." He said with a tone that was not open to discussion. Rosa was not going to argue with him and dropped her head to turn away when she felt a hand on her arm. Her first thought was the brute was going to push her down the steps, but when she looked up she saw it was the tall blond stranger looking at her with his electric steel grey eyes and a reassuring smile. Rosa felt light-headed, and if not for Marcus would have fainted on the hotel steps. "Come, my dear. Let's go in and have lunch. You look hungry." He said, staring directly at the burly doorman.

"You cannot come in with her." He almost spat out *'her'*.

"I think you will find I can," Marcus whispered, lifting the girl up and helping her towards the hotel entrance. She was not sure what was happening, or if she was in any danger from the bully or the stranger. "Keep walking," Marcus said calmly. "Nearly there."

The doorman was joined by another equally large man wearing a matching suit and sunglasses. "Where the hell are you going?" The second man asked.

Marcus replied in perfect Russian. "I was hoping to meet my friend Mr Movsesian for lunch, but if you don't want me to, then you can tell him." Both men froze on hearing Movsesian's name and then looked at each other. The first man spoke more meekly this time. "Well, in that case, I suppose we can make an exception for you and your friend, but not in the main dining room. Follow me." One of the men went through the large heavy glass double doors followed by Marcus and the girl, with the other man taking up the rear.

"It's going to be OK. What's your name?" Marcus asked the girl quietly, wanting her to focus on what was happening. She looked up, her large almond eyes almost hypnotizing Marcus. "Rosa Lala Jigarkhanian," she whispered back, "are you Russian?"

Marcus almost laughed but suppressed it. "No." He confirmed. Then added. "Whatever happens do as I say, even if you are not sure, do as I say. Do you understand?" Rosa nodded once.

"OK. You can eat in here. When Mr Movsesian arrives I will come and get you," doorman number two said. They entered the kitchen through the double swing doors, and the man called over to one of the cooks to give Marcus whatever he wanted.

The girl ate hastily at first; a bowl of soup, some fish and several bread rolls, some of which she stuffed into a pocket of her coat. Marcus sat watching this poor girl and realized the more he looked at her she was, in fact, older than he first thought, probably around twenty-seven or twenty-eight. Her eyes were bright, despite the dirt around them, and her mouth was wide and inviting. Even under her oversized garments, he could see she had a figure. Rosa saw him staring at her. "I know I look a mess. I've been travelling for weeks with my mother and brother. I have nothing but what I am wearing," she said sadly.

Before she had finished eating her fill, he had made a decision – he must help her. Maybe take her away from all this – take her back to England? *'Listen to yourself, man. Are you going soft?'* The sound of raised voices caused Marcus to refocus and to look through the glass lattice square in the kitchen door. He saw one of the burly doormen talking to two equally large men, who were definitely not hotel management by the look of their clothes. He turned to the girl. "Keep eating, say nothing. Understand?" She nodded, looking into the now finished bowl of fish soup.

Marcus stood just inside the kitchen door and placed one hand on his Walther PPL, mounted with a silencer, in his inside jacket pocket. The kitchen door opened and Marcus stepped into the man's path, distracting him from the girl. There was a fifty-fifty chance he had made a serious mistake with the girl, knowing Movsesian's liking for young girls, and the profit they make him.

"Mr Movsesian does not have an appointment with you," he snarled and reached for his concealed gun.

Marcus already had his PPL out and pointed at the man's head. "I didn't say I had an appointment, I said Mr Movsesian would be here for lunch. Now tell him I have something to sell that is so rare even he couldn't afford to pass it up. Tell him it's from Kazan."

Marcus sat down opposite Rosa. She was trembling with fear. "It's OK, I promise."

"Don't say that if you do not mean it," she answered factually. She looked away to ensure she was not being eyed by the cooks, but they were busy preparing ordered food for the restaurant. Rosa, unobserved, lifted her jacket, and Marcus glimpsed her pathetic mid-drift. She folded down the top of her skirt and revealed the gold Lira coin belt. "You can use this if you want," she offered, adding, "It is all I have."

Marcus recognized it immediately, but unless it was made with rare coins, it was not worth a great deal, especially to someone like Movsesian. "Thank you," Marcus said, genuinely touched that this girl . . . woman, would forfeit her most treasured possession. Rosa rearranged her clothes and smiled at Marcus.

"What is your name?" she asked.

"Marcus," he answered.

"And why are you here? Who is this man you want to kill?" Marcus was taken aback by the question. Rosa expanded. "You have a gun and you have asked to meet him. Is he a bad man?" she asked, almost relaxed by the sustenance.

Marcus breathed deeply. "Yes, very bad. And he will not think twice about killing me and taking you. Do you live far from here," he said, looking around the kitchen area, and for a plan B of escape.

"We lived in Turkey. I am travelling to Georgia with my mother and brother." Rosa said, suddenly feeling very frightened. Marcus closed his eyes for a moment. "I am sorry I got you into his. I won't let anything happen to you . . ." but his voice trailed off as he saw a new man come through the kitchen doors holding a gun, a machine gun.

"Come, both of you, now," he demanded.

"No. Not the girl. She stays." Marcus said with self- assurance.

"Do not argue or this can end now."

Marcus sighed and looked at Rosa. He held out his hand to escort her from the table to follow their new guide outside to a waiting car.

They were invited to get in the backseat of the first car, but not before Marcus was frisked and his PPL confiscated. One man patted the girl down and confirmed she was clean but a bit skinny for his liking. Marcus wanted to punch him but he knew he did not have the advantage, and let it pass, for now. He clenched Rosa's hand for all of the ten-minute drive to their destination, which was a small warehouse not far from where he had parked his car. Ernest Movsesian sat behind a long wooden pine table, covered with antiquities, but the lack of light made it difficult for Marcus to establish if they were fakes or not. Wooden crates stood stacked all over the place, and other tables held more objects ready to be packed in wooden crates. The low sunlight found its way through the old tiled roof and bounced across the low beams onto the floor.

Ernest Movsesian was looking older than his fifty-seven years. His rugged tan face and long wavy grey hair added another ten years at least. He wore thick-rimmed Ray-Ban's which he removed as Marcus and Rosa approached, flanked by two guards, making five in total, Marcus noted. Movsesian looked at Marcus and Rosa in turn. "Tell me why you are here in thirty seconds or they will shoot you both," he said eyeing Rosa, "but it would be such a waste."

Marcus counted to twenty. Rosa turned and stared at Marcus, seemly accepting her fate. Never to see her mother or brother again. To die a miserable death through no fault of her own. All she wanted were a few coins to buy food and move on to her new homeland, Georgia.

"Kazan . . . Our Lady of Kazan." Marcus finally said, after twenty-five seconds.

"You take me as a fool. It does not exist . . . ," he said, wondering if, for a moment, this stranger had new information. The famous gold Icon, Our Lady of Kazan has been a Holy Grail of Russian Icons since it was first discovered in the fourteenth century. Discovered then lost, and despite the legends and fables, no one knows where it is to this day.

"I would not presume to insult you by offering you the original object, although it would, of course, be a sensational discovery should it ever be found again." Marcus's words were measured, and he saw he had the war lord's attention. "What I have is the accepted copy dating from the eighteenth century. It was to be given to the Pope, John Paul V1 but on its journey from Portugal to Rome it was . . . re-patronized." Marcus said, laughing, hoping to ease the atmosphere around him.

Movsesian was looking intrigued and even relaxed a little in his high back mahogany chair. "I assume this was not made public knowledge, or I would have heard of it," he said, telling Marcus he was not going to be easy to dupe.

"Of course not. It would be an embarrassment to the Portuguese and flood the market with even more counterfeits. I can have it with you in one hour." Marcus went for the kill. Movsesian stood and came to stand in front of this stranger who had the nerve to work his way into his camp and make-believe he could offer him a priceless object. "How much are you asking?" Movsesian asked casually as if buying a new car.

Marcus did not hesitate. Dyke and his experts at the British Museum had valued the approved eighteenth-century copy at around five hundred thousand pounds. "Four hundred thousand, US dollars," he said, knowing he would never get anywhere near the actual value, even if he did have it, and could get out of this situation alive. Movsesian frowned. "You think me a fool. Even if you have it you will not get more than forty thousand on the open market."

"OK," Marcus said with a shrug, "we can negotiate around forty. Maybe throw in some firearms. I know some people in Spain in the market for some good quality merchandise." Movsesian was at least four inches shorter than Marcus so he had to look up into Marcus's steel-grey eyes, which did not flicker one bit. "The girl stays. My son and Ivan will go with you. Be back in an hour or she dies, as do you." Movsesian whispered so Rosa could not hear.

Marcus turned and spoke to Rosa, ensuring she understood what he was about to say. "I will be back, I promise. Do you understand?" and waited until she nodded.

Then facing Movsesian, "If she is touched . . . ," but Movsesian broke in. "If she is touched, it will be because you are dead. Do you understand?" Marcus nodded and turned to leave, followed by Movsesian's son, a six-foot lean young man with a boyish complexion.

"So," Movsesian's son asked as they got in the black Mercedes, "where exactly are we going?"

"Not too far, St. Mother of God's church. Do you know it?" Marcus asked.

"Of course we do," the boy replied, "but it will be packed for prayers by now," he said, looking at his watch. "It had better be there, or this is a one-way trip," young Movsesian said with a tone that was not lost on Marcus.

"So," Marcus asked, "you are the son and heir to your father's business interests, yes?"

The young man shrugged. "I suppose so. But he will have a long life. I am running it now anyway. He is too soft on moving into new business opportunities," he said, grinning. Marcus realized he may have underestimated this man. His boyish looks helped him to appear invisible, and his timid manner was just a ploy to suggest he was under his father's thumb, when in fact he was the paymaster. "What new opportunities does your father object to? Surely not protection or money laundering."

The young pretender smiled and then laughed. "No, no. We have been doing those for a long time. No, I mean women. Young women and especially babies. There is a lucrative market in the Middle East for them."

Marcus wanted to stop and take care of this sociopath then and there but remembered Rosa. She would not stand a chance if he left her behind. And what of her family. They would be worried sick about her by now and may be looking for her. Would they assume she has just disappeared or more likely been kidnapped? They knew the risks they were taking travelling through Armenia, and now they knew that price - losing a daughter, and a sister.

"Your father disapproves of this. The taking of women and children for profit?" Marcus asked, as subtly as possible. "Let's say he has no say in the matter. He is getting too old to worry about it," Movsesian junior smirked. "He is only interested in his precious antiques. Who wants those now? Guns and people are far more valuable," he snarled, showing signs of contempt for his father. Marcus realized he had touched a nerve, and that MI5 had got it wrong. Movsesian junior was running the business, not his father. "What is your name?" Marcus asked. "Endrit," he confirmed, "Endrit Movsesian."

The journey by car from Avetisyan Street to the old church should have taken no more than twenty minutes, but Ivan seemed lost. "What is the problem?" Endrit asked, becoming impatient. "I can't get any nearer. The place is full. I will park here and we will have to walk." Ivan confirmed.

Marcus noted Ivan pocketed the car keys in his right jacket pocket and had taken a pistol out of the glove compartment. Marcus was not sure if Endrit was carrying but assumed he was. "Ivan, stay here. It will be too suspicious if we all go in." Endrit said, taking control of the situation. Ivan was not pleased but obeyed his boss. They had parked in Komitas Square, a few streets away from the church. Marcus soon knew the answer as to whether Endrit was carrying. He felt the point of steel in the small of his back. "Remember your friend. She will make a good price." The boy sneered, pushing Marcus in the direction of the church. The wide imposing building dwarfed the two men as they climbed the steps to the entrance. Although dark outside, the interior was ablaze with candlelight, as well as sacred music, and the smell of incense. "Where is it?" Endrit asked impatiently.

"Safe. Under the Altar table. I hid it this morning when no one was around."

Endrit shook his head and rolled his eyes upwards. "Great. We will never get close enough."

"Perhaps you could make a donation," Marcus suggested, nodding towards the priest. Mass was nearly over and people were moving around the Nave freely, talking and shaking hands.

"Good idea, but you make the donation. Keep the priest looking away and I will find the Icon." Endrit whispered.

The two men walked slowly, side by side, towards the Altar.

Marcus reached the elderly bearded priest just before another parishioner stepped in his path. "Father," Marcus started to say, holding out his hand. "I am only here for a few days but wanted to make a small donation to the church orphanage."

The priest nodded, listening intently, and a little surprised a stranger would want to give him money. "That is most kind of you, my son. Our children are in need of much help and protection," he said, holding Marcus's hand in appreciation. The priest had his back to the altar, but Marcus could see clearly a young man standing behind the altar inspecting something he was holding, wrapped in brown paper. Marcus thought the boy would hide it under his coat and leave, but Endrit impatiently tore the paper aside and looked at the sad face of the Virgin Mary. He had not heard Marcus call out to alert the priest, as well as fellow parishioners, that there was a thief in the church, but was suddenly aware of many people advancing towards him. "Thief, thief," Marcus had shouted. "He's stealing an Icon from the church."

The priest had turned around, frowning, as he knew the church had no such Icons, although he secretly wished he had. "Stop him," Marcus shouted, rallying the congregation. The good congregation of Gyumri knew their church had no such object, but assuming one had been given to them, or more likely 'materialized' from nowhere, it was a sign that God had blessed them, and no man was going to take it away from them. Endrit looked around him, looking for an escape route, but there was none. He stared at Marcus, realizing, too late he had been duped. Endrit, seeing the crowd was in earnest, backed away, forgetting he had a gun, and gripped the precious fake in vain. The priest was now frantically trying to calm the situation. "Please, please, stop this." But no one took any notice and surrounded the now terrified Endrit. One man snatched the Icon from him, raising it above his head, before bringing it to his lips and kissing it. All was silent now, and Endrit assumed he could slip away, unnoticed. "No one steals from Our Holy Lady," someone shouted, and before Endrit could answer or defend himself, felt a hundred hands on him, pulling him away from the altar, along the long granite Nave towards the large old wooden church doors.

Marcus had exited via the east nave door, unseen amongst all the commotion. He walked swiftly in the shadows, tracing his route back to the car. Within sight of the car, he ran towards it, calling out. "Ivan, Ivan. Come quickly. The mob has gone wide."

Ivan shot out of the car, gun in hand. "What's happened?" he called over to Marcus.

"Endrit is trapped inside. There has been a riot of some sort," he panted, as if in pain, and bent down to catch his breath. Ivan didn't feel the blow when his head hit the stone pavement as Marcus flipped him up from the ankles, taking the man by surprise. Marcus grabbed the gun and retrieved the car keys from Ivan's jacket. He left the man alive in the boot of the car - he was not a target, and Marcus was not one to take a life without cause. He drove his own hired four-wheeled drive cautiously back to the warehouse giving himself time to work on a plan of escape, knowing that he may not be able to be so discerning with his targets as he had been with Ivan. He parked at the side entrance, hoping he could enter unseen. He checked the pistol he had confiscated. Six rounds and no silencer. Marcus took a deep breath and opened the car door.

He made his way stealthy to a side door entrance, praying it was open. The handle turned and he was able to see into the dimly lit warehouse.

Movsesian was sitting with his back to Marcus, looking down, reading perhaps. The three guards were to the right of the desk, all seated, playing cards. Rosa was seated in front of Movsesian and noticed the side door open. On seeing Marcus she tried to hide a smile. "What are you smiling about?" Movsesian asked with interest and looked behind him.

"Nothing. That was not a smile. I need the bathroom." Rosa replied convincingly. Movsesian shook his head. "No." The other three laughed aloud. "I'm not clearing up any of her piss, boss." Causing his companions to laugh louder. "I can pay," Rosa announced, catching everyone's attention. "Really? What with." Another gang member called over, smirking. "I can think of something," his friend offered with a wider grin.

"No, I really can," Rosa said, and stood, causing Movsesian to reach for his gun on the desk. Rosa slowly lifted the heavy braided jacket from her waist. The sight of her bare midriff caused the three men to stare longingly, forgetting their card game. Purposely, and slowly, she folded down the waist of her long bedraggled dress, exposing even more of her bare skin. Movsesian was also intrigued by now, but thought it a distraction, and was about to call a halt when Rosa slid out from her waistband the gold Lira belt. "Is this enough?" She taunted the men, holding the belt aloft, their eyes following every sway of the twelve gold coins. Marcus took his cue and crept along the inside wall until he was a few feet behind Movsesian. Rosa had seen Marcus approach and threw the belt in the direction of her guards. It had the desired effect. They each scrambled from their seats, with each of them rising in the air simultaneously reaching for the gold prize. Before they had noticed the shadow appear from out of nowhere, or registered the repetitious gunfire, each, in turn, slumped to the floor, dead.

Movsesian was slow to react in the surprise attack, and now felt the warm shaft of a fired pistol on his neck. "Who are you?" Movsesian asked calmly.

Marcus looked over to Rosa who was lying where she had fallen on hearing the gunshots. She crawled over to where her prized belt had fallen and retrieved it, inches away from one of the dead men. "Are you OK?" Marcus asked with a smile, hoping to reassure her that somehow, she was safe. Rosa nodded and stood to replace the belt where it belonged. "Where is my son?" Movsesian asked impatiently, but with a hint of fear in his voice. Marcus remained silent. He looked at Rosa and smiled gently, then, indicating with his right hand, holding the gun, to turn away whilst dressing. She jumped at the sound of the gun.

Although she suspected it, it was still alarming to hear and at the same time reassuring. "Quickly, now," were the only words he spoke. Rosa composed herself and turned to see Movsesian slumped over his desk. His thick-rimmed glasses all askew and cracked. A pool of blood stained the book he had been reading. Marcus could see she was frozen, not with fear, but with confusion. "Don't look. He was a cold calculating evil man. His reign is over." Rosa looked up from the dead man into Marcus's cold steel eyes. "There will be others. There are always others," she said, unemotionally.

"Come, we must hurry," Marcus said, picking up his gun from the desk. "The car is in the side street, and I want to get over the border to Turkey as soon as possible."

"Turkey!" Rosa questioned with alarm. "We have just come from there. I am not going back. You must find my mother and brother so we can continue to Georgia," her face was full of fear and confusion and her eyes swelled with emotion. Marcus sighed and nodded. "You are right. I am sorry. We will try and find your mother, but come now before we are discovered." And took her hand, squeezing it gently, wondering why he ever agreed to one last mission.

*

Ivan woke with a splitting headache and a sense of disorientation. It was dark, very dark. He was obviously in the trunk of his car with no apparent means of escape. He pushed with his feet at the only area that would allow him freedom - the back seat. Several hard pushes and he was in the back of the car. Quickly, he searched for his gun, but it had obviously been taken. He realized he was where he had parked, close to the church, but the streets were remarkably quiet now for early evening. No cars passed and nobody was walking by. He stumbled his way to the medieval church and towards the impressive marble entrance, flanked by two enormous brick bell towers. Ivan froze, rubbing his eyes to make sure he was seeing right. Opposite the church on the other side of the road, there was a man tied to an old cherry tree. Around the man's neck, Endrit's neck, hung a scrawled note. *'For thieving from God's house'.* Ivan stared at his friend whose arms had been tied behind his back. Ivan considered himself a man of strong character, but the sight of his friend hanging there turned his stomach, and nausea overcame him as he turned away in anger.

*

"We must get out of town now. There are bound to be others, and . . ." Marcus paused in thought.

"And what?" Rosa asked.

"One of the men who came with me, earlier, he will come back soon."

"What about the other one. The old man's son?" she asked gravely.

Marcus shook his head. "He won't be coming back. In fact, you could say he found religion. Now let's go, otherwise if we are caught they will probably take you away, and not back to your mother. Do you understand?" Marcus thought she could not possibly understand. What in hell had he got her into; all for wanting to help someone. "Yes, OK," she suddenly said. "I understand." Marcus wanted to smile reassuringly but knew it would be a false gesture.

He looked around the warehouse once more before heading for the side door. Back in the Land Cruiser he retraced his route to the old quarter to where he had originally seen Rosa begging. It was now dark and being unfamiliar with the town he was soon lost. "I am not sure where we are Rosa. Can you remember where you last saw your mother? A landmark or something." Rosa was looking anxiously out of the window for something she could recognize, but they had only been in the town a couple of days and were not familiar with any of the roads.

The headlights nearly blinded Marcus in the rear-view mirror and he had to swerve to avoid crashing. "What was that?" Rosa asked. Marcus concentrated on the road ahead, putting his foot on the accelerator. "Hang on tight. I think they have found us," he shifted into top gear and headed for the main road. "I am sorry, Rosa, but we have to leave, now." Allowing himself a glance at the terrified woman next to him, he reached out to hold her hand. "I promise I will try and find your mother and brother when it is safe." He said with as much assurance as he could under the circumstances. Rosa nodded. "OK. When it is safe," she repeated. Marcus nodded and squeezed her hand once more before notching up the speed.

Ivan had stopped a passing car and dragged the driver out. He then stopped at the warehouse to report what had happened but was not prepared for the scene that had greeted him. "He will pay for this, I promise," he spoke solemnly to his former boss and crossed himself for the second time that evening before collecting a small arsenal of firearms from the back of the warehouse. Ivan drove around the old town in the stolen car looking for anything or anyone out of the ordinary. He didn't care how long it took; he was fueled with revenge and time was not an issue. His patience paid off.

He spotted the Land Cruiser a hundred yards ahead crawling along - not making any attempt to escape. Ivan thought for a moment he was wrong about the car, but as he approached he saw the Yerevan number plate, which told him it must be a hire car. He accelerated, reaching 50, 55, 60 mph in seconds, with headlights ablaze.

Marcus headed south, out of town, towards the nearest border crossing he could find into Turkey, then, well, then what indeed. He was thinking too far ahead. His main concern now was to rid himself of this avenging warrior. They drove at breakneck speed over the flatlands of southern Gyumri before reaching the extensive Arpacay Reservoir which divided the two countries.

"I need you to get in the back and lay low. I have to stop him otherwise we will never be rid of him." Marcus said without looking at Rosa. Marcus knew he was about one minute in front of Ivan which gave him a brief window to pull over and allow Rosa to hide and position the car behind a row of waterside buildings.

Three minutes gone and there was no sign of his pursuer. Had he given up? Decided the drive was not worth it? Marcus doubted it. He would have pursued his prey until the final outcome, and he was sure Ivan was of the same mind, but where was he? Ten minutes now and Rosa was getting a stiff neck. She peered out of the window but all she could see was darkness. She curled up on the back seat again hoping this would soon be over, and if she would ever see her mother and little brother again. She could leave now, and make her own way back to town and try to find them. Who was this strange blond man she had entrusted her life with?

The past few hours had seen her in life and death situations, but he had come back for her each time and saved her. If she went with him now, where would she spend her life? How could she cope in another country, with strange customs and language?

It would be a life so different, so alien to the simple Kurdish upbringing she knew, but yet, what if she was loved and looked after, away from poverty and persecution. Surely that was worth considering.

Ivan was driving flat out and had not lost sight of the Land Cruiser's lights for eight miles. He guessed, by way of the road he was on, Marcus wanted to cross the border somewhere soon into Turkey. He could not get the image of Endrit out of his mind, trussed up on that tree with that sign.

He had stumbled across the road towards the church seeking answers. How? Why, had this happened? Ivan pushed open the tall heavy wooden doors to the main entrance and immediately saw the church was packed full to capacity. Men, women, children, young and old alike, all sitting in an eerie silence, praying. No music or chanting. No sermon or palms. Just silent prayer. Ivan walked slowly down the Nave towards the Altar where the priest was standing with his back to the congregation. No one looked at him as he walked. Everyone seemed to be staring straight ahead at someone, or something. He reached the priest. "Father, what happened here? Why was my friend killed?" he whispered.

The priest crossed himself and slowly turned to Ivan. Speaking quietly, as if in a trance. "My son, a miracle happened in our church today. The Lord gave us a symbol of his love. Look." Turning to Ivan he pointed at the icon, Our Lady of Kazan, hanging behind the altar screen.

"But, but . . . that's not real Father. It's a fake . . . you must know that." Ivan tried to make him understand, taking hold of the priest's shoulder, and shaking him. The men in the front row of the congregation made to stand, ready to protect their Sacred Icon for the second time that evening, but the priest raised his hand and they returned to their seats. "My son, they believe it is real. They believe it is Sacred. Who am I to dissuade them differently? We have never been blessed with such a significant sign from God. I cannot change our fate now even if I wanted to, as I am sure you have witnessed." Indicating to Endrit's fate. Ivan shook his head and turned to walk slowly back up along the nave. Not one man, woman or child glanced at him. Their faces beamed with the miracle that they believed had been bestowed upon them, and he was glad to have left there in one piece, but in his heart he knew nothing could ever be Sacred again after what he had witnessed that day.

Now he was within minutes of seeking the revenge his friend and boss would what. The reservoir was an ideal spot to make them disappear. He smiled at the thought. However, his guilty pleasure was short-lived as the car suddenly slowed, and spluttered to a stop. Ivan turned the ignition, stamping on the accelerator, but nothing happened. Then he saw the petrol dial was reading EMPTY.

Marcus waited another five minutes before returning to the car and easing Rosa out of the back seat, rousing her from much-needed sleep. "I think we can continue, safely now," he confirmed. Rosa leant on his shoulder and hugged him, then reached up to meet his face and kissed him on the cheek. "Thank you. I will never forget you."

Rosa turned and started to walk back to town and find her mother. "What are you doing, Rosa?" Marcus called out, astonished and surprised by her sudden actions. "I must find them. They will be looking for me," she cried without looking back. Marcus caught her arm and turned her, seeing her eyes full of tears and waning hope.

"They will take you, or worse, kill you, Rosa. You are not safe. I promised I will find your mother and brother one day, but for now, we have to get back to England, where I can make arrangements. Please understand, Rosa, this is the only outcome." He held her by the shoulders hoping he would not have to force her back in the car.

Marcus drove through the night to the nearest airport in Northern Turkey, Kars, where they boarded a flight to Istanbul. They walked through the lobby of the Hilton Hotel, past the concierge and into the lift without incident.

Rosa had never seen such a large bedroom with a separate toilet, let alone a bath. "Now," Marcus sat her on the bed looking at her so she understood, "I need to get you some papers so we can get you out of the country. This will take a few days so you must stay here."

Rosa nodded. "Where to?" she asked. "What do you mean? Where am I going?"

Marcus smiled. "Somewhere you will be safe, England."

*

Marcus knew someone he could trust in the British Consulate and arranged a temporary passport in the name of Rosa Chapel. Four days later they arrived back in England.

Marcus had bought her some clothes and other women's essentials on a rare day out shopping before they left, but all she had just now was what she was wearing, and carrying in her small suitcase. "Where are we, Marcus?" Rosa asked.

Over the last week, she had slowly accepted her new fate. She looked upon Marcus as her shining knight having rescued her from a terrible existence; fleeing her homeland to travel hundreds of miles to a supposedly better life in Georgia. She thought about her mother and brother every day and knew Marcus would find them as he had promised.

Marcus rang the bell of his own house that he shared with this step-sister, Barbara.

Barbara opened the door. "Hello my dear, you must be Rosa. Come on in." From that day on Rosa lived with Barbara and Marcus. Living and learning a new way of life. Experiencing the better things in life – things she could never have envisaged would be hers. Freedom, clothes, money, cars and importantly, love.

*

Ivan walked the thirty miles back to town. Grim determination clung to his face like a rash. The warehouse massacre scene was playing over and over in his mind as he willed himself to find out who had done this heinous act of murder.

Back at the warehouse the bodies of his friends, as well as his boss, Movsesian, had been laid out side by side. He walked slowly past each of them, crossing himself as he did so, and finally, standing in front of Movsesian, vowed his revenge.

PART TWO

Chapter One

1975

Rosa settled into her new life surprisingly well, although she yearned to know if her mother and brother were safe. She adored Barbara, and the house, and her bedroom. She had never had such a large and opulent room of her own. Her life back in Turkey was light years away from Shirley Heights. Her father, who was Russian, had died of an illness when she was ten, so was forced to work in a factory while her mother looked after her six-month-old brother. The hours were long and the pay hardly covered the price of food, so to have new clothes and a warm bed was the height of luxury for Rosa.

She thought of her mother every day, anxious at leaving her without any word. Barbara had found her the nearest Catholic Church for her to visit, and, although not Orthodox, was much comfort to her. Marcus had tried to get word to her mother before they had left Istanbul, but there was no way of knowing if the message got to her. Rosa prayed each night for God to keep them safe and that they would be reunited one day. Marcus had persuaded Richard Dyke to supply her with a new identity under the name Rosa Chapel. This was a precautionary measure should the wrong people come looking for her. It was, Marcus thought, highly unlikely, but he wanted her to be safe, especially, after the Kershaw affair.

Marcus suggested a program of learning, sharing the duties with Barbara, who was fluent in German, French and Italian, as well as knowledgeable in literature, history and art, and was also a keen watercolourist, potter and cook.

Rosa had had some basic education when she was younger. She could read and write using the Cyrillic alphabet, but now had to master reading and writing all over again if she was to stay in England. Rosa was a willing pupil. Within six months she was speaking English to a good standard, and was keen to learn other subjects that Barbara was proficient in. The first few months were like an extended holiday. Barbara took her to London to see all the sights, and of course, used any excuse to go shopping. The two women loved to shop, and although Croydon was the closest town with some good stores, London was the place to shop seriously. Oxford Street, Bond Street, Knightsbridge and Carnaby Street were all favorites, and Barbara spoilt Rosa rotten. Although Rosa was a mature twenty-eight-year-old, she was overwhelmed by the variety of shops and merchandise on offer in a city like London.

She had never thought about fashion – what to wear was whatever she could afford, or find, and could not be fussed about size, color or looks. The first time she tried on a dress she laughed out loud at her reflection – she didn't recognize herself and quickly changed back into the jeans she was more comfortable in.

If she wanted Jeans, then Barbara ensured she was wearing the right ones; FCUK, GAP or River Island, plus she would suggest more fashionable tops and accessories until Rosa eventually found her own *'look'*. Rosa was keen to ask questions and wanted to be corrected on any mistake she made, in language or etiquette. After nearly a year one aspect of the Marcus/Barbara household she was confused about was that why a brother and sister slept together. One hot August afternoon the girls were sunbathing in bikinis on the patio in their secluded garden. Barbara was reading 'Salem's Lot, by Stephen King, whilst Rosa was listening to Abba on her new cassette player, a birthday present from Marcus. Barbara went inside to answer the telephone but returned five minutes later looking very annoyed.

"What is it, Barbara? What is wrong?"

Barbara didn't answer immediately as she was still playing over the conversation she had just had with Marcus. "That was Marcus. He wants to move away from London. He's buying a cottage in the country, miles from here." And she wiped a tear from her eye.

Rosa reached out and took Barbara's hand. "You will still have me. I know what's it's like to not see your brother." Hoping in some way that was comforting. But Barbara did not look reassured. "Rosa . . . he wants *you* to go and live with him."

Rosa looked puzzled for a moment, not sure if she understood right. "Go, live with Marcus. What about you? I want to say here, with you." And Rosa felt a wave of depression come over her she had not felt since she was forced to leave her own country to look for refuge in Georgia. Barbara tried to smile. Her eyes smiled but her face was unforgiving. "You can still see me Rosa, and come and stay whenever you want to. It will be good for you. He needs you . . . he needs." But she could not find the words to express Marcus's needs.

Rosa squeezed her hand. "If that is what you want, I will obey. I will treat him like a brother like you do."

"You do not have to *'obey'*. You have a choice now; you have *'free will'*. Do you understand? As for treating him like a brother, he would like that."

"In the same way you do . . . sleeping with him." Rosa asked, coyly.

Barbara laughed out loud. "Yes, Marcus and I make love, regularly. We love each other and I would do anything for him. In a way, he saved me as well, just like you, so I look to him as a brother, friend and lover."

"In that case, I will do the same, if it is allowed, and he wants me."

"You are very attractive, Rosa. Anyone would want you, but you must learn to discriminate . . . sorry, choose carefully when it comes to a partner."

Barbara paused to see if Rosa understood her, and saw she was listening carefully. Barbara reached out to touch Rosa's belly button and gently circled it with her finger. Rosa did not object and leant back on the lounger. "Have you ever thought about a piercing?"

"No, but I would like one like yours and a tattoo perhaps."

Barbara looked thoughtful for a moment. "What about your bikini line?" she said, moving her hand slowly over Rosa's belly to the top of her bikini."

Rosa responded to the touch as Barbara had hoped. She slid one finger under the briefs and then another, and another until she found the top of her pubic hair.

"How about we start with an American cut, just to see how you like it, and progress from there," Barbara told Rosa to go for a shower, and come up to her bathroom in the en-suite bedroom.

"OK, let's start. Off with the bikini."

"All of it?" Rosa asked innocently. "It will put you in the right frame of mind and you will feel more comfortable," Barbara assured her, but also wanting to see her beautiful body. Rosa stripped and laid down on the soft bath towel. Barbara trimmed carefully and shaved evenly until she was satisfied with her creative work. "How does that feel?"

Rosa stood and looked at her new genital haircut in the bathroom mirror and smiled. "It feels good, but I don't know how it is supposed to feel."

"Well, I can remedy that." Barbara slipped off her bikini top and stepped out of her briefs and parted her thighs so Rosa could see the shaved pussy Barbara was sporting. "Mine is a little different. It's a part Brazilian. A full Brazilian is totally hairless and very sensual."

Rosa's gaze moved from Barbara's vulva to the rest of her sumptuous body. Although ten years older than Rosa she still had firm ample breasts and a shapely figure. She imagined Marcus touching her friend and caressing her soft pubic region. Rosa looked down to Barbara's open thighs and reached out to feel the soft thin hair and sensitive lips of her vagina. Barbara took her hand and Rosa thought she had misjudged her, but Barbara led her out of the bathroom into the bedroom. "It's more comfortable here."

Two hours later Rosa was cuddled up next to an exhausted Barbara. "So, what did you learn in school today?" She asked. Another two hours later, Barbara had her answer.

In the quiet of the evening and the warmth of each other's bodies washing over them, Rosa felt she was the luckiest woman in the world. She would love Marcus in every way and he will be forever grateful.

"Rosa. How would you like to go to the seaside?"

"The Ocean you mean? Yes, I love the sea."

"Not exactly the Ocean, more the English Channel. Brighton in fact - you will love it."

Chapter Two

Rosa had not travelled far out of Croydon since she had been 'rescued' by Marcus, but a visit to Brighton was exciting her as if she were a five-year-old.

"I am looking forward to seeing the sea," she said, for the hundredth time, as she looked out of the train window. The journey by train from Croydon to Brighton was far quicker and more relaxing than taking the car and gave Rosa a further insight into the southern English countryside. Her childhood memories of Turkey were vast farmlands and bleak mountains. She loved the sight of the green Sussex hills and the spread of pine forests as far as the eye could see. They walked arm in arm to the seafront, where Rosa almost ran across the busy main street, down the stone steps and onto the pebbled beach. She stood there, captivated by the sound of the heavy waves crashing on the shore. "Rosa," Barbara called from the upper-level sidewalk, "Come back. You'll get blown away down there."

They ran back into the main shopping area and found the old town, famed for its narrow 'lanes' with Bohemian shops selling everything from clothes and jewelry from India, Thailand and all places due east, to antique shops, hairdressers, coffee bars, bookshops and a tattoo parlor. "Hey, Rosa, how about a piercing with your tattoo?" Barbara said, clutching Rosa's arm. You liked mine, didn't you?"

"Will it hurt?" Rosa asked, anxiously.

"No, I promise. As long as we use a reputable shop and this is one I recommend."

Rosa followed her friend into the strange world of a tattoo parlor. The walls were decorated with hundreds of designs from Angels to Devils, waterfalls to butterflies - every conceivable subject was there for the choosing. "Rosa, this is Annuska, the best tattooist in England."

"In Europe, please," she corrected her friend, laughing aloud. "So, what can I do for you today, my dear Barbara?"

"Not me, Rosa here. She's looking for a piercing, and maybe a small design, somewhere discrete, if you know what I mean." Barbara whispered.

Annuska looked Rosa up and down. They were a similar age but there the comparison ended. Annuska was around five foot four with bright pink short hair, orange lipstick and heavy mascara, with several piercings on her ears and lower lip, plus a nose ring. "Where is the piercing to be," she asked Rosa. Rosa looked at Barbara for guidance, shrugging. "We thought," Barbara started to say, "one navel, and one may be somewhere more private. Can you do that here?"

"Yes, of course, but I need to close the shop for an hour. It will have to be during a lunch break." Annuska confirmed.

Rosa, meantime, was staring at a most beautiful tattoo design high up on the back wall of the shop. The more she looked at it, the more it seemed to come alive.

The long vertical design was intricate and colorful. A unicorn's head topped the illustration. It's long white mane cascading downwards to become entwined with ivy and roses, circling a Celtic cross rising out of an angel's golden wings. "Can I have this one, Barbara?" Rosa asked without looking away from the wall.

Both Barbara and Annuska followed her gaze to the image on the wall. "Wow! That's . . ." Barbara started to say. "Expensive," Annuska added, looking at Barbara. Rosa refocused and stood in front of Barbara like a child in a sweet shop. "Please, Barbara. I love it," she said, begging.

Barbara sighed, and Rosa knew she would have her prize. She hugged Barbara tightly and kissed her again and again.

"OK. Let's talk detail," she said, holding Rosa's hands. "How long would it take, Anna?"

"About five or six sessions. And it would not be without . . . discomfort," she said, hoping Rosa understood. Rosa nodded. "Yes, I understand. It will be with some pain, but it will be worth it," she agreed, admiring the colorful collage.

"OK, come back in an hour and I will do the piercing. Then we can arrange dates for the bodywork, OK." Anna said, pleased with her new customer, and the sale of a very expensive piece of artwork.

The two women walked around the town some more, but the early September weather was atrocious, so they took shelter in a nearby pub. "Are you OK with the tattoo?" Rosa asked, realizing only now how much it was going to cost.

"Of course, Rosa. I said you could have anything, and I meant it." Barbara confirmed, smiling confidently. "Anyway, Marcus will be paying." And she laughed aloud, which caused others to look in their direction for a moment. One customer, however, looked longer at the two women sitting and laughing together. He was wondering if they were just friends or lovers. Brighton was starting to become a magnet for gays, and the Gay Pride movement had held several small parades in the town for the past few years. "Ladies, can I buy you a drink?" The stranger asked, standing over their table.

The girls studied the handsome stranger. "Sorry, we have an appointment in ten minutes. Perhaps another time." Barbara explained, politely. "That is a shame. I was wondering if you ladies may like to . . . spend some time with me." The man said, now smirking, looking at each of them in turn. "Come on, Rosa. Time to leave I think." Barbara suggested, and they stood, ready to brace the rain once more. The man blocked Barbara's exit. "Don't be like that. I'm only trying to be friendly."

Barbara could smell stale tobacco on his breath now he was close, and she leant back to avoid the obnoxious odor. "I said we are leaving. Now stand aside or I will shout rape," she said, looking him squarely in the eyes. The man hesitated, then stepped aside. "Maybe after your appointment?" He tried one more time.

The women hurried out of the pub into the rain. "He was persistent," Barbara shouted above the wind. "Yes, but he was good looking," Rosa shouted back.

They reached the tattoo parlor just as Anna was locking up for lunch. Barbara looked back along the lane to see if they were being followed, but could not see the man from the pub. "OK, let's get piercing," Anna suggested with a smile. "Follow me."

Rosa undressed in the small back room. There was only a chair for her and a stool for Anna, so Barbara stood and watched. "What do you think? Labia or Clitoral hood?" Anna asked as if Rosa knew the difference.

"I think clitoral. It's neater and ideal for the first time. Fit her with a bar, and I will get a selection of heads." Barbara replied, looking at Rosa for approval. "If that's what you think, then OK, Barbara. I'm in your hands," she smiled and prepared herself for the procedure. It was all over very quickly. Anna was gentle and took great care to explain how to look after her new adornments, including the navel ring. "You can come here for the tattoo, or I can come to you. Where do you live?"

"Near Croydon," Barbara confirmed, "but I will pay all expenses, so I think you should come to us."

"OK. That sounds good. I will call you when I have the designs ready. The first session may take two hours, but others probably an hour at the time, with around four to six days actual tattooing." Anna suggested.

The two women returned home exhausted, but happy. As Rosa was still sore she decided to lie down for a while and dream of the body art that will soon decorate her. Barbara ran a bath and soaked herself in sweet-smelling chamomile and lavender, considering how life would be without Marcus. She knew she had plenty of pastimes to keep her busy and her business was doing well, despite the recession. She was a strong independent woman making her own decisions and living the life she had chosen, to the full. That choice also included the conscious decision not to have children. Marcus had never touched on the subject, but she had made her mind up many years ago. If her parents were alive her life would probably have taken a different path; getting married and settling down as the perfect suburban housewife, and mother. Marcus, for his part, considering his treatment at the hands of his parents would not have wanted children, and to her knowledge, has never sought to be near to or be overly friendly with them. The one thing he does do with a passion, however, is to seek justice for them whenever he sees evidence of abuse that has gone unpunished. That justice, to her knowledge, had been carried out at least four times over the past twenty years.

Barbara stirred momentarily from her relaxing slumber thinking she must check on Rosa soon, but her thoughts returned to the time when Marcus took revenge for one boy in particular; her friend's young brother, Simon Mace, back in 1969, when the justice began. Claire Mace was at boarding school with Barbara and Naomi, and was one of Ms Simone's circle of special pupils. She should have been at the reunion they had arranged for Marcus to meet Ms Simone, but she didn't come.

Later, Barbara learnt her brother was being abused by her uncle, Daniel Mace, her father's brother. On hearing this story Marcus persuaded Barbara to get Claire to arrange a meeting with the boy to hear his account of what happened. The boy was just ten years old, and Marcus thought that his looks and natural shyness probably played a part in his unforgivable mistreatment. Even though Marcus believed the boy there was no evidence to take to the police. Claire was the only family member her brother had confided in, and her parents had no idea of the trauma they were going through.

Claire argued that they would not be believed as her father got on well with his brother, and she could see that they would be punished for even suggesting such a heinous crime. Marcus was about to leave Claire and her brother, dejected at his inability to suggest an outcome, when the boy said, "Uncle Daniel had a camera."

Marcus eventually left them saying that their uncle would never hurt anyone again. It took Marcus several weeks to break-in to Daniel Mace's home to find the evidence, but he did. Hundreds of black and white photos in a shoebox, hidden on top of the wardrobe, gave Marcus all the evidence he needed to pass sentence on Daniel Mace. Marcus considered sending the photos, anonymously, to the police, but Clare Mace begged him not to, fearing what a trial would do to her father. Six months later Daniel Mace was found hanged in his own home, apparently having committed suicide. The full facts relating to his death - the macabre scene that greeted the police when they found his body, were never released to the public. The police, however, did find a box of black and white photographs hidden in his bedroom, together with all the darkroom equipment needed to develop them. The police were able to identify some of the boys in the photos, but none of them was of any family member of the Mace's, as Marcus had removed and destroyed them.

Barbara realized she had been the catalyst that had spurred Marcus to take revenge on other pathetic beings that had not been properly convicted.

She shivered again at that thought as she awoke in the now lukewarm bathwater wondering if Marcus would ever find closure to his constant nightmare. She accepted she had been complicit in all Marcus has done, both fiendish and pleasurable, remembering the many new friends they had met and engaged with over the years. What did the future now hold for her and Marcus, now he is moving to the country? Could she move on and find someone else . . . and have a normal relationship? The tears in her eyes told the answer that she already knew.

Later that evening Barbara went to Rosa's bedroom to see how she was feeling after the minor surgery. "I'm fine. Still a little sore down here," she said, sliding her hand down to her genitalia, "but it feels good. I can't wait to try it out," she whimpered, hoping Barbara would oblige.

"Later, my love. It needs to heal properly." Barbara came around the side of the bed and sat next to Rosa. "Rosa, love. You are a grown woman. A very attractive woman and it is natural that men, and I am sure other women, will find you attractive and want to get to know you." Rosa was listening with interest, but not sure what Barbara was getting at.

"That man today, for example. You thought him attractive, but he was . . . not the type you should encourage. Do you understand?" Barbara paused, looking for understanding from her friend. Rosa nodded. "I think so," Rosa said meekly, leaning her head on Barbara's shoulders. "I will not talk to a man again." She announced as if that was the answer to Barbara's concerns.

"Rosa, that's not what I am saying, my dear. It's just the type of man you must be careful of."

Rosa looked up into Barbara's eyes and smiled. "I only want you and Marcus in that case. No one else." And proceeded to caress Barbara. Her hands moving over her breasts and swiftly down her side to her soft thighs. "You are not in pain, are you?" Barbara ignored the rhetorical question and let Rosa in.

A week later Annuska visited Croydon for the first session. It was a defining moment in Rosa's life. Never before had she consciously allowed anyone to permanently mark her. She had been beaten and raped, and she had scars, both physical and mental, but this was going to be *her* scar - *her* choice - a reminder of the *free will* Marcus had taught her. Something she would look at with pride and would be a reminder that she was a stronger person now, freed from her mental scars, and in control of her life.

Chapter Three

1979 July

Chas and I don't talk much about Marcus and Rosa, but our love-making seems to have improved. Maybe the thought of Marcus or Rosa helps . . . it does me, and I am sure Chas as well if only he would admit it. Images of Rosa massaging me and Marcus caressing my thighs turn me on quicker than ever when I am making love to Chas. Should I feel guilt or gratitude? Was it a lesson in love-making or was there a more sinister motive our benefactors have not shared with us.

Naturally, my best friend Sally, who is twenty-three, going on seventeen, and two stone heavier than she should be for her age, works at the checkout next to me and wanted to know all about the holiday. "So come on, Bell, you have hardly told me anything exciting about the hols," she calls over, in-between zapping a customer's groceries.

"There's not much to tell. We drove around, looked at churches and museums, and stayed in pubs." I stopped zapping and stared at the flashing bar-code reader. "The Fox & Hounds was a nice pub," I said, still gazing. "Are you going to finish serving me, young lady?" The old woman asked. "And be careful how you pack those eggs, I had two broken last week."

I snapped out of my mini day-dream, but Sally was still interrogating me. "So . . . what about the . . . nights," she whispered and gave a teenage giggle. Some customers raised their eyes and looked bemused; pretending not to be interested in our conversation about holidays, and my bedroom activities.

Life at the check-out became as automatic as the bar code reader I was scanning, and just as monotonous. But life went on, and gradually the memory became more distant, but not forgotten. It was six months later, however, the following February, that everything changed.

1980 February

Our lives had been fairly routine since that summer encounter with Marcus and Rosa, but it was hard to put them out of my mind altogether. I sometimes played the sequence of events over in my mind, and always ended up smiling. Why have I not fancied another man, or woman come to that? Has Chas had anyone since Rosa? Does he consider we have an *'open'* relationship now? I certainly don't. Marcus and Rosa were a *'one-off'*. A special moment that cannot, and will not, be repeated. I only hope Chas knows that as well.

"What are you thinking about, Bell, as if I didn't know," Sally asked grinning, sipping her hot chocolate. We were on a break in the staff canteen of the supermarket, and I was daydreaming again.

"Oh, nothing special. Just wishing . . . thinking, there must be more to life than working here."

"I thought you liked it here. We have fun, don't we? The perks are good and the pay is . . ." she stopped and thought for a moment, "rubbish actually . . . you are right; we need a change of scenery." We sat, contemplating what we could do to improve our circumstances. Not a lot was the consensus. "We could go down the Job Centre and see what's on offer." Sally shrugged.

"Out of one boring job into another – I don't think so. I want to do something different . . . something . . . challenging."

"Hell, Bell . . . like what, drive a bus or climb a mountain." And she laughed aloud.

"No . . . but something just as stimulating." I said in thought. Sally suddenly looked serious. "Make sure I can come with you Bell . . . you will . . . won't you?"

We sat in silence for a while, knowing Sally would be here for a long time, even if I did manage to escape.

"Hey, daydreamer," she suddenly perked up. "Are we still on for your birthday bash on Friday down the Grange, and some Karaoke." And went into the opening lines of Dancing Queen.

I just smiled and realized I would be twenty-four in a few days. *It's not too late,* I told myself . . . *It's not too late.*

I have never had a dream come true. Most people wish for something better than they have; be it a job, house, car, partner . . . although I have never wished for that since I met Chas. He is also restless in his work as a painter and decorator, but he is talented and would love to be a full-time artist, but that does not pay the bills.

* * *

Marcus had had twelve previous *projects,* as Rosa called them, over the past ten years. All of them came about by chance, as did Isabel and Charlie. Ten of them were before he had met . . . found . . . Rosa, and he had pleasurable memories of all those encounters. Why he found Isabel and Charlie different he was not sure, but he kept thinking of them working away in dead-end jobs when they had more talent and ambition than they were expressing right now. Charlie was passionate about art and Isabel has expressed an interest in photography, and with the right tools, and training, could make a first-class photographer. He made a mental note to contact his friend Mike Payne whose black and white erotic work he admires a lot. Marcus put a plan in place. Set them up in a studio and see what they can do.

* * *

"Five minutes to break," Sally called over. "I'm starving."

"Nothing new there then." I quipped back. I wouldn't admit it, but I was in need of a packet of crisps and some caffeine as well. After some heated words with Chas last night I had skipped breakfast, leaving Chas in bed wondering what all the fuss was about.

I have never had cause to feel jealous, (possibly once when I saw him with Rosa) and maybe because we don't go out that much and even if I do see him talking to another woman that's fine, but last night at the pub he was more than talking – he was practically in her mouth. Chas said he was just being friendly, and besides, '*don't we have an open relationship*', since last year?' I had sat in the bathroom thinking things through. He banged on the door – but not long I remember – but it gave me time to reflect. Why was I being like this? Was being jealous a sign that our relationship was moving in a new direction. Marriage!

"Bell . . . Bell . . ." Sally was calling over. "You have a customer."

I came out of my daydream and started scanning, robotically – frozen peas, readymade pastry, pound of potatoes, frozen meal for one – "£5.25 please. Next."

I looked at the moving conveyer belt that is supposed to bring the purchases towards me, but there was nothing there. I looked up at the customer who I thought was having a joke, and stared, first in horror, then in disbelief. Marcus smiled and nodded. "Hello, Isabel. Is this what you call working?"

"Marcus!" I exclaimed too loudly, causing Sally, and various other interested busybodies, to look in my direction. "What are you doing here?" I said, flustered, looking around, for no reason but to think.

"I was in town and wanted to take you to lunch," he said, still smiling.

"Bell, who is that?" Sally called over from her till. "Your uncle?"

I ignored her or didn't hear. "Marcus, I can't go to lunch now, it's not for another two hours."

"Then how about leave now and never return," he said, but this time he was looking more resolute. I was not sure what he had meant. "Leave now? I said I can't for two hours. I am really busy, Marcus." I replied, sounding so unsure of myself I thought I was dreaming. "Isabel. Remember *Free Will*?" He said softly, so only I could hear. "I want to take you away and show you something. If you do not like it then you can return to this . . . this job, if you really want to."

"Show me what?" I finally asked. "You do mean now, don't you?" I added, seeing his unyielding expression. He nodded once and held out his hand. I took it, and a gasp of disbelief could be heard in the close proximity of my station where those lucky enough to be close to the till had witnessed the exchange. Sally nearly fainted. "Miss Kendrick!" An official voice bellowed from nearby, but I had removed my uniform tabard and was walking out of the store arm in arm with Marcus before my supervisor could get close enough for an explanation.

"Now, before I regret what I have just done – thrown my job away I think – please tell me what the hell is going on, Marcus." I pleaded, in the back of a taxi.

"I am sorry if this all seems rather dramatic, but if I gave you time to think it over you may not have agreed," he said, almost apologetically.

"Agree to what? And where are we going?" We sat in silence for a while, each of us looking out of our respective windows.

I turned to Marcus and touched his arm. "It is good to see you after so long. How are you? And Rosa. Is she with you?"

"I am fine and no, Rosa is not up this time, but I hope you will see her soon. Now, don't worry. Think of this as an adventure. A new start, if you want it," he said, patting my hand. "Ah, we are here."

I noted we had travelled towards Putney and were now in a quiet side street; almost Mews like. Tucked in between terraced houses stood what looked like a garage shutter, with a single door entrance on one side. I was about to say something to Marcus when the door opened and Chas came out. "Chas!" I called out with genuine surprise. "What are you doing here?"

"Hi, love. Has our benefactor told you anything yet?"

"Benefactor? What are you talking about?" I demanded, realizing everyone had the advantage over me.

"Come on in my dear, and I will explain everything," Marcus said, ushering us off the street, into the unknown. I looked in awe at the spacious premises we were standing in. It was empty except for a small kitchenette unit at the far end. The brick walls, painted white, gave the structure depth, and the two dormer-windows in the high ceiling threw soft dappled light onto the floor. A wooden staircase halfway down to the right led up to a mezzanine floor.

Chas looked at me and smiled as he came over and hugged me. I did not move away as I didn't want Marcus to know we had had a fight (of sorts) earlier. "Listen to what Marcus has to say, and then have your say. That's all I ask." And kissed me on the forehead. Marcus smiled and shrugged. "Come, let's walk down the other end. I should have thought to bring some chairs. Sorry about that," he said, annoyed with himself. We walked to the other end of the premises where there was a sink unit and kitchen work surface. "Hey, you can sit on this if you want, Bell." Chas offered. "I'm fine thanks, I sit all day, remember," I said, wearily.

I could tell Marcus was starting to feel some tension between us, but put it down to the anxiety of the current events. "My friends," he finally said, "I have been thinking about you both since we met that wonderful day last year, and I hope you both thought of it as a special and unique experience."

"You bet," Chas said. "We talk about it all the time, don't we Bell."

I ignored Charlie, giving him a sarcastic glance. "Please continue, Marcus."

"OK . . . yes . . . I realized you both shared ambitions over and above what you told me were dull and boring jobs. Am I right so far?" We both nodded in unison.

"Right. So I have decided to do something about it. I will purchase this Mews property, in my name for now, and will set you both up in business - Charlie doing what he loves, painting, and you, my dear, can enter the world of photography." I gasped out loud.

Charlie beamed. "Fantastic, isn't it, Bell. My own studio," he sounded elated, and could already see himself at work, under the skylights, creating colorful abstracts. I was more measured in my elation. "Marcus, have you thought this through. How can we make a living doing something we know nothing about?"

"Hey, Bell, I resent that. You've seen what I can do, and I know there is a market."

"OK, but that could take ages to come to fruition, and then there's me. I don't know anything about being a professional photographer." I said, throwing my arms in the air, hands splayed out like a statue, waiting for an answer. Marcus came closer and placed his hands on my shoulders. "Do you trust me?" he asked meekly, looking me in the eyes.

"Marcus, I don't know you. We had one night of . . . whatever, and we never heard from you again until now. Seven months later. How did you find me by the way?"

"I told him, love," Chas answered. "Marcus remembered where I worked. He called the office to find where I was working today and he came to get me. Same as he did you."

"I know this is a shock," Marcus said, "but I mean every word I have said. I think we need some lunch, and I will go over the entire proposition with you. If you both decide not to agree, and I must stress I need you BOTH to agree, you can return to your ordinary lives."

"Not bloody likely . . ." Chas was going to elaborate but was stopped by Marcus. "Charlie, Isabel and you need to hear me out, so let's get lunch and you can hear the rest of my offer."

I still looked dazed and had a hundred questions to ask. The main one being, *'How in hell am I going to get my job back'?*

Marcus took us to a quiet Italian restaurant close by. I ate half-heartily while Charlie devoured his meal, and Marcus ate thoughtfully. I think he was concerned about my reaction, but I had promised to hear him out now we were here.

"Now, my friends," he started, after the wine had been poured. "I will only drink this rather good *Nobile di Montepulciano* in a toast to your future success if you hear me out, and agree to my proposal."

"What, can't I have a sip?" Charlie said, looking rather dismayed at the prospect of not drinking.

Marcus smiled but turned to me. "I saw something in you both last year that I have not seen for some time. After you left I thought of you returning to mundane jobs you obviously don't enjoy. Am I right?"

"Too true, Marcus. I've had enough of house painting." Charlie said hastily, finishing his bread roll and then taking mine.

I frowned. "OK, I don't see it as a career job, but it does pay the bills, and that is what I am worried about, Marcus."

"You do not have to worry about money. I will finance you to what you are earning at the moment for one year, by which time I believe you will both be self-sufficient."

"That's fantastic, Marcus. What about it Bell? What do we have to lose?" Charlie asked, looking at me with more hope in his eyes than I have ever seen.

"Everything . . . if we DON'T succeed. What am I supposed to do? I know nothing of photography."

Marcus nodded. "I will supply all the equipment you need – if it makes you feel better you can pay me back when you are famous – and I want to introduce you to a man who will teach you everything. In fact, you saw his work at my house."

"Christ. David Hockney!" Charlie said, mouth full of pasta.

Marcus smiled. "I wish. No, Mike Payne."

"What!" I gasped. "You want me to take nude shots. . ." a little too loudly so other diners looked over in our direction.

"Not if you don't want to. Mike shoots almost anything, and he has agreed to take you on as a student for three months. Something he doesn't usually do by the way. After then you should be ready to work alone. It will be hard work and you will have to relocate to the Midlands, but it will be worth it." Marcus waited for another outburst from me, but none came. I sat staring at the plate of food in front of me, slowly shaking my head.

Marcus let me continue contemplating his offer and turned to Charlie. "Now, Charlie. I will do the same for you. Finance all your equipment and pay for any tuition you feel you need. I am not sure at what level you are at but you seem to know your subject. The pencil drawing you did of Rosa was exquisite."

Charlie looked at Marcus and was speechless for the first time that day. Realization seemed to have dawned on him and, although he wouldn't admit, he was full of doubts and insecurity, just the same as I was. He looked over to me for answers. A sign. Anything. But I had none.

I hated being rushed into anything. I usually took my time to analyze a situation, not go head-strong blind into the unknown. But why not? Then and there I summed up my life. 'I'm twenty-four.

Dead-end job. No money.' OR 'I'm twenty-four. Want to see more of the World. Being offered the opportunity to start a new career.'

"Isabel," Marcus said quietly. "Are you Ok?"

"Yes, Bell. What's it to be? Flip a coin or go with the flow."

I looked at Charlie and smiled and picked up my untouched glass of wine. "To the unknown." Charlie squealed out. "Yes." And grabbed his glass. "To art."

Marcus was, for the first time in a while, feeling an emotion he had not known since saving Rosa. He fought back the pride that was swelling in him and raised his glass. "To success."

* * *

For the next few days, Marcus stayed with us in our spare room and spent every waking moment going over plans; financial considerations, equipment, business plans etc. "I thought the mezzanine floor could double as a bedroom for either or both of you if working late. What do you think?" Marcus asked.

"Brilliant idea. Large bed with wrought iron bed head. I can see it now" Charlie agreed. I was more downbeat. "I thought that area was to be my studio."

"Yes, it can, but you would have more room downstairs, at the rear of the building. We can put up a dividing wall, with access to the kitchen. Charlie will work in the front unit. It has more light for his needs. What do you think?" he asked, almost rhetorically.

By the end of the week, I was ready to leave to start work with Mike Payne in Birmingham. "I'm going to miss you, Bell." Charlie sighed, hugging me.

"Me too. Look after yourself. You can always go back to your mother if you want to. But let me know."

"Hey, I'm a big boy now. I can cook." And we kissed goodbye. "See you at the weekend, Bell."

Marcus had arranged to drive me to meet Mike Payne and get me settled in at the hotel he had found close to the studio. "You can come and go as you please. Mike is not paying you but he expects you to turn up on time and approach your tuition professionally."

"Don't worry, Marcus, I won't let you down. I do want to succeed, I really do." I said, touching his leg for reassurance. He would be lying if he said he had not thought of her in a sexual way. Sleeping in their flat, next to her room, had been difficult, but he needed to keep sex and business separate – for now.

Mike Payne was different from what I had expected. Younger, almost boyish, but I knew he was in his early thirties and had been a professional photographer for over ten years. He was charming from the first introduction, and I knew I would have to be careful of this one – it was work after all.

"So, Mike, you will take care of this young lady for me, and teach her all you know in three months." Marcus said, adding, "Otherwise I may not be one of your best customers."

"Don't worry, Marcus. If she is willing to learn, then she will do just fine." Mike said assuringly as possible, looking me over. "Come, let me show you around and we can discuss a plan of action."

An hour later I had seen all there was to see of the studio and offices and had met the other members of Mike's team; Katie, who was eighteen and on work experience three days a week, when she bothered to turn up, and James, twenty-five, who was good at props and lighting.

"OK," Marcus said, holding my shoulders outside the studio, "good luck, Isabel. Call if you need anything, and don't forget to collect the hire car in the morning." I just smiled and nodded. This all seems so unreal. A week ago I was at a check-out, now I'm two hundred miles away amongst strangers, being entrusted to learn a new skill by someone who also doesn't really know me. "Thanks, I think," I said, trying to make light of the situation. "I'll try not to let you down, Marcus, I promise." And then he kissed me on the lips, warmly and lovingly, reassuring me he had not forgotten how he felt about me.

"So, shall we get to work?" Mike suddenly appeared by my side. "Yes, of course. Do I call you Mike?"

"Yes, I insist. We are one big family here and everyone is equal . . . except me," he said with a grin, but I got the message.

I spent the rest of the day familiarizing myself with some of the equipment and going through the rest of the week's workload. There was a mix of shoots coming up; private portraits (mainly female), some corporate work in Birmingham and one final calendar shoot for next year's all-male nude calendar. This could be fun after all.

*

Charlie rolled over in bed to reach for Isabel, forgetting she was not there. Not only was she not there, he was sleeping in the studio bed he had just installed to hopefully surprise her on her return at the weekend. There was still some decoration to do to the mezzanine, and some furniture to buy, but it was taking shape. Earlier in the week Charlie had gone on a spending spree and bought all the essentials he needed to start painting as a true artist. He had listened to Marcus go on about 'direction' and 'focusing', but all Charlie wanted to do was paint anything, as long as it was *abstract*. Never mind about if it will sell, Bell can take care of that side of things. Life was going to be great, thanks to Marcus. "Now," Charlie thought, "the only problem with abstract is I don't need a model, or do I?"

*

I called the house phone three times but there was no answer. "Typical." I thought. "Away just three days and he's already on the town." I sat on the hotel bed and looked around my small prison. "Shit. Why did I agree to this?" And flopped down onto the pillow, burying my head in the soft down, trying to suppress the anxiety that had suddenly overcome me. Day one had been fairly routine. Going over the equipment;

camera, lenses, filters, etc. Seeing how the lighting set-up worked, and how it is adjusted for different effects, and of course, making tea and fetching sandwiches.

Mike seemed an OK guy and was very hands-on - very tactile when it came to showing me things to do or just standing next to me. I wondered how well he knew Marcus and if he had been one of Marcus's *'friends'*, as I called them. I was sure I could get some answers over the coming weeks. After some revision on lenses, I took a meal in the hotel restaurant and headed for an early night . . . again.

Chapter Four

Mike worked long hours and expected me to do the same, especially if a publishing deadline was to be met. Most of the late work meant us being alone together, editing, cropping and mounting work for the next day's presentation.

It was also a good time to talk about my role and study the man in more depth. He would talk about lenses, lighting and perspective as if he were describing a renaissance artist's painting. His passion for photography was undeniable, and his enthusiasm rubbed onto me very quickly. He was however not so keen to talk about his private life, which I respected.

The darkroom, where he developed all his monochrome work, was the most intimate of places. Small, dark and smelling of developing fluids, I also found it claustrophobic and nauseous at first. There is no sound here and vision is reduced to viewing everything in a red haze. Other senses are heightened; those of smell and touch, and an awareness that you are being looked at judgmentally, or desirably. His breath on my shoulder was warm and inviting. His hand was on mine, steadying my hold on the tweezers holding the film paper in the developing fix. Then lifting my hand we placed the nearly exposed film into the rinse bath. Was he testing me? Did Marcus expect me to sleep with him? Did I expect to sleep with him . . . NO. If this happened it would jeopardize all I have come here to learn. There may be a time, in the future, who knows, but for now I had to be true to my dream, no matter how frustrating that was. Would he expect me to respond to his advances - I don't know, but as I didn't, Mike treated me with respect for the remainder of my stay. Well almost, but I'll come to that.

Five weeks into my training and I am actually enjoying it. I can't say the same for the occasional days I have off and spend at home. Charlie really can't look after himself. He spends most of the time in the studio and sleeps there as well, not always alone from the state of the room. His painting has been erratic at best. Dozens of canvases piled up against the wall, all looking remarkably similar; abstract - no substance to them.

"You are better than this, Charlie. Marcus said 'focus'. This is not focusing." He paced the mezzanine floor, hands-on head. "Bell, I'm finding my 'niche'. All painters go through a period of finding themselves," he tried to explain. "Come to bed, love. I miss you so much."

"Looking around here, I doubt it. Who is she?" I sounded cross and he looked confused. "Bell, you know I don't make a habit of it, and I thought we liked to have . . . other interests," he said, smiling away his excuse. "Anyway, I am sure you have been kept *occupied* with your Mr Payne. I hear he is good looking, according to Marcus."

"Marcus! What has he been saying? Does he expect me to sleep with him? What the hell."

"Hey, calm down love. Marcus popped in on his way back after he dropped you off and we talked about what he thought I should be doing etc., and I asked what this guy was like, and he said, very professional. You were in good hands."

"And how do you jump from *'very professional'* to *'good looking,'* Charlie?" I demanded. Charlie sat, bemused, and just shrugged. "It seemed natural. We agreed on other relationships, for sex that is, and I thought, assumed, you would do the same, love."

I closed my eyes and shook my head, not knowing if to hit him, or Marcus, for planting ideas in his head. I sat on the bed, a few feet away from Charlie. I wasn't in the touching mood just then. "Charlie, what we had with Marcus and Rosa was special. I'm not sure how it relates to other encounters, or whatever you want to call them. I love you, and I want to make love with you, not anyone else." I reached out to take his hand. "Please, Chas, say you understand. If you don't want me anymore then let's call it quits now, before all this goes too far."

He looked at me sheepishly before he dropped his head in thought. Then, pulling me towards him I could almost see his eyes swelling with emotion. "I love you too, Bell," he said sincerely. "I got it all wrong, didn't I?" I kissed his hand and pulled him towards me, kissing him and holding him tight. "I'll come back; leave Birmingham if that's what you want." I offered.

He caressed my face and kissed me again. "No, this means a lot to you, and I know we can make this work. I will change, I promise Bell. No more sex with strangers . . ." and he smiled coyly, "only with people we know," he laughed, as I did, slapping his arm.

"OK, perhaps with a very few select people we know." I agreed. Then, being serious again, as I wanted him to focus, "And the painting. Please see that tutor we talked about, at least get some ideas on what is selling, never mind if you don't like it just now, that can come later."

We made love most of the night, and I didn't want to leave, but I had to drive back to Birmingham early.

"Good morning, Isabel." Mike greeted me with a cup of coffee. "Thanks, is it my birthday?" I asked, sarcastically.

He frowned but said nothing. "OK, we have a private shoot today. By that I mean a paying client who wants some saucy photos of herself so she can call it art." Mike then reeled off a list of props, lighting and make-up he wanted, and of course costumes, although from what he described would not be a major priority.

The client in question was a very attractive forty-something. Shoulder-length auburn hair, hazel eyes and a young looking petite face on a mature body. My job was to settle her in the studio, relax her, talk to her and make her feel beautiful, which she was. We considered what she would wear and how far she wanted to undress. "I don't mind all the way really, as long as it is tasteful," she said, touching my hand. "OK," Mike called over, "let's start ladies."

The client started to undress behind a dividing screen, and she asked me to help select the first look. I could see she was nervous, and maybe having second thoughts now it came to the crunch. Mike was not going to wait all day. "Why not start as you are, blouse and skirt, and gradually work down from there," I suggested. She smiled at me and held my hand. "That could work. Thank you." And I lead her out to the bright lights and backdrop stage Mike had picked out. A chaise long in a Victorian room setting, complete with aspidistra.

After twenty minutes and two rolls of film she had only just removed her blouse. "This is not working," Mike whispered to me. "Do something."

I went over to the client and sat next to her. "I felt the same on my first shoot. It seems easy, undressing in front of strangers, but it's not, is it." I confided, taking her hand. "You have a wonderful figure. I would like to see it for one." I squeezed her hand, keeping eye contact.

"You would, really."

I nodded. "Let me help with your bra, and I have a pearl necklace that will look great on you." With added jewelry and her hair brushed back in a windswept look, she gained more confidence. "Well done you," Mike whispered through the lens and winked approval.

Within another fifteen minutes she had removed her skirt and looked stunning in stockings and suspenders. I didn't know who she was doing this for, but whoever it was they would not be disappointed, or so I thought. We hit another problem. "She's still not relaxed, Bell. Her posture is all wrong. I need her to look sexy and we only have an hour left."

I ran several scenarios in my mind. The only drastic one was the one that would work, or so I convinced myself. I sat next to the client on the sofa. "We need you to relax some more. Unwind. Feel sexy," she looked at me intensely, and gave a nervous shudder, although it was not cold in the studio. On the contrary, the heating was on. "You need some stimulation," I whispered. "Lean back here, legs together, head back." I had found the largest and softest sable powered brush in the box, and gently ran it over her neck, behind her ear, down her arm and across her nipples; her now very erect nipples. Her eyes were shut. "Good, very good." Mike called out, "Keep that look, and open the legs a little." I had ducked down behind the chaise long. Her hands were behind the chair and I reached up to take hold of them. "Yes," she whimpered. "Hold me. Touch me again." I wasn't part of the shoot and had no desire to be, but Mike had picked up on the situation. "Bell, lean over the back of the chair. Hide your face behind her hair and fold your arm across her breasts."

The client responded to the role-play instantly. She even moved my hand down to her panties, both our hands touching the soft moist silk. I played my part in her fantasy, although my face remained hidden throughout, and even I was surprised by the results, especially in black and white, which were certainly artistic, but more to the point, beautifully erotic. The client was over the moon with the final portfolio and purchased everything Mike had taken. She even sent me a bunch of flowers with a note, *"Come around anytime. M"*.

"Seems you have an admirer, Bell. Didn't know you were into women." Mike joked.

"There's a lot you don't know about me," I replied, wishing I hadn't sounded so vampish. "Really, how about telling me over dinner. You've earned it after that last shoot."

The thought of a change of menu seemed a good idea. "OK, thanks. I would like that."

We ate at his favourite curry house, which was one of the best ever, and I told him my life story . . . well, leaving out the part about me, Charlie, Marcus and Rosa of course. I said we had met them on holiday, and we just *'clicked'*.

"So, what are you going to focus on after your time here? Do you think you can make a living? It has taken me ten years to get this far. All I am saying, it's not an easy profession."

"I know, Mike, and you must think I am really naive, or Marcus is, thinking Charlie and me can change our working life on a whim." I took another sip of wine which was going down all too easily. I hadn't been drinking much since being here, and I was making up for lost time. "So, that's me, what about you," I said, hiccupping. We both laughed. "Sorry, not used to good wine." And we laughed some more.

"You have a wonderful smile, Bell," Mike said, looking me over with his professional eye. "I think you should have a portfolio of your own. Let me shoot you like we did the other week."

"I've heard some excuses, but that's a good one," I said, pointing my finger at him, although now not too steadily. "You are not getting in my pants, Mr Payne." And downed the remaining glass of wine in one, whilst wondering why the room was moving in a strange circle.

"I think it's time I took you home, young lady."

I must have slept all the way back as I didn't remember anything. I woke up on the chaise-long in the studio, with a blanket over me. My head hurt like something was trying to get out. "This will help." Mike was standing there with a cup of coffee and aspirins. I pushed off the blanket to stand, and then realised I was only wearing my knickers and bra, but before I could say anything Mike explained. "I couldn't let you get your dress all creased, could I, and I wasn't sure if you were going to puke all over it. And no, before you ask, we didn't."

"I will have to believe you. I wouldn't remember anyway, which is not how it would have been if it had happened . . . ever . . . which it won't . . . shit. I'm sorry Mike. I don't know what came over me."

"Forget it. Shit happens. Go back to the hotel and take the day off."

"No, I'll be fine, really. Just need coffee, lots, and I'll be ready for work."

"If you say so, Bell, but go if you want to," he said, seeing I may not last the day.

A week later we had covered a wedding, as a favor to a friend of his, but it was good experience for me, plus we shot the final page of the all nude male calendar, Mr December. Lucky me got to place the 'Star' on the top of the tree . . . trunk!

*

One weekend towards the end of my introduction to photography, I stayed over as Charlie was going to visit his Mum who had not been too well. I had not seen much of Birmingham as my working days were long and tiring, so I took myself off to the Bull Ring - Birmingham's famous shopping complex. I trolled the shops, especially the clothes shops, making a mental list of all those fabulous dresses I was going to buy when I was rich and famous.

I found myself in Debenhams department store looking at the latest fashions, and although I couldn't afford any of them, I grabbed two wonderful designer outfits, and headed for the changing rooms, just wanting to feel the luxury wash over me for a few minutes. One was a very bold print and the other a very chic Ralph Lauren wrap dress - I've always loved how easy they are to undo.

I rushed into the changing rooms knowing the store was about to close, but all four cubicles were occupied. I paced the waiting area considering buying them, but that would have been rather extreme, plus my check would have bounced for sure.

My head was full of scenarios when the door of the end compartment opened and an attractive woman in her mid-forties stepped out. "Oh, sorry," she apologized, "I haven't finished yet; I just wanted to try this blouse in another size." She obviously saw the disappointment on my face, and the two garments I was holding up so as not to crease them. "Be a darling and find me a size twelve in this, they are just around the corner, and I will hold these for you."

As the other rooms were still engaged, I gave her my dresses and went to find her white silk blouse, size twelve. I was back in a couple of minutes with the requested merchandise. "Excellent, my dear. Why don't we share? It will save you time as I know they are closing soon," she almost had her arm around my waist guiding me into the six-foot square cubicle before I could think of a reply or even object.

She was wearing a white bra and a three-quarter length beige skirt, and brown boots. We stood face to face for what seemed ages, but she then smiled and said very casually, "Let's get you undressed." She turned me around to face one of the three mirrored walls and unzipped me. That wonderful feeling of intimacy crept over me - it happens every time I find myself in a situation of being undressed for the first time - whether it's a man or a woman. Of course, I wasn't sure if she was coming on to me as we were in a very public place and therefore dismissed the idea immediately.

Seeing her reflection in the full-length mirror I took her to be in her mid-forties. Good figure - size twelve of course - but very well proportioned. I could see her breasts were full and natural under her partially laced cream bra. Her hair was dark blonde and fell in waves to her shoulders. Her ears were pierced with a single pearl which matched the single row of pearls around her neck.

"Which do you want to try first?" she asked.

"The Ralph Lauren I think," and reached for the hanger.

"Here, let me help," and she slid the dress off the hanger and unfastened the front hook. "It's beautiful - are you buying if for a special occasion?" she asked, holding the dress ready for me to slip my arms into.

"Not really. I just liked the look of it." I replied, sounding rather vague and foolish.

"Don't you know?"

Not wanting to come across as a weirdo or a shop a lifter, I just shrugged and smiled as if I was an eccentric woman on something illegal. She turned me back to face her and fasten the wrap dress at the waist and took a half step back. "You do look beautiful. It was made for you."

"Thank you. It does feel good, but I would like to try the other one." Just then an announcement came over the speakers *"The store will be closing in five minutes."*

"Damn." I blurted out. "I really wanted to try this on." And touched the other dress as if it was a rare object, my face belying my true intentions.

"I have an idea, if you agree," the woman said thoughtfully, touching my shoulder. "Buy both and you can come back to my place to try them on. If you change your mind and don't want them they can be returned another day."

"Really, can I do that?" I asked with genuine surprise, eager at the thought of owning two designer dresses, albeit for a few days.

"Of course. Come on, get that off and I'll take them to the cashier."

"Thank you, I'm Isabel," I said with a smile, letting her unhook the dress and gently remove it from my shoulders. As I turned around to pick up my own dress I could feel her eyes running over my partially naked body.

"I'll meet you outside in a moment," she said, gathering the two dresses and her purchases, leaving me alone to dress. I looked in the mirror at my reflection, standing in bra and knickers. I touched myself between my legs. It felt so warm I knew I could come if I wanted to. Reluctantly I got dressed and walked back to the cashier's desk.

My admirer was all ready to go. "You take those two bags and I'll take the rest – it's all sorted."

"What do you mean? I have to pay for them."

"I've taken care of it, my dear, on my store account. It saved time and we can discuss it back at my place," she said assertively. "Now, do you have a car?"

"No," I said. "I came into town by bus," still trying to focus on what she had done. Why would a stranger want to pay for two very expensive dresses for someone she has never met?

"Good, that will save having to follow me. The car is in the basement car park." We took the lift to the car park in silence, but she was looking at me all the time, with a satisfied grin. What was I doing – going back with a woman, an older woman, to her house to try on dresses? The past experiences have instilled in me a sense of bravado, coupled with caution, but Chas and I agreed to "go with the flow" when it comes to new experiences; although for me there had not been another experience since meeting Marcus, and I was not sure if this was going to be anything different, but the "Marcus Factor", as we call it, makes us far more curious than we used to be.

She drove a new black BMW 350 series with top of the range CD player, radio and tinted windows. "Do you like it? It was a present from my ex-husband. Probably feeling guilty for leaving me," she said, laughing. "It's only a short drive to King's Heath. Do you know it?"

"No, not really. I'm not from around here."

We drove the twenty minutes listening to a Robson & Jerome CD. "I do like these two," she said, singing along to Unchained Melody. "They have good voices. Better than some of those other pop singers of today." We turned into a long gravel driveway which led to a magnificent mock-Georgian detached house. "Do you like it?" she asked. "We have a swimming pool and games room, six bedrooms and four bathrooms, and a huge kitchen. You must see it all."

We unpacked the car and took two bags each into the hall entrance. "Let's get these upstairs, and then I will get us some drinks. Wine OK with you?"

"Yes, perfect. Thank you." I confirmed. "I don't know your name."

"Call me, Jo."

I followed her up the impressive curved stairway to the first floor. "Don't you get lonely here, being all on your own?" I asked innocently. She either didn't hear me or didn't want to answer what she assumed was a rhetorical question.

I followed Jo through double doors into her massive bedroom. As well as a Queen size bed there was a walk-in wardrobe, a two-seater sofa, dresser and still enough room for another large bed, and of course an en-suite bathroom and shower room. The bedroom was tastefully decorated in gold and cream, with red trim curtains and a beautiful red and gold duvet. The carpet must have been six inches deep, it was so soft.

"Kick off your shoes and unpack your dresses while I get the wine," she suggested, before fetching me a hanger. I sat on the bed and practically sank into it. Giggling like a schoolgirl I kicked off my shoes and reached behind to unzip my dress but I lost my balance and rolled over onto my side. "What are you doing, woman?" Jo said, mockingly, as she sat next to me.

"Don't move, let me help." She continued to unzip me, then placed her hands on my bare shoulders and gently started to massage them. "You have a lovely figure. I was your size once, but I hope you will take more care of yourself than I have."

I turned over onto my back. "You have a wonderful figure, don't be unkind to yourself," I said reassuringly, and I hoped, sincerely.

"You are very sweet." And she leant over me and kissed me on the forehead. "Now, let me see you in those dresses."

I finished removing my clothes and reached for the dress I had not tried on. On zipping me up she studied me from all angles. "No," she finally said, "the color and the print size is too large for you. You are delicate – you can't take these large patterns. Try on the other one again." Jo suggested.

I obeyed without question. I had liked that dress but her comments seemed valid. "That's better. The paler color against your complexion and the three-quarter sleeves look great. The pattern is bold, but not overbearing. What do you think?"

I looked at myself in the full-length mirror in her dressing room and nodded. "Yes, I agree. Thank you so much. I will keep this and return the other one." I said, completely forgetting I was acting out a Walter Mitty moment.

"Excellent, but I will take it back as I paid for it on my account.

Now, I have a surprise - no gift, I want you to try on."

"What are you talking about; you can't go buying presents for someone you don't know," I said, following her back into the bedroom.

"Nonsense. Anyway, I can spend my money on whosoever I want. I have no one else to spend it on."

"Don't you have children?" I asked with real interest. She sighed and smiled sweetly. "No, it was not to be, but let's not talk about me. I want you to try this on." And she held up a most unusual highly colored crochet style cotton dress. "I know the size is right. Do you like it?" she asked enthusiastically.

I looked at this dress of many colors and realized I could see right through it. I burst out laughing. "I can't wear that, it's . . . it's . . ." but couldn't find the words to describe it.

"It's daring, that's what it is. Come on. See what you think once you've tried it on," she said persuasively. She came close and unhooked the front of my dress; her left hand on my waist as if to balance me. The dress fell to the floor and I stepped out of it - her hand still holding my waist, but now feeling her fingertips pressing my flesh.

I stepped into the dress with a thousand holes. "There, you look divine."

It did feel different from what I had expected. Very lightweight and not itchy at all. The only problem was anyone could see my underwear.

"I don't think I could wear it out, it would cause a few accidents." I laughed.

"I bet," she said, thinking. "It would look even better without the bra, and darker knickers would work with it."

I stood, hands-on-hips facing the mirror wondering how not to hurt her feelings if I said it was not really me. She came behind me and started to unzip me. "What do you think? Shall we try?"

I closed my eyes and felt her soft touch on my shoulders again. I let the dress fall, and she unfastened my bra. "Are you flirting with me?" I whispered, as she gently blew warm breath on my back.

"Absolutely," she whispered back. Then taking my shoulders turned me slowly.

She looked me up and down, smiling all the time, rubbing my upper arms. This was not the first time I had been "flirted" with, but it was certainly the first time by an older woman. Jo was indeed very attractive, and I had never been with a woman her age. Why would that matter? I have been with older men . . . well, one man - nearly.

She unbuttoned the blouse she was wearing and unzipped the side of her skirt which fell to the floor. "Come, come here and lie on the bed." I sat on the edge next to her and fell backwards onto what felt like a bed of feathers. "You have been with women before, haven't you?" she said, more factually than accusingly. I nodded, yes.

I put my hand behind her neck and pulled her to my lips. We kissed, softly at first exploring each other's tongues, neck, eyes, nose and ears until she worked her way to my breasts. First, gently licking the nipple from underneath, and then taking more into her mouth, until she was able to suck me and work her tongue on my nipple at the same time. She did this alternately until I had to have some of the same. I pushed her on her side and grabbed at her bra, pulling it away to reveal her gorgeously formed breasts. "Wow." I gasped. "They're beautiful."

She finished removing her bra and I stared at the most fantastic pair of breasts I had ever seen, including Rosa's. I pushed her on her back and sucked and tongued her nipples until she moaned and sighed with ecstatic pleasure. Moving slowly down her body to her navel I worked my tongue into it, at which she wailed and panted even louder. I parted her thighs and positioned myself to give her my tongue again.

"Yes, yes . . . don't stop now," She begged.

I didn't stop. She climaxed and exploded, and still I didn't stop.

We made love thoughtfully but intensely, as Rosa had taught me – each of us discovering the other's senses and using our hands to explore peaks and valleys of the body in ways only women can. Our lovemaking seemed to go on all night, but two euphoric hours had passed before I knew it.

Kissing and caressing is probably the most loving thing a couple can do after making love. Just to lie in each other's arms for a while makes it right – makes it meaningful. I stayed the night and we made love many times. Lying in each other's arms in the morning dapple sunlight, I told her my story, and why I was in Birmingham. "This Marcus sounds wonderful. I must meet him." Jo said, practically begging me for his number.

"Jo," I said thoughtfully, "he must never know I told you about him . . . he is a very private person."

"Don't worry, my dear. I can be discreet." Jo said, giving me one of her seductive smiles. "Now, tell me more about this Mike Payne . . . he also sounds interesting. I may just have to book a sitting with him one day."

"That would be good, but please wait another week until after I have gone back to London. I don't want to be distracted by you at a photoshoot." I laughed.

We had a lazy breakfast after we showered in the largest walk-in shower I had ever seen, followed by a swim in the indoor pool. The property was so secluded we even made love on a sun-lounger under a perfect blue sky. "Stay and have lunch . . . what else do you have to do today?" Jo asked. "In fact, stay all day and night. I want to devour you, you gorgeous thing." And proceeded to nibble my neck and ear, which she had realized were just two of my most sensitive areas. "I thought you devoured me last night, I seem to remember. Or you had a really good go at it." I said, considering her offer.

"OK," I said, but I must call my man and see how things are going with him."

"Perfect!" Jo exclaimed as if she had just won a prize. "Use the office phone next to the dining room whenever you want." After another quick dip in the pool, I wrapped myself in one of Jo's luxurious toweling bathrobes and found my way to the office.

"Hi, lover," Chas said on hearing my voice. "Surprised you didn't come home this weekend, what happened . . . got a better offer?" he asked, not realizing the apparent truth in his question.

"As it happens, yes, but I'll tell you all about it when I get back. How have you been, How's the painting coming along . . . have you heard from Marcus . .?"

"Hey baby, hang on . . . so many questions, Bell. Everything is fine, except your mother keeps asking why you are in Birmingham on your own."

"Sorry, Charlie. I'll call her. Won't be long now before we start our new adventure. Are you scared? I am, Charlie . . . going into the unknown." I said, glad he could not see the trepidation on my face; the anxiety in my eyes. "Hey. Are you still there?" Charlie had gone quiet.

"Yes," he whispered back, "just missing you, babe. Let's go out next Saturday and celebrate, what do you say?"

"Sounds wonderful . . . but no Indian . . . had my fill of curry for a while." We left each other with the sound of kisses in our ears, and a suspicion in my mind Charlie was not alone.

*

Chas replaced the receiver and rolled over back on the bed where Rosa was keeping it warm. "So, why didn't you tell her I was here? That's not fair. I came thinking you were both here."

"Don't worry . . . we don't have secrets . . . I'll tell her. I just didn't want her to be jealous of me having you all to myself." He said, convincingly, and rolled over again, landing on top of the gorgeous Rosa.

*

I spent the remainder of Sunday with the mysterious Jo - why am I drawn to people like that - and after a wonderful al fresco lunch of antipasti and Cannelloni with salad, washed down with a bottle of Valpolicella, we relaxed on sunbeds in the glass conservatory, although it was not long before I felt Jo's fingers drawing circles around my belly-button.

I touched her hand and took it to my lips, kissing her fingers one by one, her breathing hastily increasing by the time I reached her thumb. "Don't stop," she said, "I have another hand and ten toes yet." I must admit, feet have not been an erogenous zone I would voluntary descend to, but I do remember Rosa taking my foot and working her tongue so expertly around each of my toes until I nearly came. Having satisfied Jo's fetish, I worked my way northward, to more satisfying territory. An hour or so later in a quiet moment I plucked up enough courage to ask her about her life . . . ex-husband *et all*.

"Simple, my dear. Married young - married rich. Good divorce settlement." Her cavalier persona was tinted with something else - regret, remorse, anger maybe. "And you've never thought of marrying again?"

"Once bitten, etc. etc.," she said, implying either her distaste for men or, more probably, enjoying her freedom as a rich, independent, intelligent woman in the prime of life.

"Will you and your Charlie get married one day?" Jo suddenly asked. My hesitation in replying caused her to frown. "Well," she asked again, turning towards me, meeting my eyes. "Well, yes, probably, one day," I said, sounding even unconvincing to myself. Why would I hesitate to say, "Yes, very soon, of course we are. I love him". That question nagged me for the rest of the evening, but I did my best to hide it until it was time to leave my sociable hostess. "I will call you soon. I Promise." I confirmed for the tenth time as she kissed me one last time before I climbed into the taxi and back to my hotel to start my last week's tuition with Mr Payne.

*

"So," Mike asked, "how was your weekend?" I couldn't help but smile, or smirk maybe, at the question. "Very good, actually, and you?" I asked, just to be polite.

"Busy, but not at work for a change." But he did not elaborate further. "So, you have one more week with me, and there are two things I want you to do." I looked on with interest, hoping my last week would be a tad more relaxing.

"One, you may remember, I asked if I could shoot you, and secondly I am going to give you an assignment. Call it a passing out exam. Choose any subject, anything you like, and let me see what you have learnt. You can use any of the equipment and darkroom, of course."

"Can I do them in any order?" I smiled, knowing I wasn't going to get away with not doing the shoot.

"Yes, I don't see why not. We can schedule the shoot for Thursday morning. And what about the assignment - any thoughts?"

"I think so, but I may need to go back home for one day if that is allowed," I asked hopefully - an idea already forming in my mind, which I knew he would love. I called Rosa to see if she could come up to the studio for a day, which she was happy to do, especially to see me. I explained the photoshoot I had in mind, and she thought it a great idea. Not only would I be behind the lens, but I will be in the photo as well.

Having Charlie around for what I had in mind would be a distraction - for him, so I persuaded him to go out for the day. Charlie gone. Door locked. I set to work. Rosa's body tattoo was the central theme and would be the key to balancing the finished frame. Rosa was to be naked of course, back to the camera. Her arms entwined with another woman, whose face was not in shot, with one hand touching Rosa's bottom, and the other her shoulder. Rosa's head would be thrown back; her black hair having been moistened would shimmer in the light. I set the camera on the tripod and took some Polaroid's to establish the correct light meter settings. The self-timer was set for ten-second intervals. I took my position in front of Rosa and untied my robe. We posed maybe a dozen times, I can't remember exactly, but we ended up in bed having the best sex ever. Charlie returned later in the afternoon, and predictably wanted to join us, which he did.

I returned to the Birmingham studio the following day and developed my films. I mounted them in a set of five shots. The largest was A3, the full-length image of Rosa's stunning tattoo, complete with unknown lover, and four smaller seven by five inch images; two each side with close up detail of the tattoo, plus one close up of her wearing her double pearl thong with her hand covering her shaven pussy, and a final detail of her pierced belly button, shimmering with water droplets, all in monochrome.

"Well," Mike said after a lengthy study of my work, "well done, Isabel. These are very good, I love the shading on the back of the tattoo, and the detail in the close-ups is very good. The contrast of skin colors between you and your friend works well."

"How did you know it was me?" I asked, looking at the photo again to see if I could identify myself.

"After three months, Bell, I've seen you enough, sometimes in a state of semi-undress, to know that is you," he said, smiling. "Is this the subject matter you want to work with, because if it is you will do well?"

"I'm not sure, Mike, but I have learnt a lot thanks to you, and I have several options I want to explore when I get back home."

I spent the evening packing my bags, although that didn't take too long when I heard a knock on the door. "Mike," I exclaimed. "What are you doing here?"

"I thought I could take you to dinner as it's your last night in town," he said convincingly.

I stood, staring at his gorgeous face longer than I should have. "Then, why have you a bottle of wine in your hand?" I asked, suspiciously. He stepped a few paces into my small bedroom I had considered my home the past twelve weeks and placed the bottle of vino on the dressing table. "That's for after," he replied, and turned to stand in front of me; his six-foot-two-inch frame towering over me. "After . . . what?" I said, not completely naively - with my voice quivering and my heart pounding.

Twelve weeks of pent-up sexual desire came to the surface quicker than Carl Lewis ran the 100-meter sprint at the last Olympics. This was not the *love-making* Marcus and Rosa spoke of, this was raw hot passion. We tore at each other's clothes, kissing all the while. Mouths wet with desire, tongues desperate to explore. In a brief moment of hesitancy, he pushed me gently onto the bed and finished undressing me. He knelt at the end of the bed and ran his fingers up the side of my legs to remove my knickers, then glanced towards me, as if waiting for something. I was resting on my elbows watching his every move; legs parted, head cocked.

"Don't bloody stop now." I hissed, feeling that wonderful rush of adrenaline wash over me again like it had only a week ago with Jo.

After an hour, and a couple of glasses of wine, we resumed our sexual activities but now with more consideration and tenderness – love-making, as I like it.

Our earlier passion was the result of mixed emotions and frustrated desires - he thrust into me - turned me over and over, backwards and forwards, in many positions I had not experienced; all the time taking control. He had not been over assertive, but the force behind the passion, although strong, was controlled and never hurtful. The eventual climax was powerful, and we came together in a blissful combination of choral satisfaction and mind-blowing acrobatics, that probably shook the hotel to its foundations.

Mike left in the early hours of Friday morning, leaving me a note on the dresser. *'Don't hurry in . . . xx"*

I took his advice and finished my packing, showered, and had a good breakfast in the hotel restaurant, although I kept imagining people staring at me, silently accusing me of being responsible for the earthquake the West Midlands experienced during the night.

Before I left, Mike gave me a portfolio case complete with a dozen mounted photos he had taken of me earlier. "Thanks, Mike, they are great. Marcus will love them." I hugged Mike and kissed him goodbye. "Don't forget to come and see me when you are famous," he said, kissing me once more. I was sure our paths would cross again, as I now knew we both had sexual chemistry.

Chapter Five

1983

Marcus von Hartstein . . . the name was still haunting him after all these years. He would lie on his bed, trying to remember how he killed his mother. Everyone says he did, but the actual memory of the act was not there, just blurred visions and noises coming from the corridor outside the bedroom where he was hiding until the army found him, shivering and afraid.

Why now? He asked himself. Why now, after forty years or more was he having these nightmares, or *dunkle Traum*, as he preferred in his original language - a 'dark dream'. Being alone for many years in his parents' house, without his brother or other children to play with, was not just lonely but detrimental to his mental stability.

Early home life had been good he always recalled. Marcus's home was a large house with ten acres of land including a swimming pool, tennis court, and a lake in southern Austria. His mother, Vivienne, loved it, but she also longed to be nearer to Vienna where all her socialite friends lived, and where all the grand parties took place. To make up for it, she would throw a large party every mid-summer day when the weather was guaranteed to be good, and house guests could swim and play tennis or croquet.

His mother and father were attentive parents, and he wanted for nothing - except his brother. Marius was ten years older, and Marcus could, if he concentrated hard enough, remember playing with his brother in the vast grounds. Playing hide-and-seek in the wooded copse, or racing twigs in the brook that ran the border of their property. Then one day he was gone and Marcus was alone. He stayed in his room for days on end, not eating, just crying.

"Don't be sad, Marcus. He will be home for the holidays." His mother would say, trying to comfort him. Not even his nanny, Liza, could console him, although he remembered her as being kind and caring . . . and protective.

Marcus became withdrawn and took to exploring the grand old Schloss with its many rooms and dark hiding places. He found closets and secret compartments, not even his parents or the servants knew about or had forgotten. Alone, in his secreted world, Marcus would pretend his brother was with him, and play hide-and- seek, sleeping lions and pick-up sticks, just as they used to.

From the ages of six to nine he was educated at home by a very old and frightening matron his mother had employed. He was tutored from 8.00am to 4.00pm with a break for lunch at 12.30, and then took piano lessons from 4.30pm to 6.0pm. Lateness or any wrong-doing, which included getting an answer wrong, was punishable by the 'strop' across the bottom or a 'cane' across the hand.

Marcus's mother, and Liza, were initially fretful for the boy, but her husband, Herbert, insisted he had to have discipline, and backbone if he was to be a soldier like his father. With Marius at boarding school in England, he was alone those four long years to fend for himself. Marius should have been there. He would not have allowed those things to happen. The beatings and . . . worse . . . things he did not want to remember, but could not forget.

Marcus was aware of the war being fought in faraway places, not knowing it would change his life forever and tear his family apart, but by then he would be glad - glad of the chance to escape the abuse, and maybe find his brother.

The abuse was not apparent to a trusting six-year-old from a loving home. Marcus told himself the attention he received was because his brother was away and his mother felt guilty whenever he had been given the cane.

His mother spent more and more time with him and gradually took over from Liza to supervise his bath time, making him feel he was the only son she had. His father was away from home all the time and the servants had been reduced to just two, plus the cook. The large house became a prison. Shutters were nearly always closed and the windows had crosses taped on them to stop them shattering. Unused rooms were locked up, and he and his mother used just the sitting room and the dining room, and her bedroom. She said it was more practical to use just one bedroom, as it saved on cleaning, but Marcus was happy to share his mother's bed and snuggle up next to her where he was warm and safe.

On his ninth birthday in August 1944, Marcus's father came home for his birthday party and showered him with presents, but the best present he had was seeing Marius come into the living room smiling, with arms spread wide. Marcus ran over to his brother and let himself be swept up and hugged as he had never been before.

Most of the selected guests were close friends of his parents, except for Fritz and Anna, who were nine and twelve respectively. They ate cakes and played games, and then his father gave him a present. Marcus eagerly unwrapped the brown paper parcel and stared, speechless, at the content before him. "Come, my son. Go put it on and let us all see you in your new uniform."

Liza took his hand. "Come, birthday boy. Let's see what your new present looks like on." And lead him upstairs to her bedroom. Marcus looked around the small sparse attic room as if he had never entered it previously. Liza's single bed was neatly made and her small dresser was laid out with a hairbrush, clothes brush and comb, plus a black and white unframed photo of an older woman. There was also a small bottle containing amber liquid, but Marcus could not read the label as it was in French. Liza sat on her bed with Marcus facing her. "Come now, let's get you undressed," she smiled reassuringly.

Liza had been employed by the von Hartstein's for three years when Marcus's mother was taken ill and could not look after him. Marcus had got on so well with Liza that he begged his parents to keep her on six months later when his mother had fully recovered. Liza's own birthday had been just five days ago. She was twenty. No one knew. No one brought her presents or made her a cake. She was just a servant without any friends. Mrs Hartstein had said she could go home to her parents in the west to see how they were, but she was too scared to travel since the war started, and bombings were getting more frequent now. The occasional letter did get through and she was relieved to hear her parents were safe, but her elder brother had joined the Nazi Party. Liza knew nothing of war. She was a simple country girl, loving horses and dogs, cooking and laughing, but she had not laughed much now for nearly two years, and was frightened for herself and young Marcus, especially as she knew, or suspected, what was happening to him.

"There," she said smiling, "you do look handsome." She turned him around so he could see himself in the mirror, hanging from the door. Marcus frowned. "I don't like it," he snarled, his eyes swelling with tears. Liza turned him back to face her and looked him in the face. "Marcus, you only have to wear it today to please your Father. Can you do that for me?" Marcus looked down at his feet and rubbed his shoulder which was itching against the new starched brown shirt, and nodded yes.

"Good boy. Now we will go downstairs and show you off to everyone, OK?" Liza knew he would be expected to wear the Nazi Youth uniform regularly, but she wanted to get him through this day and help him not to dwell on the future. Everyone applauded when they entered the drawing-room. Liza held back so Marcus could be the birthday boy again as he walked to his father. "Thank you, father. It is very nice," he said clearly, and everyone clapped again and nodded their approval of the latest recruit to Hitler's Youth Army.

Most of the guests had left by eight o'clock, keen to arrive home before dark, although the two couples with children near to Marcus's age stayed behind. Marcus could not understand why Anna was at his party as they had never been friends. The three children sat on the window seat around the bay-window, watching Marcus's mother talking to Liza.

"Liza," Mrs Hartstein said with assertiveness, "please make up two of the guest rooms for Mr & Mrs Muller, and Mr & Mrs Linzer. Their children can sleep with them. I'm sorry its last minute but they have too far to drive now, so it's safer if they stay the night," she concluded, not expecting any complaints from her employee. "Ma'am," Liza said, almost startling Marcus's mother. "Marcus can stay in my room tonight as Mr Hartstein is home," she said, hoping the woman would understand - after all, she had not slept with her husband for nearly a year.

"That's . . . thoughtful, Liza." Mrs Hartstein said, surprised at the suggestion, but realising this young girl after all was not to know of their sleeping arrangements. "Yes . . . that is very thoughtful of you. Of course he can, for tonight only mind you." Liza smiled her thanks and went about preparing the guest rooms, hoping she could somehow talk to Marcus and dismiss her suspicions.

Marcus had known Fritz at Kindergarten for two years before he was tutored at home but had only seen Anna a few times previously. She was pretty for a girl, he thought. Blonde hair with pigtails, large blue eyes and old enough to wear a bra. "I'm going to summer camp soon," Anna said with pride in her voice. The two boys looked bemused. "What happens there?" Fritz asked.

"We have fun . . . and . . ." but Anna was suddenly interrupted by her mother.

"Anna. Come on up. Our room is ready." Anna walked away without saying goodnight. "She is very rude, that girl," Fritz said, following her every step until she was out-of-sight. Marcus half-smiled at his friend's observation but said nothing. He was thinking about his brother and where he was and hoping he could stay for more than one day. His thoughts were interrupted by Liza. "Fritz, your parent's room is ready. You are sleeping on the folding bed in their room. Marcus, you are in my room tonight. Is that OK?"

Marcus looked at Liza and smiled, then nodded. "Lucky man," Fritz said, sounding jealous, but Marcus didn't understand.

Upstairs, Mr & Mrs von Hartstein were preparing for bed. "Herbert, you promised me Marius would not have to fight." Wiping away a tear.

"Vivienne my dear. Every young man has to do his duty. I kept him in office as long as possible on his return from England, but even I have superiors," he explained, sounding frustrated at having to explain these matters to his wife. Herbert von Hartstein was a large, well-built man and his very presence made mere mortals flinch, but his wife had always stood her ground and been a strong partner in all matters of marriage and family. But the thought of losing a son was too much. "Please, Herbert. Tell me where he is going," she begged.

"Don't ask me, my dear. You know I can't tell you. All I can say is, he is not going to the Front." Hoping that would pacify his distraught wife. Vivienne sniffed and wiped another tear from her eye. "Thank you, Herbert."

Marcus looked at the single bed in Liza's room. "Where will you sleep?" he asked Liza, but before she could answer there was a tap on the bedroom door. Marius peered in. "Marius!"

Marcus's face beamed. "Hello, brother. Are you stealing my girl?"

Marcus looked surprised, not really knowing what he had meant. Marius scuffed his brother's hair and leant over to kiss Liza on the cheek.

"OK," he said suddenly, "sleeping arrangements." He took the thick bedspread off Liza's bed and placed it on the floor, adding one of the pillows. "There you are, young man. Fit for a King." Marcus looked bewildered. "But where are you sleeping, Marius?"

Liza had already undressed and was wearing her thin woollen dressing gown her mother had sent her recently. "Marius is going to keep me warm, Marcus. It's our secret. Is that OK with you?" she asked, not knowing if Marcus understood or not. "Of course he can keep a secret, can't you Marcus?" Marius said, "He's a big boy now."

Marcus had removed the itchy uniform and knelt on the bedspread on the floor. "I suppose I can." He was not sure how they could sleep in such a small space, but he remembered how happy they looked lying in each other's arms. "Remember, brother, not a word to mum or dad, OK."

Liza opened the bedroom door. "I'll be back in a minute," she whispered and walked to the bathroom across the hallway. She locked the door and leant back on it, closing her eyes. What if I'm wrong, she asked herself for the tenth time. Why had his mother taken over from her at bath-time, and insisted on seeing him to bed? She still wasn't sure, but a gut feeling told her otherwise. Even if she had proof, what could she do with it, a girl in her position? Who would listen to her fanciful notions of child molesting at the respected von Hartstein's? Liza sighed and resigned herself to the fact that she was not as brave as she thought. Her only friend and ally was Marius, and even he might rebuke her for suggesting what she was thinking. Is there anyone a child can trust, and be believed? Surely there is a way - there has to be.

Liza tiptoed across the hallway back to her room but froze on hearing voices from the landing below. She stood at the top of the landing stairs and peered down to the second floor where the voices were coming from. Her floor was in darkness due to the black-out, but she could see a dim light coming from a torch, and Mr von Hartstein in his dressing gown talking to Mrs Linser. Her daughter Anna was with her, still in her party dress. Mr Hartstein was looking at Anna and smiling whilst talking to her mother, but Liza could not make out what he was saying. Then, without provocation, Anna followed him into his bedroom, and Mrs Linser returned to her room.

Liza's mind was racing. Why would Anna go into the von Hartstein's bedroom, wearing her party dress? She placed one foot on the stairs but decided it was too risky to venture down. She returned to her room as quietly as possible and slipped into bed alongside Marius. "You are shivering. Come, cuddle up with me and get warm." Lisa cuddled into Marius's shoulder and felt the warmth of his body instantly thaw her. She felt his hand slide under her dressing gown which she had not removed, and cup her left breast. She placed her hand on his and whispered in his ear. "I need to talk to you tomorrow before you go."

Marius crept out of Liza's bedroom at 6.0am to go back to his room for an hour before dressing. As he reached his bedroom door on the second floor, his parent's door opened and young Anna emerged looking sheepish and tired. On seeing Marius she hung her head and ran back along the landing to her parents' bedroom.

Marcus had stirred when his brother left the room and looked up from his make-shift bed to see Liza staring at him. "Hi," he whispered. "Hi," she replied, smiling. "Want to come in here for a while?" she asked, pulling back the eiderdown. Marcus knelt, then shuffled towards the bed and raised himself into the warm space left by his brother. Liza was quiet for a moment and Marcus thought she had fallen asleep again, but she was still fighting the dilemma of what she wanted to know.

All she could think about was young Anna entering that bedroom, and what was happening to her. "Marcus, when your mother washes you in the bath or cuddles you in bed like this, does she . . . touch you anywhere you think is wrong?"

Rosa shook Marcus gently, then firmer. "Marcus, Marcus . . . wake up." She tried not to raise her voice but he was not responding. "Marcus!"

Marcus, still with eyes closed, was shaking his head from side to side, wanting to erase a memory. "Liza, Liza . . . ," he called out.

"Marcus!" Rosa tried again, shaking his shoulders. Marcus opened his eyes and smiled. "Your face is all I want to see when I wake up," he whispered, touching her face.

"You called out a name . . . Liza. Who is she, and should I be jealous?" Rosa asked, wiping his brow.

Marcus sat up and pulled Rosa to his side, holding her close. "I am still trying to figure out what happened to me a long time ago. You know some of it . . . but . . . there was more . . ." Marcus hesitated, not sure if Rosa should be told the truth. How would she react knowing he had killed his mother? "Liza was someone who looked after me when I was very young and worked for my mother. She . . . she . . . knew my brother. . . Marius."

"When you say *knew*, what do you mean, Marcus. In what way?"

"I'm not sure . . . it was a long time ago and my memory is blurred. Something happened to my mother . . . she died a horrible death and I am still trying to fit together all the pieces."

"What happened to your brother, and this Liza?" Rosa asked, wanting to know more.

"I don't know. He was in the army, but I don't know if he survived the war or was taken prisoner when the allies arrived in Austria. As for Liza . . ." Marcus shrugged and sighed. "She probably went back to her parent's home or . . ."

"Or what, Marcus?"

"I don't know . . . I was just thinking aloud. I think she and Marius were close. I remember him sharing her bed one night while I slept on the floor, but that needn't mean anything . . . need it?" he asked, looking at Rosa for an answer.

"Maybe not . . . maybe yes . . . if you want answers Marcus, you must get some help. What does Barbara say?"

"She has mentioned hypnosis, but I am not sure I want to reveal everything about myself to a complete stranger," he said, but not dismissing the idea completely.

They made love with the evening sun setting across the Forrest of Dean, throwing dappled sunlight through the lattice windows. For all his bravado, working for MI5 and his wiliness to take revenge for a friend's miscarriage of justice, Marcus realized he was hiding from the outside world, cocooned in his own safe environment, here in a remote country village.

He cuddled Rosa from behind after the lovemaking and traced his finger across the Unicorn tattoo from her shoulder blades down her spine to the small of the back, where she let out a purr of sensual delight. *"Unicorn"* he whispered.

"Yes, it's a Unicorn." Rosa agreed, half asleep.

"Yes . . . of course . . . a Unicorn." Dyke had suggested a Unicorn as his code name, saying it represents, amongst other things, someone or something that does not exist. Was he referring to me or . . . my brother? Was it possible Dyke knew Marius?

Chapter Six

1984

The daily jog had shortened to once or twice a week recently, not because he didn't want to jog, but his body was telling him something, and he had to listen. Marcus stopped at his favorite spot overlooking the golf course and reflected on life, love and death as he often did. His life was good. His lovers were good. That just left Death. He had lived with Death for many years now, and he challenged Death to take him whenever *It* wanted to, but it always seemed to keep its distance. Was that because of the undertakings Marcus had carried out over the past twenty years; inflicting punishment on the wicked and perverse? Was Death giving him a final chance to fulfil some unknown destiny? Whatever the reason, Death seemed to be good company just now.

Marcus surveyed the horizon and smiled inwardly, satisfied his path was true and solid. In that moment of complacency, he could not have known about the eyes upon him from five hundred yards away. Eyes peering through high-powered binoculars. Eyes full of satisfaction and joy. "Yes. I have you now Mr Hartstein."

It had taken Ivan seven years to find the man who killed his friend and boss, but it had been worth the wait, and trouble, in tracking this assassin across Europe. After his aborted car chase out of Gyumri, Ivan had made it his life's goal to revenge his friends. After the funerals and a period of mourning with the victims' families, Ivan bought a map and traced out all of the possible routes Marcus could have taken on the road to Turkey, and to where he could have flown out of the country. There were several airports they could have taken, but his research showed that Kars was the closest on their route out of Armenia, and it had direct flights to Istanbul. Ivan visited Kars airport and asked staff if they had seen a tall blond man travelling with a Kurdish woman two weeks ago. Ivan bribed several people for information before being told of a couple that arrived early one morning and boarded the first flight out, to Istanbul. The woman at the ticket counter remembered Marcus particularly as he was so very good looking, and thought it strange he was with that shabby looking girl half his age. For a few Lira extra, Ivan hit the jackpot - they travelled under the names Marcus Hartstein and Rosa Chapel.

Marcus made his way back home feeling rejuvenated, and ready to face Barbara about funding for a new exhibition center in Berlin. Money was not the problem - it was more the logistics of the whole idea. The London gallery had prospered over the years, and Barbara was a rising star in the art world, but now she needed to be seen in other important cities; Berlin, New York, Tokyo and Rome.

Marcus was a *'sleeping'* partner, in more ways than one, and was happy to let Barbara run with the business although she wanted his backing and approval when it came to important decisions like expanding the business.

They had touched on the subject the previous evening, but Marcus, having spoken his mind, left the room, leaving Barbara deflated and annoyed. In all the time they had known each other they had never had a row or raised their voices to each other.

Rosa had been out for the evening but noticed the sudden chill in the air when she arrived home. "What's going on, Barbara. You look so sad," she said, hugging her friend.

"Nothing really. Just a silly disagreement with Marcus over the business. Nothing for you to worry about." Barbara said, reaching up to kiss Rosa's cheek.

"Have you had a good evening?" she asked, wanting to change the subject before she dwelled on it too long.

Rosa sat next to Barbara and held her hand. "I met a man," Rosa said, a little too excitedly. Barbara flinched, not meaning to, but the statement took her by surprise. "What man?" she asked, trying not to sound overly alarmed. "He was at the evening class, learning Portuguese as well," Rosa answered eagerly. "And guess what, he is from Georgia."

Ivan had wanted to leave his home-town in Northern Armenia sooner, but in 1980 before he had completed his plans to go to England, he was enlisted in the Army and sent into conflicts all along the country's borders with Turkey, Georgia and Azerbaijan.

Many of his comrades died in conflicts during those bad years, and Ivan considered one more would not be noticed. He made his way to Georgia and eventually to Turkey, working at odd jobs to buy food, and for travelling further afield. By March 1983 he had reached Istanbul and had enough money to buy a new identity and the means to get to London. Once in England, he contacted the Georgian communities in London, quickly identifying who could help him track a Kurdish woman called Rosa Chapel. It was a long-shot, but the members of the community were happy to help, once they had heard Ivan's story - well, his version of events. The word was spread far and wide, and all Ivan could do was to wait and be patient. Stories started coming back to the Kurdish HQ in London of women who could be the missing Rosa Chapel. Photos were sent to help with the identification, but Ivan did not recognize any of them, even allowing for a change of hair color and a new identity.

"She will not be in a Kurdish community." Ivan kept telling his helpers. "She was abducted. She could be living anywhere as a servant or slave, or even worse," he would cry out, ensuring his words would be understood, and the search continued in earnest. Then, in early September a photo arrived of a woman smartly dressed with black shoulder-length hair and stunning features. Ivan stared at the photo longer than he had any of the others. "Yes," he whispered. Then louder. "Yes! I am sure it is her. Tell me where this is."

Rosa had befriended another Kurdish woman around her age at evening classes in Croydon where she was learning Portuguese as she wanted to travel to South America one day. Her friend was studying Arabic. They had met in the canteen during a break one week and started talking.

Her friend had told Rosa about the Kurdish community in the UK, and that she should come and meet others that had found sanctuary here. Rosa listened with longing and sadness to the stories of home, and the Kurdish struggle, and felt guilty she was not contributing anything towards their plight.

Ivan enrolled in the course halfway through the term but was not concerned about learning another language, but he would act the part to meet his needs, no matter how long it took. It took exactly two weeks. Like Rosa, Ivan met Miska in the canteen, and he was introduced to Rosa, but to both the woman he was known as Albert. All three became very friendly in a short space of time; talking of home and the terrible times that the Kurdish people were having out there. Ivan, although not Kurdish, played the role well, and when he related his story about the earthquake, he had them eating out the palm of his hand. After another week, Rosa let Ivan see her home on the tram to Shirley, and she pointed out the house she lived in, with her friends, Marcus and Barbara.

Rosa had kept Albert a secret up to now, although she could not explain why precisely. Barbara and Marcus were protective of her, and Barbara had taught her to be 'aware' of different men, but Albert was different, he was kindred. "Why do you not want to come in and meet my friends?" Rosa asked him one night, as he walked her to the edge of the Cul-de-sac. "I am not sure how they would greet me, Rosa. I have no job or prospects really, but I am looking," he said convincingly.

"Perhaps Marcus could find you a job, I am sure of it. Please let me ask him, and then you can meet him." She pleaded, wanting to show him off. "OK, but I meet him alone. If I am with you I will get, how they say, tied in a tongue. .?"

"Tongue-tied . . . OK. You can see him alone." And they kissed deeply, and for a brief moment, Ivan felt a longing he had not felt for a long while. Perhaps when this was over, Rosa would come away with him and start a new life. Perhaps they could live here, in this grand house. She certainly was not living in peril, or as a slave, and he was pleased for her, but nonetheless he had to do what he had come there to do.

Marcus arrived back at the house by 8.15am, showered and made breakfast. There was a note on the table from Barbara saying she had gone to the office, and that Rosa had some news for him. Intrigued, Marcus called up to see if Rosa was awake. He poured her a cup of black coffee, just as she likes it and turned to go upstairs. Marcus's recall was perfect, and he recognized Ivan the driver immediately, although he looked as if he had aged a good deal, and his hair had been cut short and he was now clean-shaven. "I have waited a long time for this moment, Marcus Hartstein," Ivan said in Russian.

"You will now pay for murdering my friend and boss in cold blood." Marcus remained calm, weighing his options. "Actually, I did not kill Endrit. The mob did that."

"Liar!" Ivan shouted. "You were with him. You must have tricked the mob into thinking Endrit was stealing the Icon, and they attacked him. Did you see what they did to him?" He spat venom, recalling clearly that awful scene outside the church where they strung up his friend. Marcus sighed in sympathy.

"Yes. And it was tragic, but I did not kill him, and I did not kill you, Ivan. Have you forgotten that?" Marcus's tone had changed to being more assertive, causing Ivan to consider if he should be thankful or not. "Yes, I was grateful for that, you could have shot me, but when I saw what you had done to Movsesian and the others, I vowed revenge."

Marcus realized Ivan was not armed - at least he saw no gun or knife. If he did get into a fight Ivan would probably be the fitter of the two men, but Marcus did not want to put that theory to the test if he could avoid it. "Where is Rosa? Is she safe?"

Ivan squinted - the low morning sun had breached the kitchen blinds and Marcus saw his chance. He threw the hot coffee into Ivan's face followed by his right fist. Ivan went down on one knee, realizing this old man did not have the punching power that he did. "Is Rosa OK?" Marcus asked again, but Ivan just sat on the floor smiling. "You like her, don't you? I thought at first you had kidnapped her for your play-thing, but I see that is not the case." Marcus readied another fist, but Ivan stayed put. "She could have returned to Georgia, or wherever she is from," he continued, waving a hand in the air. "But she decided to stay with you, here in this wonderful house, with fine clothes and jewelry."

"She is free to do whatever she wants to do!" Marcus interrupted. "I have not kept her here, imprisoned, against her will as Movsesian did with his women." His voice was quivering with anger, and he could feel for the first time he was losing control of himself. Ivan steadied himself on one knee before standing up and wiping a trickle of warm blood from his lip. "I wanted you to know I am here. I now know where you live, and who you love. One day I will be back, but I will not come to talk." Ivan turned and retraced his steps to the backdoor, and was out of the house before Marcus could retaliate or challenge him. He sat on a kitchen stool and rested his hands in his face, feeling the overnight stubble that was waiting to be shaved, but he knew his hand would not be still enough for a while. Rosa appeared in the doorway wearing a pink toweling dressing gown.

"Marcus! Are you OK," she asked, seeing his face, and the stained floor. "I thought I heard voices."

*

The following week Rosa returned from the last lesson of the year looking dejected. "Hola, Rosa," Barbara called over to her friend as she came through to the living room. "Hey, what's up? You look sad."

Rosa sat on the sofa and let a tear run down her cheek. "He's gone. Albert. The man I told you about. No one knows his number or address. He's just gone." Rosa closed her eyes and hung her head. "I wanted to hear more about my homeland and maybe go back with him one day to find my mother and brother." She looked up to Barbara who was listening sympathetically. "What do I do now, Barbara? He's gone."

Barbara hugged her friend and rocked her gently, knowing exactly why her Albert had left her.

Chapter Seven

1985

Marcus invited us to two days of his 50th birthday celebrations; well, actually Barbara and Rosa did. Marcus was happy to have guests but he did not necessarily want to be reminded of his age. Apparently, they would invite couples they had befriended, in the same way they met us . . . and indulge in food, drink and lovemaking over a long weekend, but because it was a special occasion they had invited the very first couple they *found* nearly twenty years ago, another couple from ten years ago, and Charlie and me, apparently the last of their initiations. I gave Marcus a present of the original photo I took of Rosa and myself after completing my tuition period with Mike Payne. "It will hang in my private gallery. It is beautiful, Isabel," he said with pride.

It was also the first time we had met Barbara. I was immediately taken with her. She was vivacious, confident, beautiful, and reminded me of the lovely Jo I had met in Birmingham. We all got on really well, and I was so absorbed with talking to Giles and Fiona, the *first* couple to meet Marcus and Barbara, I almost forgot we were there for what others would term *an orgy*. But was it? I don't really know the definition. It was a birthday dinner with nine friends, all tuned in on the same wavelength, there to enjoy a weekend of intimate pleasure. That sounds a lot better than an orgy, doesn't it?

Barbara sat next to me on the sofa and held my hand. "I see you are trying to sum-up our guests. Let me fill in the blanks." She said, leaning into me, her voice soft and sweet. "You met Giles, 42, and Fiona, 39. They met us back in 1965 in Lloret de Mar. He runs a successful car mechanic franchise with two garages in Sterling, and she is a physiotherapist. Steve, over there is 37 and his wife, Claire is 36. They met us whilst touring in France ten years ago. Steve and Claire own a 3 star Michelin restaurant in Derby."

I was impressed and overwhelmed by these people who had also been helped to find their way in life, like Charlie and me. "Now," Barbara said, touching my arm, "who do you fancy first, and it doesn't have to be me, but I am free if you are," she said, laughing. I felt myself blushing, which I never do, although perhaps it was more of a feeling of expectation, knowing, or not knowing, what the next twenty-four hours would bring. I often recall the feelings I experienced when I first met Marcus and Rosa that day, just six years ago. Those feelings were returning, except they are now entombed in a new mature body belonging to a more fulfilled and confident woman and I found I was yearning to be touched and held by a stranger, and immerse myself in a new sensual experience, once again.

That evening, and the following day, I made love to everyone present, including Marcus, which was, in fact, the first time we had made love to each other. It was about two in the morning. I was lying with Charlie and Rosa when Marcus crept into the bedroom. On seeing Marcus, Rosa took Charlie by the hand. "Come, lover. Let's find Claire."

Marcus laid next to me on his side, his hand caressing my thigh. "How are you?" he asked. I laughed. "Exhausted, almost." I said, "But not *that* exhausted." I quickly added, in case he changed his mind.

Trepidation engulfed me, but my free will motivated me. We faced each other and I kissed him on the mouth, fully, longingly, thankfully. He turned on his back as I reach his neck, and moaned softly as I moved purposely downwards to his clean-shaven chest, still moist and musky with the aroma of sex. I licked and bit his nipples until he recoiled with both pain and pleasure. This, I remembered, was the *giving*, not the taking, he had taught me, and I was grateful for it. My body was on fire just with the thought of Marcus lying under me. Ensuring he was fully erect I sat across him and fed him into me. He caressed my nipples and touched my face tenderly, then, without realizing, he took over the *giving*.

He held my hands firmly and thrust into me, gently at first, then increasing the rhythm until we were one in motion, rising and descending in time to a silent song only we knew.

I awoke, entwined in his arms as the first shards of sunlight broke through the curtains. I lay there, staring at him. The age didn't matter a toss to me - it was the *man* that mattered and what was inside of him. I kissed my fingers and laid them gently on his heart, just as a tear formed and rolled down my cheek. I didn't want to leave him alone, but I knew he would understand - that is the kind of person he is - was. The rest of the house was quiet, and in the semi-darkness made my way to the closest bedroom, where Claire and Giles were entwined. Then to the next bedroom across the hallway where I found Barbara and Charlie. I slipped into bed behind Charlie and hugged his waist. Barbara stirred and rolled over. "How are you?" he whispered. "Wonderful." I replied, truthfully, "and you?"

Charlie turned to face me, kissing me as our lips met. "I love you. Have I said that recently?" he said, staring into my eyes. "You don't have to . . . but it's nice to hear . . . love is an emotion, an expression of our feelings for each other . . . that can manifest in many different ways, not just verbally." I smiled, realizing then I wanted to spend the rest of my life with Charlie. We kissed again and he reached for my waist, just as Barbara turned back to face us. "Can I express an emotion to you both," she asked, one eye open and grinning like a Cheshire cat.

In a quiet moment later that morning I found Marcus at his desk in the conservatory, reading. "Sorry, didn't mean to disturb you," I said, apologizing for my presence.

"Nonsense. Come and sit next to me," he said, offering his hand. I pulled up a chair and rested my head on his shoulder. I don't know why, but I had always thought of Marcus as ageless.

Anyone would say he was ten years younger for sure. "What are you reading?" I asked out of interest. He turned the book cover over, and I was startled to see the title, *Ulysses*, by James Joyce. "You looked surprised."

"Sorry, no . . . well, just a little." I stammered.

"I have always been happier reading seasoned authors, Huxley, Hemingway and Salinger for example. Modern fiction, I find, is too shallow and unimaginative, for the most part. There are exceptions, of course, Rushdie and le Carré for example. What do you like to read, Isabel?"

I'm not a book worm. The last book I read was probably The Famous Five. "I'm not a book worm like you, Marcus," I replied, hoping to press him further on other interests. "What about hobbies? What do you do when you are not working . . . and not recruiting friends?"

Marcus looked puzzled by my question at first and then smiled. "You were the last, you and Charlie, back in '79. Barbara, Rosa and I have met some wonderful friends over the past twenty years, and we have been blessed with their friendship and love." He leant over and kissed my forehead. "You were . . . are . . . special though. You have a gift for sensing out the pleasure in others, and for how to use it. One day, when I am no longer here, I would like to think you, Rosa and Barbara will continue the quest, and find other couples willing to benefit from our experience."

"What do you mean, when you are no longer here . . . are you going away, or," I sat up and turned to face him, "are you ill, Marcus. Why are you talking about leaving?" I said, my voice sounding faint with fear. Don't judge me. I didn't think of Marcus in a fatherly way. It's hard to explain. We have been with him no more than three or four times since we met, but I feel an emotional connection . . . not love as I love Charlie, but a love for what he is, and for what he has done for us.

"Isabel," he smiled slightly, "you know me as one person, but my life is complicated. You and Charlie must not be connected with me in any way."

"I don't understand," I said, with concern in my voice that even worried me.

"Barbara and Rosa are the only ones who know my life story, and maybe one day, when I am no longer around, they will tell you all about it, and you can then decide if I am still the man you think I am." He leant over and kissed my face, eyes and lips, as gentle as that first time we met. "I don't think of myself as a bad person, but as a victim looking for answers, and in looking for those answers I have done some bad things."

A tear trickled down my cheek and he gently brushed it away. "Don't cry for me yet, my dear Isabel. Wait until you know what you are crying for."

Chas and I drove home knowing that experience would probably never be repeated, but I alone knew there was more to Marcus than I had ever imagined, and was humbled to be held in his confidence, no matter the circumstances.

*

There was a time when Marcus could have just left, and had nothing more to do with Rosemary and Nathan Star, and their beautiful daughter, Barbara. He was out of Austria - a free man, he could go anywhere and build a new life. He had read of the cold and wild Highlands of Scotland which sounded a lot like home. There a man could hide forever; maybe get married and have a family. Maybe fate had a hand in him not running away; not deserting Barbara when her parents were murdered - maybe *fate* had been his savior after all?

Marcus opened his black leather A5 portfolio. Under *Investments* he had written; Isabel - Photographic equipment £5,000. Charlie - Artist equipment £5,000. Under *Property* he wrote; Freehold on Mews property, 2a The Cut, Putney. £185,000.

In the preceding thirty years he and Barbara, and lately Rosa, had met and become *friends* with eleven other couples, all of whom had benefitted from his generosity. He would *invest* in new businesses and acquire property, and when the couple had gained enough experience to make a living on their own, he would sign over any property he had purchased so not to have his name linked with anyone. These business investments, with their *pleasurable* attachments, had worked well, and Marcus even surprised himself sometimes at what he had achieved, all because *fate* had intervened all those years ago.

Over time he had invested over a million pounds in people and property, plus the houses he had bought for Barbara and Rosa. Money he had worked hard for - well, not all of it.

Life back in the detention camp, after the war, was made more bearable by Dr Nathan Star, whom Marcus had come to trust. Some evenings when Dr Star wanted to get the young Marcus to open-up some more about what had happened to him, they would play chess together, and Dr Star would give him chocolates and coffee. "It's a good job we are not gambling, young man, otherwise you would owe me a lot of money," Nathan said, jokingly after he had beaten young Marcus several games in a row. Marcus's face broke into a faint grin which was not lost on the doctor; he had never seen the boy smile since his arrival, and why should he? "Was that a smile I saw, Marcus?" Nathan asked gently. Marcus dropped his head again, and then looked up to meet Nathan's eyes. "My father was a *Kunstoffizier*. He has a lot of money at home."

Nathan Star stared at the boy and blinked, trying to remember if he had heard correctly. His German was good, but he had seldom heard the word before; *Kunstoffizier* - Art Officer, someone who searches out and takes valuable art or objects for the *Führer* under the direction of Goring himself. Nathan Star studied the boy, wondering if it was just a word he had heard by a visiting friend, or if his father actually was an Art Officer. "How do you know this, Marcus?" Nathan probed.

"Father gave lots of jewelry to mother, and hid some in a safe place . . ." Marcus stopped and wondered if Marius knew about the safe place, and if the English or Russians had found it.

"I can show you if you want." Marcus volunteered, relishing a chance to see his home once more. Nathan sat back in his chair and thought out the possible scenarios. It would be a risk, but it could work. He had always dreamed of his own practice back home, and additional funds would be an asset to get it off the ground when he returned home in the next few weeks. One day a week he would drive out of the camp to visit other military posts in the area, and have some private time to sketch or fish. "Marcus, I can't take you with me, but if you tell me what you know then I will visit your home and see what I can bring back with me," Nathan said, as reassuringly as possible.

"But I must go with you." Marcus barked. "You will never find it alone."

"It's not allowed, Marcus. I will find it if you give me a detailed layout of the house. Do you understand?" Nathan said, offering the boy little option.

After an hour Marcus had drawn the entire layout of the house, indicating where he knew his father hid the most valuable objects. "There is also my mother's jewelry box if it has not been taken," Marcus added, hoping to change the good doctor's mind about taking him along.

"Now, not a word to anyone, Marcus. I will be going there in two days."

Dr Star pondered the risks of searching an abandoned house alone. His options were few. Go alone and risk being caught stealing, for which the penalty is a court-martial, or worse, firing squad, or persuade Major Ferris to let him take a driver for the day, and on the way back collect some personal possessions for the young Marcus von Hartstein - it sounded plausible.

"No. Absolutely not, Doctor. I do not have spare chauffeurs to take you out on a sightseeing tour of the local countryside." Ferris bellowed at the humble-looking doctor standing before him.

"OK, I understand personnel are short, but I need permission to call in at the von Hartstein's place to collect clothing for the young boy. It was winter when he came here, and he has no lightweight clothes. Please, Major, it would be the compassionate thing to do."

"Yes, yes, OK," Ferris said, waving away an annoying situation. Then suddenly he stopped writing and looked up as Dr Star was leaving. "Take my Staff Sergeant with you. He could do with a change of scenery."

Nathan Star froze, cursing under his breath. "Thank you, Major," he said, turning. "That is most generous of you." And gave the faintest of smiles.

Staff sergeant Kershaw would not have been Nathan Star's first choice of companion, but beggars cannot be choosers - unfortunately. Kershaw drove the doctor without conversation for two hours, stopping only to visit another medical center to collect some much-needed supplies, and catch-up on the outside World from fellow professionals. After lunch, the two odd fellows journeyed back towards camp, but not before stopping off at the von Hartstein's *Schloss*.

"I won't be long, sergeant," Star informed his driver. "No need to come in."

"Sorry, doctor. Major's instructions. Must accompany you in case of looters." Kershaw said with a deadpan expression. Star tried not to look too disappointed.

"Sergeant. See that fishing rod I was given by Commander Peebles." The Sergeant frowned, glancing at the bundle of cane resting on the back seat of the Jeep.

125

"That is a *Pezon et Michel* fly rod. 6ft 6in of precession feather-light cane made by one of the world's most famous manufacturers of cane rods. It is a present to your Commander. If it was to go missing I would not like to be in the shoes of whoever was supposed to guard it." Star said, feeling the thespian coming out in him. Sergeant Kershaw weighed up the options but felt he had no choice but to guard the precious cargo. Doctor Star drew his service revolver. "I will be just fine, sergeant. I have my side-arm."

Grabbing his surgical bag Nathan Star tentatively entered the imposing Schloss; his revolver raised. The kitchen had been cleaned of all bloodstains, although much of the downstairs had been ransacked, and Star felt he was too late.

He was sickened by the stories he had heard of looting and desecration. Those soldiers were not discriminate as to whether they looted enemy soldiers' houses or innocent civilians. Even if he found Marcus's mother's jewelry, Nathan was not prepared to take it, no matter how valuable it was. He would never be able to tell if it was stolen from innocent victims of the Nazis, or unlikely, brought and paid for. Nathan made his way upstairs to the master bedroom, following Marcus's drawing. He found his mother's dressing room, where Marcus was discovered and was astonished at the number of dresses, coats and shoes his mother possessed. He knew he could not let sentiment get in the way of his mission and knelt at the end of the room, looking for the hidden panel. Tapping lightly, he discovered the false panel and removed it with one sharp push. Using a torch Nathan squinted into the vortex, wondering how much time he had left. Having adjusted to the semi-darkness, he realized the space behind the wall was much larger than he had first thought. Squeezing through on all fours, Nathan made his way into the unknown. The small torch gave out little illumination, so he had to feel his way around; groping for anything tangible.

After smoking two cigarettes, sergeant Kershaw was getting impatient, and a little embarrassed at having to guard a fishing rod, no matter who it was for. "Hello. Doctor. Are you OK?" he called out from the hallway, not wanting to stray any further and lose sight of the Jeep with its cargo.

Doctor Star could not respond to the sergeant's call even if he had heard it. He was not sure if Marcus really knew what his father was hiding, but he knew it was a secret, and all secrets have a value. In this case, a bag containing ten bars of gold - pure unblemished, unmarked gold. Nathan didn't know how long he had sat staring at the bullion but was suddenly aware of someone shouting his name. He shot out of the concealed room and reached the bedroom door as he heard Kershaw call out again.

"OK, sergeant. Nearly done. Couldn't find his room, but all OK now. Down in a minute."

Nathan dashed back and reached into the hole with one arm pulling on the gold hoard. It was heavy, but slowly he dragged it out into the daylight. Quickly opening his surgical bag he lifted the gold into it and tried to lift it, which was difficult. Standing up straight he took a firm grip on the leather handles and lifted the bag, trying to show no emotional strain at all. Leaving the bag in the hallway he darted to the third room along which Marcus had identified as his. Nathan quickly located a handful of boys clothing and rushed back to his bag, placing the clothing on top of the gold. "Sorry to keep you, sergeant, but we can now go. By the way, I thought you may like this little number for your girl." Nathan had grabbed a dark blue evening gown off the rails as a diversion in case his driver became suspicious. But on seeing the dress Kershaw smiled. "Thank you, sir. Most thoughtful."

"Of course, sergeant. That's between you and me." Nathan said, winking."

"Absolutely, sir," Kershaw replied with a salute.

"Sergeant, why don't you give the Commander his present. I am sure he will appreciate it." Nathan suggested, giving him a chance to return to his own quarters and pour himself a large whisky.

With the gold well hidden, Nathan went to find Marcus. "Hello, young man. I have some new clothes for you." Marcus was overjoyed at seeing something that actually belonged to him. He immediately discarded the second-hand jumper he was wearing and slipped on a bright orange short-sleeved shirt from the pile of garments the doctor handed him. His thoughts were so wrapped up on his new appearance, he totally forgot the other reason Doctor Star went to his house for.

After the unfortunate death of Herr Rosenberg, Nathan Star took the bold decision to smuggle Marcus out of the camp on a stretcher. He wrapped his face in bandages and placed the gold bars at regular intervals on each side of the boy to balance the weight. When one of the medical orderly's commented on the weight of the patient, Nathan replied assertively, "Those are ice packs, Private, to keep the patient cool whilst in transit. Do you have any further medical observations?"

"No, sir." The orderly replied sheepishly and carried the stretcher to the waiting transport.

During the flight to England, Nathan removed the gold bars into his medical case. He had given Marcus a sedative to calm him during the long journey and prayed he would not regret his actions.

Nathan kept their secret, even from his wife, and hid the gold for many years in an old tin box in his garden shed, where no one but he ever ventured.

After he resigned from the Army Nathan Star was offered a prominent position at the new National Heart Hospital in London, where ground-breaking advances in heart surgery were taking place. It was an offer he could not refuse, and all thoughts of opening his own Practice were forgotten.

Eight years later Nathan Star and his family were run off the road and he and his wife tragically died. Their ten-year-old daughter, Barbara was taken into care by her Grandparents. Marcus had virtually forgotten about the gold, but after Nathan's death, his solicitor sent him a letter on instructions from his client if he should suddenly die.

'The sweets are in the old tin in my shed, under the bench . . . keep safe. NS'

He knew what Nathan was telling him.

That evening he visited the old shed and found his tin of 'Sweets'. He looked down at the polished gold bars and hoped he could put them to good use, in memory of his friend and savior, Nathan Star. Marcus stayed in his adopted home until the funeral. The next day he packed a suitcase and some personal belongings, including a photo of the Stars and himself on holiday, and left for London.

Marcus closed the leather journal and slipped it back into the desk drawer, and turned the key, thanking his friend and savior once again, as he did every time he made an entry.

Chapter Eight

2001

I shivered as I stirred from my memories, plus the late August evening temperature was now much cooler. Charlie must have placed a wrap over my shoulders and let me dream, as he always does. I rose wearily and stepped back into the lounge, following the smell of coffee. "Hi, sleepyhead," Chas said, greeting me with a cup of my favorite blend. "You were dreaming about him again, I could tell."

I was indeed, as I do from time to time, wondering how our lives would be now if we had not accepted that invitation for drinks, on that hot summer night back in 1979. You might say we were naive and foolish to have stayed in that cottage back then, and be seduced . . . if it happened now it would be called *Sexual Harassment*, and he would have been arrested. But we were not children - we knew what we were doing and I for one am glad to have been fulfilled, and rescued by Marcus.

"I wonder where he is now," I asked, rhetorically. Chas kissed my forehead and stroked my neck, which he knows sends sensual Goosebumps down my spine. Putting down his coffee he walked over to the Chair and sat on the edge of the crimson seat. Without saying a word he held out his hand to me. Smiling, knowingly, I slipped off my shoes and walked over to my husband. Reaching for my hands he guided me closer and sat me on his left leg, supporting my back. A wave of ecstasy and passion washed over me and my legs parted voluntarily, and I felt my breasts swell. Our faces were nearly touching, and I could already feel the excitement and apprehension vibrating from my body. He placed a hand on my leg, and our lips met.

I hope somewhere Marcus is watching over us and is pleased that his *Pleasurable* work is being carried on in his memory. If there was another side to him, then I am innocent of all its details, and only wish to remember him in the way *we* knew him – friend and lover.

PART THREE

Chapter One

1995

Marcus read all the national daily papers from front to back, although he seldom read all of the sports columns. His interests lay in other human stories of the day. Harry Wentworth's story filled the front pages in most of the tabloids. There was public outrage, and the papers had had a field day. Here was a man convicted of rape and abduction of young boys and he walks free. Marcus shook his head, reading the sad revelations of the two victims of the Catholic school where Wentworth was a caretaker. One was just eight and the other nine, and their evidence was shot to pieces by the defense, and Wentworth went free. The defense claimed the boys' abusers wore a mask so it was impossible to identify his client. There was also no DNA in his car or at his home connecting him to the boys. A clear case of injustice.

Harry Wentworth lived alone, like most pedophiles, and Marcus had to be sure of this to succeed. Most pedophiles have a similar profile; Loners. Quiet mannered. Unkempt appearance, working in low paid jobs with no self-esteem and probably been abused themselves as a child. Marcus, although not religious, prayed occasionally he had been saved by Barbara, sexually, for there was no telling if he would have taken a different path.

There was also a profile of abusers at the other end of the social spectrum. Those who thought they were untouchable - sacrosanct. Well-healed public figures in politics, the law, the church and the entertainment industry – all too important to touch, but Marcus knew their day would come. For now, all he could do was right some wrongs for those who could not fight back for themselves.

It is not easy to make friends with a pedophile. They are automatically suspicious of any sudden new acquaintances, so approaching Wentworth had to be one-on-one and direct. Marcus drove his hire car to within half a mile of Wentworth's house; a small pre-war end-terraced house in a cul-de-sac not far from the school where he used to be caretaker. He turned up his jacket collar on the cold November evening and surveyed the street. It was 9.00pm. Three teenagers on bikes charged past him shouting some abuse, but other than that no one seems to be out. Guy Fawkes Night had come and gone so there was no other reason to be out in the cold. Two street lamps threw some light on each end of the cul-de-sac, but the middle of the street was dark. Marcus took a deep breath and checked his side pocket, then gripped hard on the black sports bag he was carrying. He always got an adrenaline rush before he went in, no matter how calm he professed to be.

He walked the short path to the front door and looked around once more. A cat ran along the boundary wall before jumping off.

Litter was strewn across the unkempt front garden, and a sorry state of disrepair was evident across the rest of the property. The front curtains were loosely drawn, and the ghostly flicker from a television made the dark room seem surreal. He knocked once, firmly. "Yes." A guarded voice called from the other side of the door. "Police," Marcus replied, not too loudly, but heard the chain being released and two bolts slide open. Harry Wentworth fell to his knees as soon as the Taser touched his exposed flesh. Marcus pushed him backwards with his right foot then swiftly and silently closed the door, and re-bolted it. Marcus was pleased with his new purchase. The GL404 Taser was one of the best. It was lighter and easier to conceal than the twelve-inch cattle-prod he had used on previous occasions.

The first time had been twenty-six years ago after hearing a story from Barbara about a young boy who had been abused by his uncle. It took Marcus several weeks to track his prey and plan his retribution, but he did, and he did it in such a way that the authorities would get the message. There would be no copycats, not the way Marcus left his wretched victims.

Since that first act of reckoning, Marcus made a pact to himself that whenever possible he would take revenge against injustice, and was prepared to face the consequences if necessary. Planning an audacious and deadly attack is one thing – carrying it out was another. Before the first one, he had ordered a cattle- prod from a farming magazine. The twelve-inch stick is battery powered and has two one inch prongs at one end. The result is not deadly, but when the steel prongs are in contact with a living beast it can render enough shock to put a grown man off balance. Marcus tested this technique several times, on himself, until he was satisfied with the area on a human that would give him maximum effect needed to restrain his victim. This unique apparatus was used with maximum effect on three occasions until he saw the availability of a new invention – the Taser. This had several advantages over the cattle-prod; it was smaller, more powerful and could reduce a man comatose if applied in the correct manner.

Harry Wentworth collapsed from the knees. His back arched, his face frozen in astonishment. Marcus stood still and listened to ensure no one else was in the house. Satisfied, he cupped his hands under each shoulder blade and hauled the man backwards onto the first run of the staircase; slippers fell from Wentworth's feet onto the stairs one by one as he was hauled up the frayed carpeted stairs. Marcus was still fit for his age and in general good health, but years on from his first quarry, dragging a fifteen stone man up a flight of stairs was not getting any easier. At the top of the stairs, he took two short lengths of rope from the bag and secured Wentworth's hands and feet then applied a strip of Duct tape to his mouth. Looking up, he saw the trap door to the loft and half-smiled. Plan B would have been an inconvenience. Unfortunately, this loft did not have a loft ladder, so Marcus went downstairs and found a dining room chair. Placing it under the loft opening he threw the larger length of rope into the dark hole and propelled himself after it.

Lofts are either empty, housing an old iron water tank and not much else, or they are packed with unwanted paraphernalia – old memories and unwanted junk.

What they all had, however, were strong wooden beams. The center cross beam is usually six inches square and ideally situated right above the loft door. Marcus carefully swung the rope around the beam and secured it with a timber hitch knot, dropping the remaining length to the landing floor below.

By now Harry Wentworth was struggling to come to terms with his situation and to attempt escape. "Keep still, Harry, you may hurt yourself," Marcus whispered in his ear. Wentworth froze, staring at Marcus trying to figure out what was happening to him. He mumbled as if to say something. "Sorry, Harry, can't remove the tape. You may make a noise which would not be good." Marcus stated factually. He remembered the first one. He had removed the tape from Daniel Mace's mouth seeing he wanted to say something, and he nearly screamed the house down. Marcus panicked and in the struggle to put the tape back on, Mace slipped off the bannister and the deed was done too early. Wentworth struggled again to make himself heard but to no avail. Marcus knelt on the threadbare landing carpet and looked into Harry Wentworth's eyes. "Harry Wentworth," Marcus stated slowly and quietly, "you are accused of rape and indecent assault on two boys from the school you were employed at as caretaker. You stood trial but the law failed to deliver the correct verdict." Marcus stopped talking to ensure his audience was paying attention. By now they usually were. He remembered the second one however in 1971, who started to sob uncontrollably, shaking his head back and forth and wet himself, realizing the fate that awaited him. They usually calmed down when Marcus started to relate who he was. Marcus sat crossed legged facing his quarry and leant back into the wooden bannister railings to make himself comfortable.

"Harry, you deserve to know who I am and why I am doing this. My name is Marcus von Hartstein and I was abused as a child by my mother. I was born in Austria, although back then during the war Austria did not exist – we were all German – but not all Nazis. Well, my father was. I was left to be brought up by my mother in the country. Life was good at first. I didn't go to school, but was taught at home." Marcus paused, as he usually did at this point in the story and closed his eyes, not for effect but to recall the unpleasant memories he was reciting. "However, when I was nine my father brought me a Hitler Youth uniform. I couldn't join the movement until I was ten, but he wanted me to be prepared, and wear the uniform every day for the next year."

Marcus rubbed his eyes, covering his face with his hands. "Sorry, Harry, every time I tell my story it still hurts. Thought it would get easier as time went by, but it doesn't. The pain inside my mind is still there." Marcus said, tapping his right temple with a finger. Wentworth seemed intrigued and was listening, shaking his head in disbelieve, and wanting to say 'poor bastard'.

"Soon after my father left again, mother started to take more interest in me than usual. She would wash and dress me in my uniform, and smile at me as if I was something immortal. Soon she began lessons in what she called 'preparing me for the League of German Girls' – Hitler's breeding stock.

I was abused not only by my mother, but she later invited her 'close friends' to help 'educate' me, or *fiends*, as I prefer."

And he leant closer staring into Wentworth's eyes, "both male and female raping me until the end of the war."

Marcus was almost shaking at the recollections and realized he was holding Wentworth's arm tightly. "Damn," he cursed silently and removed his grip as if he had touched a white-hot surface. DNA was always a risk, but he was wearing two pairs of latex gloves and was confident he never left any traces that could be used to identify him.

"So, Harry, how did I escape you may well ask. Well, I shall tell you. I killed my mother. Father had been captured and shot at the end of the war, and everyone assumed she could not face the future alone, especially as he had been a Nazi officer. I spent a couple of years in a camp for displaced children, but eventually escaped and found my way to England." Marcus sighed and half-smiled. "I decided, Harry, early on, I would never let anyone abuse me ever again, and I would exact punishment on anyone found guilty of crimes against young innocent children, such as you have done."

Marcus stood up slowly continuing to look directly at Wentworth. "It's time Harry," he said, almost reverently. Wentworth lashed out with his legs but Marcus stepped out of the way. Wentworth continued to try and talk, making it clear he really had something to say, but Marcus could not take any chances. He lifted the bound and gagged man to his feet, and standing behind him lifted his legs over the top of the bannister rail and steadied him in a seated position. "Don't fall yet, Harry." Marcus picked up the end of the hanging rope which was already tied with a hangman's knot and placed it over the man's head. Wentworth continued to struggle and Marcus had to hold him firmly. He wanted Wentworth to go when he was ready - not fall and deny him gratification. Wentworth, facing the realization of what was to come, repeatedly shook his head, and Marcus saw tears were running down his face. Wentworth turned his head to face Marcus and slowly mumbled 'please'.

Marcus stared at this sorry individual and told himself yet again, he must not change his routine, no matter how pathetic they look, or how repentant. Marcus blinked to refocus. "OK, but just this once." Still holding Wentworth across the shoulders, he slowly peeled away part of the Duct tape. Wentworth was calm now, maybe accepting he was not going to be rescued at the eleventh hour. He leant into Marcus and whispered into his ear. *"Father Dunfold is no Saint. I can prove it."*

Marcus looked into Wentworth's eyes, and having seen men brag, lie and cheat during those years after the war, he knew Wentworth was telling the truth. "What evidence do you have?" Marcus asked cautiously. "Plenty, but I have to show you where it is." Wentworth insisted, trying not to lose balance on the wooden bannister rail.

Marcus smiled. "Good try, Harry, but I don't think so."

"Wait, please. Whoever you are you must be interested in someone else. We worked together. I was paid to keep quiet about him. It's the honest truth. On my life."

Wentworth was pleading, and Marcus could see some logic in the story. Why would he lie now? He knew he wasn't going to get out of his situation, and saw Marcus as someone who would listen to his last confession, like a priest.

"OK, say I believe you. Where is this evidence?"

"I can show you. I have to take you to it. It's not in the house." Wentworth was talking fast now, feeling he was getting through to his executioner. "It's not far. In the garage."

The duct tape was still partly covering Wentworth's lips and he kept pushing it away with his tongue, whilst talking. Marcus replaced the adhesive gag fully, and Wentworth panicked, nearly falling off the ledge. "Hold on, Harry. I'm going to lift you off." And Marcus took position behind the bound and gagged man and lifted him over the wooden bannister onto the floor, as he had had him previously. Marcus removed the duct tape completely this time but not the noose. "OK, Harry, you have one minute to tell me where and what this evidence is, and I will go for it myself."

Harry shook his head a hundred miles an hour. "No, no, no. That's no good, you will never find it," he spat out the words in desperation. "I am telling you, I have to go with you."

"Harry," Marcus whispered, trying to calm the man down. "That's not going to happen, believe me."

And looked deep into Harry's eyes to impress to him he was serious on the subject.

Harry hung his head and Marcus thought he was going to cry. That would be a problem in these small houses. Neighbors have exceptionally good hearing when they want to, and the sound of crying could raise someone's curiosity. Instead, Harry shook his head slowly, and then raised it, looking at Marcus. "OK, they deserve to go down. But only I can show you where the evidence is."

"They? You said '*they*', Harry. Who else was involved?" Marcus had picked up on the plural. "No one. I meant him." Harry said, looking away, which told Marcus he was lying. "I can take you. You will never find it alone." Harry insisted, desperation painted on his face the likes of which Marcus had never seen before. Marcus weighed up the risks. He could start running, start shouting - or both. But if this evidence does exist then it could be vital in identifying others, and just maybe save a child's distress or even a life. "OK," Marcus said slowly. "I will gag you and tie your hands until we are there. Do you understand?" Wentworth nodded. "Yes, yes, OK." Thinking he had earned enough points to save his life.

Gagged and hands bound, Wentworth hobbled down the flight of stairs but stopped at the bottom nodding to Marcus he wanted something. Marcus peeled back the Duct tape again.

"Shoes. It's wet and cold out there, and a jacket." Marcus placed an overcoat over Wentworth's shoulders and found a pair of black lace-ups near the front door.

Wentworth slipped his bare feet into the shoes but Marcus did not volunteer to tie the laces. Gagged again, the two men walked slowly along the hallway to the kitchen at the back of the house.

Wentworth nodded again, and Marcus pulled on the gag so he could speak. "Must I have this on? It's going to take much longer this way. I promise not to call out," he begged.

"If you utter anything than answer my questions you will not make it back in the house." Wentworth nodded thankfully. "The key you want is in the drawer, behind you."

Marcus found the key and a torch, then opened the back door and immediately fended off the bitterly cold wind that chilled their bones, searching for lost souls. "In the garage," Wentworth indicated with a nod. Inside the garage was pitch black. Marcus turned on the torch and nearly fell into the deep concrete inspection pit. Marcus turned on his prisoner. "You could have told me about that," he said sternly. Wentworth just shrugged. "OK, enough games, where is this evidence?" Marcus asked with extra malice. Harry Wentworth was still playing all his options over and over, but none of them seemed to have the outcome he was hoping for. "Down here," he indicated with a nod. Marcus shone the torch into the eight-foot-deep pit and shook his head. "If this is a dead-end, then you will not see the outside of this garage. Is that clear, Harry?"

"Of course. I just want to help you. It's down there behind the far wall." Marcus shone the touch on the end wall. "Where Harry?"

"Two of the breeze blocks are loose, and behind them, there is a safe. That's what the key is for."

Marcus was not keen to drop down into the unknown. He would have to gag and tie Harry, but he could still cause a disturbance. It wasn't that late yet, but if what is in the safe is as good as Harry proclaims, then it would be worth the risk.

Marcus shook his head at the thought of a priest being a pedophile. Are there any people in society which children look up to, and respect, who are not wretched and perverted? How can a child trust his own parents – he knows all too well about that – and how do they see other adults they are supposed to look up to, respect and learn from if they are being groomed for the gratification of these vile monsters. Marcus knew the arrest and conviction rate was low. Many children are looked on with suspicion when they cry 'wolf', as the police are reluctant to arrest an adult known to the child, let alone a figure in authority - a public figure such as a clergyman, entertainer or politician. The press would have a field day if these high profile cases were lost, and children would be even more reluctant to come forward in the future, leaving them abandoned, frightened and withdrawn, and at the mercy of their evil pursuers. What does the future hold for these poor souls?

The new Childline initiative was a start, set up nine years ago by TV personality Esther Rantzen, where children can call the hotline twenty-four hours a day and report abuse. It was a start, but Marcus was concerned for the future. What part would this new technology, the World Wide Web, have to do with catching pedophiles? Hopefully someone other than he will have the foresight to protect our young generation of innocents, as he felt he was getting too old to continue alone.

He looked at his watch. Half-past midnight. "Damn," he cursed to himself. Decision time. "OK, Harry, you are going down and retrieve what is in the safe. No arguments." Marcus untied his hands and gave him the key. "Now go."

Wentworth climbed down the narrow gantry steps to the belly of the pit - his every movement being watched under the spotlight of the torch. Slowly he took five paces to the end and gently pushed on one, then another of the rough grey bricks. Marcus saw they could be removed easily, and Wentworth laid them on the ground. He fumbled with the safe key in his cold hands and dropped it. The torch found it for him, but it was balanced precariously on the edge of the iron gutter rail used for maneuvering heavy engines in place. If the key dropped between the rails his fate was sealed, and no one would ever know what secrets he had to barter with. The clock was ticking. "Focus, man, focus," Marcus called down to him. He knelt down, hands shaking, focusing on the key. He inched forward slowly, using two fingers to catch the end of it, and lifted it to safety.

Marcus took a deep breath, as did Wentworth. "Now hurry, man. It's cold up here." Marcus said, wanting to know what this safe contained that would save a man's life. Wentworth put the key into the safe and opened the door, and removed a folded A4 brown envelope, and two black video boxes. He took the contents and held them above his head. "See. See. I told you I had something you would like." Wentworth said excitedly, assured his freedom was now secure.

Back in the house, Marcus removed the overcoat Harry had been wearing and marched him upstairs. Bound and gagged securely, sitting on the floor, Marcus left him and returned to the lounge downstairs. He was numb from the cold, and shivering from the adrenaline at having this new tangible evidence in his hands, but all that evaporated as soon as he opened the brown manila envelope. He was holding images of boys as young as seven or eight, either naked or dressed in robes. Marcus closed his eyes and his arm went limp, letting the photographs fall to the floor. A tear formed in his eye and fell on to the monochrome images. In all of the twenty years since he had first vowed to revenge the innocent, he had only read of the horrors they endured, mainly from court transcripts and newspaper reports. This, however, was the first time he had seen first-hand evidence in such graphic detail. He opened one of the video cassettes. The only marking was a date, written in hand on the label; 21st July 1979. Marcus opened the second video box. Again, a handwritten date; 3rd May 1983. Forcing himself to confront his worst fears, he placed the first video in the video player under the TV and pressed play.

Harry Wentworth started rocking back and forth on the floor, faster and faster - agitated with fear. He knew what his persecutor was watching, and he now feared the worse.

Black and white images appeared on the TV, and as he watched the scenes unfold he felt a shiver down his spine and Goosebumps down his arms. A man in a monk's robe was holding a cane. The camera panned to the left and four boys, all naked, were kneeling in front of the monk. Marcus turned the video off and ejected it. He hadn't planned for this - seeing these horrors brought it all back to him. The brutality, the beatings, the rape.

Marcus ran upstairs, two steps at a time. Wentworth was rocking even faster seeing the rage in Marcus's eyes as he came closer and closer. He started yelling into the Duct tape, but he only heard his desperate pleas over and over in his mind, not from his lips – not then or ever again. He struggled repeatedly as Marcus picked him up and sat him on the bannister ledge, just for a millisecond. With the palm of his right hand pressed firmly between Wentworth's shoulder blades he pushed. The deed was done.

The fall was not a long one, but the height and the weight was enough to provide the fatal pressure needed on the neck.

Marcus looked down at the swinging corpse and shook his head. He had to refocus, time was running out. He looked around the landing and was satisfied he had not left anything, and started downstairs. He looked up at Wentworth's sullen face. His tongue, almost purple, was partially protruding, and his sunken eyes were wide open with thin lines of blood leaking from the capillaries. In a few hours the face would go pale as the blood drains to the lowest point of gravity, then he could perform the final act, but not this time, it was too late. Marcus thought about untying his bindings which would give the impression he had committed suicide – unable to live with the guilt of his crimes. Marcus did not want that. He wanted to leave a message; a visual message.

He gathered the videos, photos, torch and the safe key, and put everything in the bag. He turned off the downstairs lights and the television and left the house at 3.15am.

At fifty-nine years of age, Marcus wondered how long he had left or could go on doing this alone. To bring someone else in would be dangerous and risky. Perhaps he had done enough. Five acts of revenge would never make up for the torment he received from his mother, but perhaps it was time to move on – time to enjoy the rest of his life with people he loved and trusted. The temperature in the street was almost freezing as he headed back to his car, but he was already too numb to notice. The twenty-minute walk had done him good. His blood was flowing now and his heart was back to an even rhythm until that was he placed his hands on the steering wheel, and realized he had not removed his latex gloves since leaving the house.

*

Marcus caught the first London train with only a few minutes to spare. His breathing was heavy and his head was pounding. He sunk back into a corner seat and closed his eyes, hopeful for sleep, but he could not stop playing the events of the past few hours over and over in his mind. He drifted into a half-sleep. His retina behind his closed eyelids picking out the lights from the rain-soaked glass. Flicker, flicker. Flash, flash . . . flashlight shining in his eyes.

"Marcus, listen to me," he heard a woman's voice whispering in dark, the flashlight too close for him to see her. "Stay here, in this room. Hide in the dressing room but be very quiet until I come for you. You will be safe, I promise." The woman's voice was anxious but familiar. "Liza . . . is that you?" He called out. "Where are you? Don't leave me."

*

Barbara was waiting for him at the station as planned. "You look exhausted," she said, her concern matching her desire. "Are you ill, Marcus?"

Marcus shook his head. "I'm fine. Please get me back. I have something to do."

Marcus slept some more during the forty-five-minute drive back to Shirley Heights. "You were mumbling. What's going on? What happened?" Barbara asked again, pushing him for an answer, but Marcus got out of the car without answering.

He knew he would have to tell Barbara eventually - he had never lied or kept her in the dark about anything in his life. They were after all 'soul-mates'. When he came back into the lounge after a shower and a change of clothes, Barbara was sitting on the sofa. She looked relaxed but inquisitive. She also looked as beautiful as ever. Marcus considered himself a fortunate man considering where he could have been living if Richard Dyke had not been so accommodating.

"Why are you smiling?" Barbara asked. "You looked like shit a while ago."

Marcus sat next to his life-long friend and covered her hand with his. "I was remembering why I love you so much. You are always there for me and you do everything I have ever asked of you." He lifted her hand and kissed it gently. Barbara remained silent as she had learnt to do. Pressing Marcus did not produce results, and Marcus had seen through this tactic for many years. "OK, you win," he smiled. Marcus refreshed his brandy and poured one for Barbara. His hand shook ever so slightly as he gave her the glass. "Marcus, for Gods' sake, are you ill?"

"No, no," he said, preferring to stand but decided to sit again. Turning to Barbara he re-told the dream he had on the train.

Barbara listened with interest, and with some reservation. "Marcus, considering what you did last night and the trauma it must have caused you - relating your story again to that ghastly man . . . it's bound to have had an effect on you, but a dream is not the same as a recollection."

Marcus shook his head.

"Barbara, this was *not* a dream. I now remember why I was found in my mother's dressing room.

Liza told me to go there." Marcus stopped and stared at the roaring fire. "Liza and Marius . . . they must have eloped together . . . they could still be alive."

Barbara wanted so much for Marcus to be right, but she could not for one moment think his brother would leave a sibling to be arrested or to be taken by occupying troops. "Marcus," she said, touching his face and gently moving his head back to meet her eyes. "Marcus, why would they leave you to be taken by the British, knowing *you* would be blamed for her death?"

"I . . . I . . . don't know." Marcus stammered, feeling deflated. "But I want to find out. I want to know the truth, and I think there is one man who knows it."

Chapter Two

1995

Christine Ling had left Hong Kong in 1983 for England with a deep desire to join the police force. She would have preferred to have stayed in Hong Kong and follow her father in the Islands police force, but it was not to be. Harry Ling was a respected detective based in Kowloon, but he knew it was a hard and dangerous life for a police officer in the British colony, and no one could predict what it would be like after the 'handover' in 1997. After many loud and often public arguments, Christine walked out of the family home and headed for the UK. It was a decision she never regretted but longed to see her father again.

At forty, Christine Ling was one of the few women Detective Sergeants' in the force. She was however not fazed by that statistic. She was assertive, determined and focused. She knew she could make the grade, and take anything her foul-mouthed colleagues threw at her. She had completed her statutory three years 'on the beat' and applied immediately to take the exams for Detective Constable. That was back in 1987.

The briefing room was full. Smoke filled the air and foul perspiration filled her nostrils. There were twenty or more men in the room, plus Sheila, the Chief Superintendent's PA, there to take notes.

"OK, listen up everyone." Chief Superintendent James Jarvis opened the meeting. "DCI Crane will go through this briefing.

Take notice. Take notes." And he nodded to DCI Mike Crane to proceed. Crane was suited to his name, over six feet tall with the physique of a rugby player. *Not a man to cross,* thought Christine as she studied her boss, remembering when they met.

She had spoken to him only once back at the interview in 1987, and he was prepared to dismiss her out of hand, for no other reason than she was a woman.

"Why do you want to join CID, Miss Ling?" he asked indifferently.

"To catch bad people and lock them up, sir."

Crane suppressed a grin. "And you can't do that in uniform?"

"No, sir."

"You do realize there are no other women in the squad. How do you feel about that?"

"I can give as good as I get, sir." Christine knew there had been other women trainees, but they usually only lasted six months before the torments and sexual harassment got to them. DI Crane, as he was then, was hard-pressed to find a reason not to accept her, plus the fact it was being noticed that women officers were far and few between. Her grades were excellent and she seemed a tough cookie. He also knew her father had been a detective in Hong Kong, so he had some sympathy with her on that score – when it's in the blood it's hard to deny anyone a chance – just like he had followed his father into the force.

"OK," Crane said, bringing Christine back to the present. "Listen up. We have a murder of a man, age fifty-one. Found hanged in his own home at approximately 1.00am yesterday morning in Beamish Gardens, Springwell. He could well have been hanging there for days or even weeks, but some boys threw a brick at the front door this morning and broke the glass panels. A few hours later they ventured back to see if anyone was still there and saw a body hanging over the stairs. The deceased is Harry Wentworth. I am sure you are familiar with the name. Previous includes attempted kidnapping of a boy aged nine, two years ago, and four counts of rape on young boys between 1983 to 1992.

All charges dropped due to lack of evidence and unreliable witness statements." Crane looked at his silent audience.

"OK. Let's focus here." Crane continued. "Regardless of your feelings towards such men, we will conduct this investigation professionally and without prejudice," he looked around the room for a reaction, but none came, which he knew would be the case. "What we may have here is an act of revenge or vigilante killing. We need to check records of all known pedophiles who were NOT convicted on the principle charges of rape or assault over the past ten years." Christine Ling listened intensely. She had her own theories she wanted to put to her boss. "Also," Crane added, "we are cross-referencing the database for same or similar killings across the country. Any questions?" Christine bit her lip. "OK then. We split into three teams. Team leaders are DI Morgan, O'Brian, and Ross. Let's catch this bastard."

The detectives picked up their notepads and jackets and talked amongst themselves while slowly drifting off into the operations room. DCI Crane was still in the room talking to Micky Ross when he noticed Christine standing, waiting. "DS Ling," he called over to her. "You are on door-to-door with DI Ross and his team." Christine smiled and nodded. "Yes, Sir. Can I have a word, please?"

"Sir," DS Ling started to say but was interrupted by her boss's phone. "That was the Super." DCI Crane said, lifting his eyes upwards to indicate where his boss's office was. "Wanted to know where we were on the Wentworth case. Suggested it was a suicide."

"Sir," Christine started again, "it was *not* a suicide. The guy's hands were tied and there was Duct tape over his mouth. He can't be serious."

"I agree. I can't see him doing that himself, but leave the Super to me for now. Tell me what you are thinking, Christine."

"I have been following several cases known as *The Rope Killer*, but again the official line is suicide. You may remember one of them a few years ago, Shaun O'Neil. He was hung in his own house, but he, like others, had his . . . penis removed." DCI Crane frowned, remembering the O'Neil case.

"But Wentworth was intact, wasn't he? Why do you think they're connected?" Christine leant forward in her chair. "Sir, I know it's the same guy. I have been following these cases since 1971. There have been four cases with the exact MO.

Why he changed the MO on Wentworth I don't know yet, but I am willing to put my job on the line to prove it, sir." Christine swallowed and hoped she hadn't been too hasty in offering her job as collateral. "Give me a team and Clive Moran, the new profiler, and I can get him, sir." Crane was impressed, but he knew the Super would not approve it. "OK. I'll give you three officers and Moran, but only until the New Year. No results by then, it's back to normal duties, understand Ling."

Christine smiled. "Thank you, sir. I appreciate your trust in me."

It had been ten years since the last 'rope killing', that of Shaun O'Neill in 1985 in Newcastle, which was Christine's first case as a DC. It was also the beginning of a personal undertaking to solve the case of the 'rope killer'. She had established a link to the 1973 killing of Jamie Atkins in Exeter, and of Chris Searle in 1971 in Wolverhampton. These, coupled with the first such reported incident back in 1969, and the 1985 case, made for *'serial killer'* status. Now, in 1995, he has struck again. Harry Wentworth was found hanged in his own house. Her superior said it was not the 'rope killer' as there was one vital difference about the crime scene, his penis had not been removed - a fact that has never been made public from the previous four killings.

Christine was not convinced. Everything else fitted. Wentworth was a convicted pedophile. He had escaped a long jail sentence.

He lived alone. He was found hanging from the loft rafters - but why hadn't their man finished the job this time and mutilated the body? Forensics had not come up with any DNA other than Wentworth's, other to say there had been evidence of someone else in the house at some point. She studied the reports of the previous killings and wondered why the time of death was so different in this case than the preceding hangings. Was it a copy-cat, not knowing all the vital facts, or did the murderer do something different this time?

The old police station in Bell Street, Newcastle had been outgrown, and in 1990 everyone was relocated to a modern five-story glass 'egg-box' as it was locally called, in the center of town. The additional benefit of this move was to recruit additional staff in specialist areas. One of these specialist areas was *'police profiling'*. Christine, unlike some of her colleagues, embraced any new advance in technology or expert help that resulted in more arrests. Clive Moran looked younger than thirty-one. However, his muscular build and height, at nearly six-foot, gave him a look of authority. Christine Ling thought his conservative appearance, usually dark grey suit, white shirt and plain blue tie, also gave him a look of maturity that demanded attention. And as a physiological profiler, perhaps this was a trait he had adopted on purpose, but either way, it was one which Christine admired.

Clive Moran had been updated on the *'rope killer'* murders, as well as that of Harry Wentworth, by Christine, and now they sat together in the briefing room considering what, if any, new evidence they had, and if Moran's methods were creative enough to make progress in a case she desperately wanted to finish.

The long white case board was filled with images of the four victims, together with details of date of death, location of death and their ages. There was no photo of Daniel Mace, just an outline of a face with his name underneath it punctuated with a question mark.

"None of these guys, on appearance, seem to have had anything in common. They didn't know each other and didn't live near each other, except for O'Neil and Mace." Moran stated factually. "Records show that no connection has been made between them, although the 1969 records were not as comprehensive as they should have been. The new National Crime Computer was introduced that year, but it took a long time for information to be added, and checked for accuracy."

Christine Ling was impressed, even if she didn't show it. Moran continued summarizing. "The *only* concrete connection is that four out the five were known pedophiles . . . pedophiles who did not serve a term of imprisonment for one or more known offences, including murder, and that all were released due to a technicality or lack of witnesses. The first victim, Daniel Mace, had no convictions, which is where we need to start. We need to know why he killed Mace if he *wasn't* a pedophile, and why it gave your man a springboard to go on killing in the same manner, albeit over a twenty-six year period."

Christine Ling nodded thoughtfully. "I take your point, but let's concentrate on what we know about the latest case for a moment." She suggested. She walked over to the dry-wipe board and took a blue felt pen from the tray. "One," she started to write, "recently released due to lack of evidence."

Released after Trial - Lack of evidence
Lived alone
Time of death around 3.45am
Penis NOT removed

"According to the autopsy reports of the previous deaths, time of death has always been between 11.30pm and 1.00am the latest. The consensus from the pathology lab is that the time frame needed to remove the penis without a great deal of blood loss, would be three to six hours after mortality depending on the weight of the victim." Christine looked towards Moran for his approval of her analysis. Moran nodded thoughtfully and took up the thread.

"So, why is the time of death, in this case, the time he usually carries out his act of amputation, two to three hours later?" Moran rose and picked up a red felt pen and circled item No.4 on the board. "Because," he continued thoughtfully, "he either did not have time to wait another three hours or so, *or* he was engaged in doing something else during that time."

Christine raised an eyebrow at the conjecture. "Something else? Such as talking him to death?" They both smiled at the quip, but Moran gave the idea some credence.

"Or similar?" he said. "Perhaps Wentworth was trying to talk *his* way out of ending up at the end of a rope . . . plea bargaining, for instance. We know he was in as the neighbors say they heard the TV all evening."

"That is an interesting thought." Christine agreed. "What about the killer himself. Have you had time to form a profile?"

Morgan glanced at his notes. "From what little we have, and given the timescale of his work which covers five deaths over twenty-six years, I feel he is a vigilante, but a selective vigilante."

Christine nodded slowly. "Yes, I was afraid of that," she agreed. "He, for some reason, picks victims that have escaped justice, in his eyes, and has judged them to be executed." Christine rose from her desk and walked around to stand in front of Moran. "But what I need from you, Clive, is what sort of man is he, our mystery killer. Assuming he was, say in his mid-twenties when he killed Daniel Mace, he is now in his mid-fifties. Does he work alone? What type of work does he do? Where would he live? And more importantly, what drove him to do this."

Clive Moran tapped his pen on the notepad and underlined the last of Christine's considerations. "Yes, and that is the key to all of this. I know is a cliché," he said standing to face Christine, "but we will find it all stems back to his childhood and his parents. He was probably abused as a child by his father, hence the removal of the penis." Ling and Moran looked at the whiteboard of notes and crime scene information again. "The problem is, Christine, he is picking random victims each time, and that makes it very difficult to predict his next move unless he gets sloppy and leaves a clue."

Christine drew an outline of a face on the whiteboard with a question mark in the middle of it, and wrote next to it, 'male, white, mid-fifties'.

"Yes," she replied thoughtfully, "we need a break. Let's hope you're right." Christine looked at her watch. "I have to go soon, but let's pick up on this tomorrow morning, and I'll get DC Taylor to check out Daniel Mace's background and see if there are any relatives still alive."

Moran nodded, smiling. "A date?" he said, without knowing why, and regretting it. Christine showed him a look. "Sorry. Out of order," he said, raising his hand in defense.

"It's OK. No, just a drink with an old friend . . . in fact you are welcome to join us. She is the attractive one." Christine added, smiling.

"I can't believe that."

"It's true . . . there's always one female out of two that is always better looking than the other . . . haven't you ever noticed that?" Moran was now blushing and trying to back-track.

"Well, in that case, I am sure the two of you have broken the myth." He said, feeling pleased with his get-out. "Good night. Enjoy your drink, Christine."

Christine looked at her watch again. "Hell, she's going to kill me . . . again."

Chapter Three

Although in good health, Marcus knew his limitations. After the Harry Wentworth case, he had planned to spend the rest of his life enjoying the benefits of good friends, beautiful surroundings and a comfortable financial position.

He smiled at his reminiscences and the people he had let into his life. All had played a part, all had performed a role, and he was more than satisfied he had led a meaningful and rewarding life. There was, however, one final encounter he now had to undertake. The words Wentworth had whispered to him could not go unchallenged.

His quarry was Father Peter Dunfold. Last known whereabouts; assistant to the Dean in Gateshead – in the same area where Harry Wentworth lived, and linked to St. Martin's Catholic School for boys, where Wentworth worked as caretaker. Wentworth's pathetic plea had tormented Marcus. *"Father Dunfold is no saint."* He had played the scene over and over in his mind a thousand times, and always came up with the same conclusion – he had to find the priest now he had viewed both of the videos. Although he shared everything with Barbara, he was convinced he did not want her to see this sordid material. Rosa had visited some friends in Brighton for the night so he was alone in the cottage. Fearing the worst from the few minutes he had witnessed in Wentworth's house, he placed the first tape in the player and sat back, waiting for the horror to start.

It was over two hours before Marcus could bring himself to view the second tape, but he knew he must. He had to be one hundred per cent positive before he took action, which, he knew, must be water-tight. The second tape was different in content but just as distressing, and in many ways more degrading, if that were possible. Its forty-minute content showed just one boy, aged about eleven, being physically abused by a man. The camera must have been on a tri-pod as it only recorded events from one angle, and Marcus assumed, therefore, no one else was in the room. The camera was also positioned so it only showed the perpetrators body from the neck down, so identification was difficult, but not impossible. Marcus noticed a large mole on the man's left thigh. The boy, however, was in full view throughout his ordeal. Marcus wiped his eyes yet again before closing them and willed himself to sleep, hoping to erase the images now imprinted over his own.

Marcus woke where he had fallen asleep. The television was delivering a fuzzy muted vision of snowy interference, and the video had ejected itself. After a shower, which he hoped would wash some of the guilt away for watching the tapes, he obtained the number for the Deanery covering Gateshead and spoke to the Dean's secretary.

"Good morning, I am trying to contact Father Dunfold. I believe he works for the Dean."

The secretary put him on hold for five minutes. "I am putting you through to the Dean, Father Nicolas." A man's voice sounding too chirpy asked how he could help.

"Dean, I am trying to contact Father Dunfold."

"Why?" Came the demanding reply.

"I was a teacher at St. Martin's school and knew Peter. I retired three years ago and have only just returned from travelling, and wanted to look him up."

"Father Dunfold no longer works for me. He too has taken a sabbatical and I have no idea where he is. I am sorry I cannot help further, but if you leave your name and number I will call you if I hear anything . . . hello . . . are you there?"

Marcus had hung up. He knew when he was being fobbed off, and doubted if the sabbatical story was true. He took a train the following day to Gateshead, and booked into the Station Hotel. He knew he needed to do some research on Father Dunfold - in particular, what exactly did Harry Wentworth mean? Were they partners in a Paedophile ring? Marcus had read all the trial reports and Father Dunfold's name had not been mentioned once, anywhere; in fact, no other person was connected to Wentworth at all. Marcus had the photos and videotapes from Wentworth's garage, but there was nothing on them to show who the masked man was, or where they were filmed.

The next morning he headed for the local newspaper offices in Park Street. "Hi. Can I help you? You asked for someone from the crime desk. I'm Mandy Silver." Marcus was not expecting a woman, but his day seemed a little brighter for it. Ms Silver was mid-forties, dark blonde hair with brown eyes, and was wearing a figure-hugging blouse and pencil skirt. Marcus smiled and shook her hand. "I wondered if you worked on the Harry Wentworth trial a couple of years back." Mandy Silver looked Marcus up and down thinking, and hoping, he wasn't married. She smiled. "I did, but what do you want to know Mr . . ?"

"Marcus," he said, smiling. "I am doing some research on pedophiles and wanted some background information that may not have been prevalent at the trial."

She gazed sideways. "What information would that be?"

Marcus looked coy and frowned; as if not sure he wanted to say what he wanted in public. "It's delicate." Then adding as if he had just thought of it. "Could we meet somewhere else and I will tell you what I am looking for." And smiled, hopefully.

Mandy Silver thought a moment too long. "OK. I'll get my coat and bag."

Marcus was not expecting her to respond that quickly. An evening meal maybe or a drink somewhere quiet, later in the day.

"I know just the place where we will not be overheard," Mandy said, hailing a taxi outside her office.

*

"Come on in Marcus. It's small but it is home." Mandy had taken him back to her apartment two miles away. "Can I get you a drink? Only got beer or Gin," she offered, walking into the kitchen.

Marcus looked around the sparse room. "Beer is fine. You don't have a lot of furniture," he observed. "No, not yet. Only moved in six months ago. Still deciding if I like it. But I have the essentials. Cooker, TV and a bed." She handed Marcus a cold beer and sat on the brown leather stool, sipping her gin and tonic. "So, what do you want to know, and what exactly is this research you are doing?"

Marcus sat on the only other chair in the room, keeping a respectable distance between them. He realized she was flirting, and he was flattered, but first things first. "I'm taking a sociology and psychology course at the Open University. It may seem late in life, but I have time on my hands and I like the subjects. Always been interested in human behavior." He sounded convincing.

"You have a faint accent. Where are you from originally?"

Marcus shrugged. "I travelled a lot so I have probably picked up a 'twang' from everywhere," he laughed, hoping to move on. "I studied high profile cases from Roman Polanski to Mary Bell, but now want to focus on pedophiles in the UK over the last decade, especially those who escaped justice in the eyes of the public, and particularly those in the clergy. I followed the Wentworth case, which was fascinating insofar that he was acquitted, and then recently committed suicide. I'm trying to check if there are any other similar cases." He said persuasively.

Mandy sat silent for a while, still summing up this handsome stranger. Was he telling the truth or - *or what*? Mandy gave a weak grin but said nothing. Marcus, however, picked up on it. "What was that? You don't believe he committed suicide?" He cast the line out. Will she bite?

Mandy shook her head slowly. "It's what we were told by the police, so it has to be."

"Since when does a crime reporter believe everything they hear, especially from the police? They are known for keeping something back, even from the press – especially the press."

Mandy shrugged again. Another beer?"

"No thanks. So what makes you suspicious about his death, Mandy?"

"I'm not suspicious, and I don't think I have anything else to add," she said, making it sound final. Why did she do that? Half an hour ago she had high hopes of bedding the guy, now all she wants to do is get him to leave. Why have alarm bells sounded, she kept asking herself? Maybe she can get more answers from her close friend, Christine Ling.

"I really must be getting back now. Can I drop you off anywhere – your hotel perhaps?" Mandy asked, hopefully.

Marcus ignored the suggestion. "Mandy, have you come across the name Father Peter Dunfold. He worked for the Dean in Gateshead?" he asked, looking her in the eyes, hoping to find a hint of deceitfulness.

She cocked her head in thought. "No," and Marcus could see was telling the truth, "but I have only been with the paper three years. I have heard rumors of naughty priests of course, but no one takes them seriously, do they, I mean they are priests for God's sake," she said, leaning back in thought.

Marcus realized this was going nowhere and smiled. "Of course. It was a long shot, but to answer your question, no thank you. I can get a cab."

Mandy said goodbye outside her block of flats and hailed a taxi. She looked back at Marcus through the rear window as it drove off and sighed. Why did she play hard to get? Must be losing her touch, she thought.

Time was now of the essence. He needed to get out of Gateshead before he met too many people. He was pretty sure Mandy Silver had not heard the name Dunfold before, so he was not going to get any further there. His only option was what he wanted to avoid, but there was no other choice. He hailed a taxi. "Do you know the Dean's residence?"

It was approaching 6.15pm when Marcus stood outside the Dean's large mock Georgian residence complete with white sash windows and a large black double door. Marcus banged the brass knocker loudly. A few moments later the door was opened by the Dean's valet. "I need to speak to the Dean, it's most urgent." Marcus pleaded, breathlessly, for effect.

The valet looked him up and down and nodded for Marcus to come on in. It was obvious he was distraught and in need of some advice. "What is the problem Mr?"

"Hartstein . . . I have some important news concerning one of his parishioners – it is very important." Marcus coughed, for more effect. "Wait here. I will see if the Dean is available."

Marcus stood when he saw the valet walk back towards him. "The Dean will see you, but he has to leave in fifteen minutes."

Marcus smiled. "Thank you. It will not take that long, I am sure."

He followed the man down a carpeted hallway, with many doors on either side. Some had copperplate engraved name – Assistant to the Dean, or Diocese Treasurer. The Dean's office was at the end of the hall. The valet opened the door and gestured for Marcus to enter. "Father, this is Mr Hartstein," and left the room closing the door behind him. Marcus turned to face the door and quickly and quietly turned the key in the lock. The Dean looked up from his notes behind his desk. "What is it? What did you do? Who are you?"

"So many questions, Dean. But I only have one for you and I want the truth." Marcus was by the Dean's side before he finished the last syllable, and pushed the Dean back onto his large leather chair. "Where is Father Dunfold?"

The Dean appeared confused, as he might be. A stranger makes his way into the private office of the Dean and demands information. This is unprecedented. The Dean looked at Marcus with suspicion, playing for time. "Was it you who called yesterday, wanting to know about Father Dunfold?" He asked, leaning back in the chair, not knowing how violent his intruder could be.

"Yes, Dean, it was. Now I am here in person and I need to know where you have hidden him."

"Hidden. What do you mean? He has gone on a sabbatical – that's all I know." The Dean offered, trying to sound assertive.

Marcus was no stranger to interrogation. He had endured it at the age of ten when he was liberated by the British in his native Austria.

They wanted to know how his mother had hanged herself - and how could she with her hands missing. They questioned him for days but he said nothing. Because of his age they stopped short of beating him up, but the mental torture was just as bad.

Marcus placed his hand into his inner jacket pocket and looked poised to pull out a weapon. The Dean was now perspiring badly and leant further back in his chair as Marcus came even closer to his face until eventually, they were eye to eye with each other.

Still, with this hand on the non-existent weapon, Marcus repeated the question with more menace than earlier. "Where is Father Dunfold hiding? You have five seconds."

The Dean gasped for breath and shook his head. "What do you expect to achieve? The man is out of harm's way."

"Out of harm's way! Is that how you repay his victims, Dean? Rape, torture, imprisonment . . . you knew what he was doing for all those years in the orphanage and you turned a blind eye."

The Dean stammered. "We . . . I . . . did not know, that is the truth, and the police have not charged him," he said, defiantly, as if that was all that needed to be said.

"And what of Harry Wentworth, Dean. Did the Church pay him off to keep quiet? Well, let me tell you something. He confessed just before he jumped. His actual words were *'Father Dunfold is no Saint'*." Marcus said, remembering that night. "Once more, Dean. Where IS HE?" Marcus raised his voice which was something he was hoping to avoid. Suddenly there was heavy knocking on the office door.

"Dean. Are you OK? The door is locked." A concerned voice called out.

"Last chance, Dean." And Marcus made to pull out a weapon from his coat. "OK. OK. He was transferred to Kingshampton-on-Sea, Norfolk. That's the truth." The Dean said in a panicking and ashamed tone, dipping his head as if praying.

"Thank you, Dean, and if I find anything that connects you as well to Dunfold and Wentworth, I will be back for you."

Marcus walked briskly to the office door, unlocked it and pushed past the man hovering in front of him. He picked up pace and exited the front door and jogged around the corner, removing the latex gloves as he ran out of sight, before hailing a taxi to the station.

*

Christine was twenty minutes late, as usual, and Mandy was on her second glass of Pinot Grigio, when she came in all apologetic.

"Sorry, Man. You know this job." The two friends kissed and Christine picked up the glass of wine that was ready and waiting for her, albeit now at room temperature. "Boy, do I need this." And proceeded to take a good swig of the vino nectar.

"So, what's keeping you busy?" Mandy asked, hoping for gossip.

"Hey, we are both off duty. That's official. And I'm starving." Christine said, but was smiling as she said it. Mandy sat back and fingered the rim of her wine glass, thinking if she should tell Christine about her visitor. "Hey, why the long face. Thinking of someone are we?" Christine asked, mockingly.

Mandy finished her second glass and poured another. "Hey girl, save some for me," Christine said sarcastically.

"I'll get us another one soon," Mandy promised and took a deep breath. "Chris, have you come across the name Father Dunfold?"

"I thought we were here to enjoy ourselves, not talk shop," Christine replied, keeping her tone even, wondering where that came from.

Mandy gave her friend a perceptive look. "You do, don't you," she said, determined not to be brushed off. "Come on, tell-all," she demanded, not realizing what she was asking.

"Mandy, you know better to ask such a question, and anyway, where did you get that name from?" Her friend inquired, feeling slightly uneasy as to where this conversation was going.

"Well, this rather handsome . . ."

"I thought there would be a man involved somewhere."

"Do you want to know or not." Mandy teased. Christine said nothing. "OK, so this guy came to the office this morning asking if I knew a priest called Father Dunfold. He said he was doing research for a degree at the Open Uni." Mandy paused, taking a sip of wine.

"Sounds plausible." Christine offered.

"Yes, but he also mentioned Harry Wentworth – you remember him I believe – the guy who apparently hanged himself very recently."

Christine was now all ears. "Why did he mention him, and why did you say *apparently*, as if he didn't."

"Well, he said the police usually hold something back – did you . . . sorry, did *they*, hold something back about his death."

Christine was looking worried. He could just be fishing, but to mention Wentworth and Dunfold together was a concern. "Mandy, could you identify this guy, and what was his name?"

"I'm sure I would know him if I saw him. Cute eyes and a very sexy smile, and gorgeous derriere. Bit older than me though."

"Hasn't stopped you in the past." Christine threw in.

Mandy ignored that. "Said his name was, Marcus. Didn't give his last name." Christine looked wide-eyed at her friend. "German, perhaps. Did he have an accent?"

"Not sure." Mandy tried to remember. "Maybe, but not very noticeable, and when I asked about it, he sidestepped the question."

"Fine detective you would make," Christine said, looking anxious. "I can check with the Open University of course, and check if he is a UK resident . . ."

Mandy interrupted. "Hey, you are avoiding the question. Do you know a Father Dunfold, Christine?"

Christine was fully aware of Father Dunfold, and the allegations at St Mary's orphanage, but no evidence could be found, and it was assumed the boys had made up the allegations because the orphanage had been run very strictly over twenty years; plus the Dean and Superintendent Jarvis are two of the trustees. Dunfold had suddenly left the Deanery a couple of years back, just about the time Wentworth was arrested. Christine was just about to answer her friend, truthfully, when her mobile rang. "Yes, Taylor, you know I'm off duty . . . what . . . when . . . OK, I'll go straight there. Yes, I've only had half a glass, unfortunately."

She finished the other half glass of wine and looked forlorn at Mandy. "Got to rush love. There's been an incident at the Dean's house."

"OK, but why have *you* got to go."

"Because he asked for me. He was Father Dunfold's boss."

Chapter Four

Christine fumbled with her car keys as she tried to start the engine. "Shit," she exclaimed. "Shit." Again she attempted to insert the key into the ignition, but her hand was shaking. "Chris, calm down." Mandy pleaded. "Why are you like this? What's happened?"

DS Ling leant back in her seat and sighed. "Mandy, the man you met today, this Marcus guy. He may be a killer."

"Holy shit," Mandy gasped. "But what's that got to do with the Dean asking for you?" she asked.

"I can't say any more now. Sorry, Mandy, but I will as soon as I can, I promise." Christine said, touching her friend's hand, and hoping she could figure out the story herself first. She started the car on the third attempt. "I'll drop you off on the way there."

"Like Hell, you will. I'm with you girl and no arguing." Mandy said, more forcefully than if she hadn't had half a bottle of wine.

Several police officers were already there, and as Christine got out of the car she was met by her colleague, DC John Taylor. "OK, Taylor, what happened here?"

Taylor stamped out his cigarette and stepped into stride with his boss as they walked the short gravel drive to the front door. "Well, it seems a man telephoned yesterday asking for the whereabouts of Father Dunfold, and when he was told he was not here by the Dean, this man showed up in person this evening and threatened the Dean. Forensics are in the Dean's office so you can talk to him in the library."

Taylor introduced Christine Ling to the Dean. "Yes, Taylor, the Dean and I are acquainted. Go and see how forensics are getting on, and see if we can trace all calls to the Dean's office over the past twenty-four hours. And a cup of coffee would be good."

Christine Ling sat opposite the Dean on a very uncomfortable high back chair. "So, Dean, why would his man be interested in Father Dunfold now, so soon after Wentworth's death?"

The Dean sipped the brandy he had been given by his valet, to calm his nerves. He had had an hour to get his story right, but even now he was not sure what to say that would sound plausible to Ms Ling. He knew Father Dunfold's name was mentioned, by someone, when Wentworth was first arrested, but the police, quite rightly in the Dean's opinion, were reluctant to act against a priest without evidence. Both the Dean and Father Dunfold were among the trustees of the Church's half-way house and took the responsibilities of caring and educating young boys very seriously. Some were wild and angry when they first came into their care, but with a firm hand and a strict regime, they quickly fell into a subservient role. They had to be educated.

They had to be respectful, and above all, they had to be obedient. Wentworth's arrest was an anxious time. When the police first came to interview the Dean about Father Dunfold it was a very sober affair. Everyone was treading on egg-shells. Ling had been told in no uncertain terms to *'go easy'* with the church - *'nobody wants to be seen accusing the church - if we are wrong, imagine the headlines',* her boss explained, ensuring she got the message. Now the Dean was not so sure how DS Ling would empathize with him over this latest episode but hoped she would keep the same objectiveness she had shown previously.

"Ms Ling, thank you for coming so quickly. I asked for you because you are acquainted with the previous encounter regarding Father Dunfold, and therefore know how sensitive these lines of enquiry can be," he said, finishing his brandy.

Christine Ling was all too familiar with the Wentworth case and Father Dunfold, but she sensed the Dean was worried about something, or someone, due to the intrusion by his attacker. "Dean, tell me about this man. Did he tell you his name?"

"Hartstein or Hartsteen . . . I can't remember exactly. Have you heard of it before?" He asked.

"No," Christine confirmed, but mentally pleased she now had a name. "Why would he give you his name? It doesn't make sense," she asked almost rhetorically. "What did he want, Dean? He wasn't here to rob you, was he?"

The Dean sighed. "He wanted to know where Farther Dunfold was. He was very insistent, and threatened me with a gun." The Dean said, feeling even more agitated at the memory.

Christine was curious. Why would he expose himself like this? He must have a damn good reason to threaten the Dean. "Where did you send Father Dunfold, Dean? His life may in danger."

Just as the Dean was about to reply, Taylor came in with the coffee. "Sorry, got talking to the Dean's valet." Ling didn't respond to the intrusion but kept looking directly at the Dean. "Well, Dean. Where is he?"

"My dear lady, I don't know where he is. He is on a sabbatical, which is precisely what I told this Hartstein chap. He panicked when Charles, my valet, started banging on the door, which had been locked from the inside."

"That's what the valet confirmed, gov. The intruder opened the locked door and barged past him and out of the front door in seconds." Taylor confirmed. "Also, no forensics yet, anywhere."

"OK, Taylor. Finish taking statements and I'll meet you outside." Ling instructed.

Alone again with the Dean, Christine pushed him once more. "Dean, if you know something then please tell me. I have reason to believe this man is dangerous, very dangerous."

The Dean sighed and shrugged. "I am sorry my dear, but as I have said, I cannot help you. I would, however, urge you to treat this as a burglary that went wrong.

The Church, and your superiors, would not want a spotlight on a member of the clergy that could be embarrassing for all concerned."

Outside the Dean's residence, Christine Ling was furious. "Damn that man," she cursed. Taylor was about to query her outburst when Mandy came over. "Christine, what happened? Is the Dean OK?"

"He's fine, Mandy, just fine." And walked away towards her car, leaving Mandy and Taylor staring at each other, bemused. They caught up with her at the car. "Taylor, I trust you have a description of this man."

"Yes," Taylor replied.

"Well, do tell us," Christine asked impatiently.

DC Taylor took out his notebook and began to read. "Approx. six foot. Dark blond hair. Blue eyes. Average build. That's all I got from the valet and the Dean."

Christine turned to her friend. "Mandy, can you add anything to that?"

"I'd say the eyes were more grey than blue, and he had a glorious . . ."

"OK, Mandy. That part of the description is not necessary." Christine smirked.

Christine explained to Taylor. "Ms Silver, here, also had an encounter with our intruder today, although on a more social level." She said with a mocking smile. "Mandy, you will have to come down to the station and give us a statement, and tell us exactly what was said, and Taylor will arrange a sketch artist tomorrow."

*

"Are you OK now, Dean?" Charles, the Dean's valet and friend, asked with concern for his employer.

"Yes, thank you, Charles. It was an ordeal, but no bones were broken. The police were very understanding. I am sure they will catch him soon." He replied, reassuring his trusted friend that the excitement was all over, adding, "Ask Martin to come in first thing in the morning so I can brief him on what to tell the press."

"Yes, Dean. Goodnight then."

"Goodnight, Charles." And the Dean was alone again in this study, sitting at the same chair he had been attacked in just a few hours ago. He smiled thoughtfully. Letting Hartstein have Dunfold's whereabouts was not a bad decision, especially if he is as dangerous as DS Ling had suggested. Perhaps, in time, his *'loose end'* would be a loose end no more.

Just then his private telephone rang. "Dean," a man's voice said, "Glad you were not hurt. I assume everything is under control?"

Chapter Five

Christine and Mandy drove back towards town in silence, until it got too much for Mandy. "Well, that was intense," Mandy said. "I must get back to the office to file a report for the paper," she said thoughtfully, trying to remember all the names involved.

"Mandy," Christine started to say. "You know I can't give you all the details, as much as I would like to. And far as we are concerned, it was a break-in that went wrong."

Mandy touched her friend's knee. "It's OK, babe, I won't embarrass you, I promise." Christine dropped Mandy off at her flat promising to call her in the morning with any additional news, although she was sure there would not be any. Driving back towards her flat, Christine kept wondering why this Marcus guy would make such a bold attempt on the Dean's life, and leave empty-handed. What if the Dean had not been honest with her? Was he hiding something . . . something to do with Wentworth? At the traffic lights she checked her watch, 1.45am. "Oh, shit. Why not?" She made a sharp right turn cutting in front of the last city bus. The driver slammed on his breaks but Christine was gone before he could figure out what had happened.

As she approached Wentworth's house, snow was falling and the temperature had dropped several degrees since she had left the Dean's house. She checked the glove compartment for her woolen mittens. "Thank you, thank you," she whispered to her spiritual guide. Christine parked opposite the house and sat looking at the sad corner terrace property, now masked off with police crime scene tape, although it had been torn away in several places by local's, just for spite. She noticed several windows had also been broken since her visit yesterday, probably on the news that the resident's real name was

Wentworth - a convicted child molester. News travels fast in small communities, and the two local 'bobby's' who got the short straw to guard the property, thought better to turn a blind eye than protect it from an angry mob.

Christine surveyed the street looking for the police car assigned to the house but saw nothing. She took out her two-way radio mike and pressed the red button." DS Ling here. Checking on surveillance outside Beamish Gardens. No sign of our boys."

"No, ma'am. Pulled away at midnight. DCI's orders ma'am. Are you there now?"

"Yes," she replied. "I was in the area. Seen some damage to property and wondered why our boys were not here, that's was all."

"OK, ma'am. I'll log it. Goodnight."

Christine swore under her breath. Her boss, DCI Crane was always going on about budgets and having two men on night duty was going to dig into his budget. She leant back and closed her eyes, letting the negative events wash over her.

She had been taught a long time ago by her father how to handle tense situations, and how to control the body's inner angst by relaxing and breathing deeply. It always worked, and she always thanked her father for it. She stared at the house again and heard an inner voice say *'go home, it's late'*.

She stepped over what was left of the police barrier tape and noticed there were no footprints in the snow, so whatever happened, happened earlier in the evening. Not having a key to the property she worked her way around the side of the house along a narrow path next to the garage. She tried the back-door but it was locked. She shone her torch through one of the six panes of glass into the kitchen, not really knowing what to expect. The only way in was to break a pane of glass. Another broken door would not be out of keeping as the front windows had been stoned earlier. She took a deep breath and tapped the square panel with the back of the torch. A large crack ran diagonally across the dirty surface. She tapped again and this time it shattered inwards. Christine carefully put one woolen mitten hand through the door and unlocked it. Gingerly she made her way from the kitchen to the hall. The rope that took Wentworth's life had been removed for further analysis to see if the maker or supplier could be identified. She moved first into the living room in the front of the house. Thankfully the curtains were drawn so she was less vulnerable to unwanted attention, but the damaged windows chilled the room and she stood there shivering, wishing she had listened to her inner voice. She panned her torch around the sparse room; just a threadbare two-seater settee and a wooden coffee table, plus a television with a VCR unit underneath. The TV was switched off, but she noticed the green indicator light on the VCR, showing it was still in the ON mode. Instinctively she felt the top of the recorder. It was cool to the touch so it had not been used that recently, but why was it switched on?

Back in the hallway, she noticed a pair of slippers, an umbrella and a long overcoat hanging near the front door. She shone the torch upwards illuminating the top of the stairs. Hours earlier she had seen Wentworth hanging there, lifeless, but *plene integrum*. That's the part of this crime that worried her. Why had he been left *untouched* - if it was the same killer? Christine was convinced it was the *Rope Killer* and not a copycat, as some of her colleagues seem content to believe. She gingerly trod the stairs making her way to the top landing. The loft door was still open where the rope had been attached, and a chill breeze covered the landing, causing her to shiver yet again. Knowing the area had been fully covered by forensics, she sat down on the landing near the top of the stairs and closed her eyes.

Within her mind's eye blackness was all she visualized. Gradually an image came into view. She saw Wentworth opening the front door. She saw him collapsed on the floor. Previous autopsy reports had indicated two small burn marks on the victim's neck or upper torso, which was consistent with some sort of restraining device. She visualized Wentworth sitting next to her, his knees tucked under his chin. His wrists were bound with rope and he was rocking back and forth in an aggravated manner.

Christine came out of her self-induced trance and looked around her, expecting to see Wentworth sitting there. She was about to pull herself up from the floor when she noticed something strange about the carpet near where she had been sitting. Leaning closer with the torch fully square on the area in question, she cocked her head and then smiled. There was no other explanation. She carefully sat against the wall behind the marks in the carpet and removed her shoes. She placed the balls of her feet into the two uniform ridges - they fitted like a glove. Her heart rate jumped. She then moved one pace to the side of where she was sitting and assumed the same position. She pushed several times with the balls of her feet on the carpet, but no impression was made. Remembering seeing Wentworth's slippers downstairs near the front door, and that he had been found hanging, wearing outdoor shoes with the laces untied, she then knew his killer must have allowed him out of the house . . . but what for, and to where?

Chapter Six

A sudden surge of adrenaline had warmed Christine no end. Her heart rate was still way above normal but she knew she was onto something. Her watch showed 2.55am. She took out her mobile and was about to call DC Taylor when she heard a noise outside. Listening carefully to pinpoint the direction she cocked her head and waited. Again, a muffled sound from the side of the house near the back-door. Could be looters coming back. *Damn Crane for pulling the patrol*, she cursed. Now in the dark, she carefully made her way downstairs, armed only with a six-inch torch, although enough moonlight was entering the kitchen to allow Christine to see her way to the back-door. She stood at the door listening for further sounds of someone out there. This wasn't going to look good, she thought, if she ends up in hospital, or worse. Her boss is likely to shout her down for any reason she tries to give him tomorrow. Why wasn't she tucked up in bed with a good book, or with . . . suddenly she heard a sound. Someone was trying to open the side door of the garage. Her instinct was to tackle the intruder, but she had no idea how many there were, or if they were armed. If there was to be a vote for arming police in the UK, then she was in favor. For too long the police have been tackling violent crime unarmed, and it was surely time for a rethink. Her present predicament was a case in point, as all she had was a six-inch metal torch for protection.

Her options were few, and it was too cold to make any rational decisions, so she planned to use the only weapon she had - the torch. Rush out and shine it in their face and take them by surprise. That was the theory. Christine moved stealthy closer to the door but before she realized, made a very serious error - she stepped on the shards of broken glass she herself put there an hour ago. She froze and swore in Chinese under her breath. There was nothing to do but continue with her plan and confront whoever was there. In the split second the intruder heard the sound from inside the house he panicked and turned tail heading for the end of the road and through an alley to a waiting car. Christine was out of the back door shining her torch all around looking for signs of life but only saw footprints in the snow going both ways. She moved quickly, trying to keep her balance on the slippery pathway, reaching for her mobile phone at the same time. Heavy cold breath filled the air around her as she looked from side to side, but there was no sign of life. She pocketed the phone. She had not seen anyone to give a description about, and felt annoyed with herself for a bungled attempt at an arrest.

3.30am. Christine sat in her car with the heater on full blast deciding her options. The house needed to be watched but she was too cold and tired to do that alone. She flicked through her mobile phone address book and dialed Clive Moran's number.

*

Clive Moran pulled up behind Christine's car at 4.10am. "Here, thought you would like something warming," he said, handing Christine a Thermos flask.

"Also got a spare blanket." Christine smiled and appreciated the coffee. She was colder than she realized. "Now, what the hell are you doing out here in this weather?" Moran's tone had changed, and it took Christine by surprise. The two stared at each other for some moments in silence, until Moran relented. "Sorry, that's not my business, is it," he said, apologetically.

"It's OK. You are right. I should have called for backup, but I thought we had a patrol car here watching out for the house, but when I got here no one was around. The duty desk told me Crane had pulled them due to budget cuts." Christine did not hold back on venting her anger.

"Hey, I understand the dilemma. On the face of it, it looks like a suicide, of sorts, so I suppose he thought . . . well, it's not a priority. But you are going to tell me different aren't you, otherwise I really will be pissed-off at getting out of a warm bed at 3.45 in the morning." Moran dipped his head waiting for a reply, hoping this was not a wasted journey.

"I got a call this evening around nine. I was in a pub with a friend when I was told the Dean's house had had an intruder, and the Dean had asked for me to come over." Moran interrupted her. "Why did he ask for you?"

"I had met him during the Wentworth case. He was keen to ensure the Church was not implicated in anything to do with Wentworth."

"Why would it be?"

"Because Wentworth worked not only at the school where he was caretaker but was groundsman at the half-way house for re-housing youngsters, which is owned and run by the Church." Christine sipped some coffee, which was now lukewarm, but still welcome. "Anyway, it seemed like a bungled burglary. No one was hurt, and the intruder took nothing, which was odd. The Dean's valet told me the Dean's door had been locked from the inside, so the intruder and the Dean were alone for around fifteen minutes. What were they doing?" Christine sighed heavily and shook her head. "It doesn't add up."

"OK," Moran said, "but that doesn't explain what you are doing *here*."

Christine looked at Moran. *Who else would have come out in the middle of the night*, she thought. Mandy maybe . . . but then again, probably not. "I'm sorry to have dragged you out Clive, but I think I have made a breakthrough," she turned slightly in her seat to face Moran. "After I left the Dean's house I dropped my friend off and intended to go home, but found myself driving over here. When I discovered the patrols had been cancelled I just felt I had to check out the house again. See if I had missed anything from yesterday." Moran was listening and didn't interrupt her flow.

"I managed to enter via the back door, and checked out the downstairs lounge first. The VCR had been left on, which was not noted previously. I closed my eyes and imagined what might have happened. I saw Wentworth open the front door and immediately fall to the ground. He had two burn marks on his neck as we saw from the post-mortem report, and I assumed it was from a Taser or similar device.

He was then on the upstairs landing, in a sitting position, but I remembered he was wearing outdoor shoes when we found him, which I thought strange.

I sat where he could have sat and found two distinct marks in the carpet consistent with someone pushing their heels into the carpet. He could not have done that with bare feet."

Christine paused, waiting for a response. Moran nodded as if understanding what he was being told. "So, if I think I have you correct, you believe, because he was wearing outdoor shoes?"

"With laces untied . . ." Christine interrupted for clarity.

"With laces untied . . ." Clive repeated, "he was taken outside before he was hung."

"Yes, exactly," Christine said eagerly. "The time-lapse fits. Wentworth was negotiating with his killer. You were right earlier this evening after all. He must have had a bargaining tool, but what?"

Chapter Seven

Abuse of children, especially young boys, was not a crime the authorities took as seriously as they do today. We now know abuse was widespread in all parts of the UK and Ireland, with many, but not exclusively, carried out in the fields of entertainment, government and the church. Educational and child-care facilities also faced multiple accusations of abusing children, and local authorities, in turn, were accused of not policing their own welfare staff who were carrying out vile acts of sadistic power. Not all abuse is sexual. Torture, slavery and deprivation were commonplace in these institutions.

Marcus, now reaching an age when most people would be thinking of retirement, kept himself fit. He jogged daily and swam at the nearby leisure center three times a week. Walking back home through the lush green meadows and ancient farmland, he reflected on his life and how lucky he had been to escape the horror of war-torn Europe in 1946. He would be ever thankful to Nathan Star for his trust and friendship, and, although perverse to some people, for the opportunity to have acquired the love and devotion of their daughter, Barbara.

Thoughts of returning to his homeland, especially to see his old home, had diminished many years ago, although he secretly knew he could have travelled incognito thanks to his covert training. So why had he not taken the opportunity, even if only to see if the old house was still there? Could he bring himself to cross that threshold again, and enter the place that hid so many secrets, and confront his fears and try and remember who locked him in his mother's bedroom? Disturbed sleep of flashing images had worried Marcus recently so he booked an appointment with his consultant in Harley Street, London, for a full medical.

"Marcus, you are fitter than me, and ten years older. Whatever you are seeing is not a physical ailment." Dr Patrick Holt confirmed.

"Then what, if not physical, mental?" Marcus asked, looking concerned. Dr Holt shrugged behind his large modern glass top desk. "I don't know, Marcus. I've known you for forty years and I still don't know you, do I?"

Marcus smiled. "Are you sure you didn't want to be a shrink, Patrick?" The doctor laughed politely realizing he would only know anything about Marcus, if Marcus wanted to tell him.

"We can arrange an MRI scan but I don't see that producing any results. If you are suppressing something that happened long ago then I suggest you think about hypnosis."

Marcus looked at his doctor and friend with mixed feelings. Hypnosis would be . . . risky. What if it revealed his shadowy life and the people he knew . . . his friends, Barbara, Rosa, Isabel . . . too many risks, too much to lose.

"It's an interesting idea, Patrick. Let me think about it further."

Chapter Eight

Christine had nodded off with the car blanket tucked around her neck, and Clive Moran watched her as she slept. He had always made a rule never to mix work with pleasure, but he was drawn to Ms Ling, and he hoped the feeling was mutual. She was everything in a woman he admired - attractive, clever, fit, good listener and available. For all his experience in *'people profiling',* he had never managed to have a long-lasting relationship that was not based on just sex. He knew he wasn't getting any younger, and yes, he wanted a family, wanted kids and all that went with it. Now, looking at Christine, he felt a surge of hope. He just had to make sure he didn't miss the opportunity.

Moran gently shook Christine on the shoulder. "Sun's up. Going to be a bright, chilly day."

"What's the time?" she responded, blinking, and remembering the reason she was sitting in her car next to Clive Moran, and who, on reflection, was her shining knight.

"Seven. Shall we take a look at what you found, if you are feeling up to it?"

"Absolutely. I need a stretch. My knees are stiff as wax."

The earlier snow had melted, and consequently, any footprints left were now turning to slush. Christine and Clive edged along the side of the house as she had done a few hours previously until they reached the garage side door. "This was what the intruder was trying to open, I'm sure of it."

"The CSI boys can check the garage out later. Let's check upstairs." Moran suggested.

Christine, now wearing blue crime scene gloves, turned the back-door handle and stepped over the broken glass she had laid down earlier. She pointed to the slippers near the front door. They tiptoed upstairs. "There, in the carpet. Heel marks made by his outdoor shoes. The forensic team will confirm that I am sure."

Clive Moran squatted on his haunches and studied the marks in the carpet. Smiling, he looked up at Christine. "It certainly looks that way. I think you need to call this in and get your team here ASAP."

*

Returning to the police station they were looking forward to a hot breakfast, but a constable caught her eye as they entered the canteen. "Sorry, ma'am, Superintendent Jarvis has asked to see you as soon as you arrived."

"Damn," she said, under her breath. "You go ahead, Clive. Save me some bacon."

Christine took the lift to the fourth-floor wishing she had had time to refresh herself and check her make-up. Chief Superintendent Jarvis was an old war-horse, and as far as Christine was concerned, *'old-school'*. He sucked up to politicians and businessmen, and never missed a photo opportunity if it helped his cause - obtaining a bigger budget.

Christine knocked and entered the large plush office overlooking the five-ways roundabout. Also present, sitting close to the Super's large smoked-glass desk, was her boss, DCI Crane. "Ms Ling, please, have a seat," Jarvis said, indicating her to sit down without any further formalities.

"I'll get to the point, sergeant. You returned to the property of the deceased Harry Wentworth who took his own life yesterday. Why?" Jarvis asked, unemotionally. DCI Crane was looking at his prodigy, hoping she had all the right answers.

"Sir, I was called out to the Dean's residents last night, at his request. There was . . . an attempted break-in. In fact, an intruder threatened the Dean, requesting information on one of his former assistants."

"Who was that?" DCI Crane asked. "Father Dunfold, sir."

"Yes, I heard about the break-in, sergeant, but why did you go on to the Wentworth house afterwards, when it was declared a closed case." The Superintendent asked, sounding agitated.

"I have been working with Clive Moran, the case-profiler, and we believe we have evidence to suggest Wentworth's death was not a suicide, but by the same killer as four previous killings over the past twenty-six years. I went back last night or early this morning, sir, to ascertain if we missed anything the first time around."

"And did you?" Jarvis asked, sternly.

"Yes, sir. When forensics confirms it, we have heel marks in the carpet which are consistent with someone digging them in, in frustration. Wentworth was wearing outdoor shoes when we found him, and no socks, which makes me think he put these on and was taken outside of the house to look for something, maybe in the garage . . . possibly a bargaining chip, hoping he could use it to plead for his life."

"Well, sergeant, we know that didn't work out for him. Did it?"

"No, sir." Christine agreed, feeling she was not getting the support from her boss she expected.

"Is that all you have?" Crane asked.

"No, sir. As I was about to leave, an intruder attempted to break into the garage. He fled on hearing me." Christine said, feeling stupid at admitting her inadequacy. Superintendent Jarvis's face moved ever so slightly on hearing this news. "Did you get a good look at him?" he asked, almost charitably.

"No, sir. Not at all. I decided to stay close to the premises until I could call DCI Crane this morning and arrange CSI to attend. They are combing the garage now." Both men sat in judgment over her. Her boss, playing both sides of the fence as usual, and Superintendent James Jarvis considering his best option without losing face.

"Wait outside, DS Ling." Christine stood and looked at her boss who would not meet her stare, and left the room.

"Well, Clive, does she have a case on Wentworth, or not?"

"We will know soon enough when the CSI boys report back, sir."

"OK, but keep her on a short lead. I don't want any embarrassing press announcements we cannot substantiate."

"No, sir. I understand." DCI Crane left the room pondering on the future of DS Ling. Christine was waiting for him by the lift and wasted no time in unleashing her pent-up frustration on him. "So, sir, are you on board with this, or not, or do you still agree with the Super it was suicide, which it was most defiantly not." Her boss looked slightly amused at her outburst, but before he could respond, his mobile rang. He nodded a few times and mostly listened. "Are you sure? OK, I'll tell them."

"In answer to your question Christine, yes, I am with you on this. CSI have found a safe in the inspection pit at Wentworth's garage, which is good, but it was empty."

Christine closed her eyes and exhaled deeply. "And the contents of the safe was most likely a video, hence the VCR player being left on. Our killer watched what he had found and took it with him," she said with some excitement in her voice.

"Hold on there. Let's not jump ahead of ourselves. Continue your investigation on this Marcus chap, and we will have a conference at 6.0pm."

DCI Crane went back to his boss's office to give him the updated information.

Christine took the lift down to her floor and immediately found Clive Moran and DC Taylor. "Taylor, get the team in here now for a briefing. Ten minutes later they were joined by three other detectives and DS Ling brought them all up to date with the information from the crime scene. "However, we need to find out about this Marcus Hartstein - not sure how it's spelt, but look at all alternatives. It's the first break in this case for twenty-six years - let's not lose it." Ling surveyed the room. Everyone was nodding silent approval. "OK. Drake and Taylor do the background checks on this guy, the works, including Interpol. He sounds European so we must check everywhere. Taylor, I also want to see the original case file for Daniel Mace. Christ knows where it is after twenty-six years, but I need it." Taylor nodded he understood. "Thompson, I want Wentworth's and the Dean's phone records including any mobiles. I need to see who he has been speaking to. OK, back here for de-briefing at 6.0pm."

Clive Moran followed Christine back to her office and closed the door behind him. "Have you wondered why he volunteered his name after all these years?"

"Of course," she said, leaning back, stretching in her chair. "He's getting too old and wants to be caught."

"If that was the case, he could hand himself in. No, I think he wants to get close to you for some reason. I don't think he intends to get caught, Christine. He is very clever and resourceful. You must remember that."

*

The Dean was enjoying a glass of his favorite sherry before supper when his private phone rang. He listened without interruption and replaced the receiver ninety seconds later, his face drained of color; now closer to the color of the pale sherry he was usually so fond of.

Chapter Nine

1996

There was an air of calmness in the house that January morning when Marcus asked Barbara and Rosa to sit with him around the dining table.

Light snow had started to fall, and he was looking forward to taking a walk in the fresh crisp air after he had concluded his business. The New Year festivities had been and gone and some routines were beginning to reappear. Barbara had visited the gallery twice that week to check the progress of a new installation, and Rosa had attended her Yoga class and been swimming at the local gym. Marcus was glad the New Year revelry was over. He had never been comfortable at parties, even when he had known everyone there. Had it not been for his 'girls', he would have considered himself a total recluse. Work had been his salvation. He had worked long and hard in the City, in the financial markets, amassing a fortune, which in time would be redistributed to good causes, after he was satisfied all his 'friends' were financially viable. Barbara and Rosa already had each of the houses in their names; Barbara, the one here in Shirley and Rosa the country cottage in Gloucester. Marcus's concern was a property he had purchased for Isabel and Charlie - the studio in Putney. He now had to ensure the deeds were transferred to them before too long - just in case DS Ling became too inquisitive, or lucky enough to make a connection.

Barbara had always been Marcus's closest and only confidant since they started living together, especially after the Daniel Mace affair. Marcus had confided in Barbara after each killing, and he often asked himself why *after* the event. Was he afraid she would have talked him out of it? He dismissed the rhetorical question and focused on the matter at hand.

He opened a buff folder and placed five newspaper cuttings in front of Rosa and Barbara. "Rosa, Barbara and I have no secrets between us. I have always been 100% honest with her, and she has supported me in every way over the years. You know the circumstances of her living with me after her parents were murdered, but you do not know anything else about my other activities over the past thirty years."

Rosa listened carefully, pushing her knowledge of English to the limit. Although fluent, she still had to mentally understand what was being said and hoped she understood the implications of what Marcus was saying. She looked at Marcus with a puzzled expression, and then glanced at the newspaper cuttings in front of her. Barbara reached over and held her hand; for assurance - for guidance - for an unpredictable reaction? She wasn't sure, but Rosa hardly felt her touch as she started to read the stories of five men who had apparently hung themselves, out of guilt. Without taking her eyes off the papers she said, "Did these men all commit suicide?"

Marcus had been dubious at first about Rosa staying with them when he returned to England with her. She should have found somewhere to stay in the Kurdish community in London - *not here with us*, Marcus would argue with Barbara.

But Barbara saw the vulnerability in her and persuaded Marcus she should stay, and he was pleased she had, and that his misapprehensions' were unfounded. She had grown strong in stature as well as mind, body and soul.

"Look at me, Rosa," he asked quietly. She raised her head. Her heart was beating faster and she felt a surge of panic wash over her. Barbara was still holding her hand, but now she could feel the pressure in her fingers, and she entwined hers around them tightly. "No, they did not." Rosa looked away from Marcus's gaze back down to the newspapers, then back up to Marcus's piercing eyes.

"You remember the men who tried to kill us in Armenia. They were bad people who could not be arrested and put on trial for their crimes. These men were bad people who *were* put on trial for their crimes - very bad crimes involving young children, young boys in particular." Rosa bit her lower lip and a tear formed in her left eye. "No one protected these boys, as I protected you, Rosa. They were abused and hurt - both physically and mentally, probably for life. Some died. These men, their abusers, were never punished. They escaped justice." Rosa looked briefly at Barbara who nodded her reassurance that everything Marcus had said was true, then looked at the photos of the men again, but this time with revulsion that overwhelmed her. The one tear was followed by another, and another.

She wiped her cheek with the back of her free hand and looked back at Marcus. "I told you I was to be married, and showed you my gold Lira belt I said was a wedding present." Marcus nodded. "Yes, I remember," he answered. Rosa took a deep breath, and her captive audience could see she was struggling to relate a deeply personal secret. "One week before the wedding his brother raped me." Barbara inhaled a breath of surprise, but Marcus kept his eyes focused on Rosa. "Tell me. What happened," he asked sympathetically.

Rosa nodded. "I told my fiancé, but he did not believe me, and called me a liar. He said I wanted to get out of the marriage, but that was untrue. His brother finally told him it was true, but he still left me," she hung her head and closed her eyes as another tear traced a line on her cheek. "He did not want me as I was not a virgin anymore, and blamed me, not his brother, who was never punished." Rosa looked up again. Her eyes glistened with tears but they were now wide open, and Marcus could see the hate and the horror in them, and he knew then she understood.

"Thank you," Marcus eventually said, "for sharing that with us. I know how difficult it must have been. We are now truly bonded, and no one can break that bond." Marcus let the silence wash over them until he was ready to continue his plan.

"Now you are up-to-date with events, Rosa, I have one last undertaking to accomplish before I . . .retire."

Rosa looked at Barbara, not understanding what Marcus was saying. "What does he mean, retire?" Are you going away, Marcus?" Her tone was tinged with fear, as well as concern, as she looked back to him for an answer.

"Do not be worried, Rosa. I will be around for a long time, I promise. But I do have to go away after, and if, my plan works out." Marcus reached over and took Rosa's hand. "If we can accomplish what I have planned, then we will all live a long and peaceful life together." Marcus collected four of the newspaper cuttings, leaving just the one about Harry Wentworth. He then went on to tell Rosa all about the Harry Wentworth case, and how he planned to catch-up with Father Peter Dunfold.

*

DS Ling had had, for the most part, a lonely New Year. Her good friend, Mandy Silver had invited her over to celebrate and the two of them sat in front of the TV drinking champagne cocktails all night until they fell asleep in each other's arms on the sofa. The 1st January is supposed to be a holiday, but Christine had other plans. After two cups of strong black coffee, she drove into town. It was nearly 2.0pm and the city center was buzzing with shoppers searching for that non-existent bargain. The CID office was empty as she had expected; *'lazy bunch'* she told herself, but didn't mean it. They were a good team and knew she could have done worse, considering she was a woman. She seemed to have their respect, which was halfway there to getting results, although she was still not sure about her immediate boss, DCI Crane. She had proved herself as a DC in solving two murders in quick succession, which had impressed Crane, so he put her up for promotion. She had passed her Detective Sergeant's examine with flying colors, and was now on the road to that converted DCI title - well that was her plan. Superintendent James Jarvis was the fly in her ointment. Bigoted, homophobic, chauvinist and all-round creep, was how she once described him to her friend Mandy Silver, under the influence, and swore to kill her if she ever repeated it. All Christine could do was to get results, and then she couldn't be ignored - by anyone.

Wondering if she had made the right decision by coming into the office, she headed for her desk at the end of the incident room. Any right-minded person would be at home with their family and loved ones. Suddenly she wondered what Clive Moran was doing. Did he have a family or partner? Christ! She realised she hardly knew anything about him but was *thinking* about him. Before she could analyze any further thoughts of a relationship, she saw a slim brown paper parcel on her desk, addressed to DS Christine Ling. She picked up the phone and called the front desk. "Yes, ma'am. Came by courier late on the 30th." The duty officer confirmed. Christine unwrapped the package and inhaled a gasp of delight at seeing the faded blue file. On it was typed *'Case Notes. Daniel Mace. 1969'*

*

Kingshampton is a small coastal village on the north Norfolk coastline, remote enough to be forgotten by the outside world, and small enough to know everyone living there.

Father Dunfold had settled in well over the past year, and although he did miss the hustle and bustle of a large city, he found the tranquility of the countryside agreeable.

He missed his *'boys'*, but he had the memories. The chances of *befriending* in his new parish were slim, but he had some good choir boys who he thought he could nurture when the time was right - for now, however, he had to appear squeaky clean.

The small church of St. Clair's was well attended, and Father Dunfold had made his mark with the ageing catholic folks of Kingshampton, as he went through the motions, robotically almost, at Sunday Communion, looking forward to his roast dinner at the local pub. As custom dictated, he stood at the church door and shook hands with the exiting congregation who mostly stopped to say how nice the service had been, and how good the choir was now, under his supervision. One Sunday in late January he noticed a well-dressed lady that was new to his congregation.

Not only was she well-dressed in Sunday best, but she was also very attractive, and alone. "Good morning. I don't believe we have met." Dunfold said, shaking her hand. Barbara felt the clamminess of his hand instantly and had to stop herself from pulling back. "No, Father. I am here for a few days visiting my sister."

Father Dunfold looked forlorn. "That is a shame. I was hoping we had a new face in the church," he said, still holding Barbara's hand. Barbara took the initiative and retrieved her moist hand. "I am sure I will be back again, one day. It's such a beautiful village, especially in the summer."

Enough small talk. "It was nice meeting you, Mrs . . ."

"Star, Barbara Star. And you are Father . . . Dunfold is it?"

"Yes, it is. Goodbye, for now, Barbara."

Barbara walked slowly along the old flagstones to the church boundary and breathed a sigh of relief that was over. Mission accomplished; *'Marcus, you can deal with the slime-bag now'* she said under her breath, heading for the station.

Marcus now had positive proof of Dunfold's description and location. He made plans to visit Kingshampton. He packed a bag with the required accessories; rope, duct tape, Taser and Latex gloves, and that afternoon drove to Norfolk.

*

Christine's initial euphoria turned to disappointment on seeing the thickness of the file. She read the case notes with interest and was surprised to find the report of the crime scene was virtually identical to all the other cases she knew about.

Time of death: 23.45 - 00.45

Cause of death: Strangulation by rope (being hung from approx. sixteen feet)

Other notes: The body was in an advanced state of rigor mortis before amputation of the penis was made with a sharp instrument, possibly a Stanley Knife. Little blood was detected from the amputation indicating rigor mortis had been reached.

Christine skimmed the pages looking for the photo evidence. There was one photo of the victim hanging in the same manner, from the loft rafters, and several of him laid out after he had been removed. Christine studied the photos but nothing stood out that was an obvious case solver. She read that Daniel Mace had been a barrister, was single and lived in the family home. He had cared for his ageing and blind mother for several years until she died in 1966. He had no criminal convictions and no arrests, not even a parking fine. So why was Daniel Mace singled out for execution by this Hartstein guy?

She then read the DCI's report which shed more light on to that question:

On searching the deceased premises 135 photographs were found in a shoebox on top of a wardrobe in the master bedroom. Analysis of the photographs shows evidence of at least twelve different boys, with between seven and eleven photos of each boy. The subjects (boys) in question were aged between eight and eleven. There was no identification on the backs of the photos. Five of the boys have been traced and gave evidence against Mace. The content of the photographs ranged from posing in swimming costumes to standing fully naked, facing front. Some photographs depicted two boys naked together.

Christine shook her head and realized she was crying and wiped away a tear with her sleeve. 'Poor bastards', she said, with respect for the lost boys. Nothing in the file made any suggestion of a vigilante or revenge attack from any of the boy's relatives. The only names associated with the victim were other members of the family, who had all been interviewed out of procedure.

Brother: Michael Mace
Sister in Law: Sylvia Mace
Niece: Claire Mace, aged twenty-two
Niece: Rachel Mace, aged eighteen
Nephew: Frank Mace, aged ten

Michael Mace had been interviewed under caution, in the belief he knew his brother was a pedophile and may have killed him in revenge for molesting his nephew, Frank. However, after several days of questioning the DCI had no concrete evidence and released his only suspect.

DS Ling re-read the slender file again, but still, nothing jumped out at her, except one thing . . . maybe. The investigating officer noted that the heating in Daniel Mace's house was turned up high, which was odd for the time of year - mid-July. Christine grabbed the case notes for the Wentworth investigation and looked for a similar entry, then stopped. Wentworth was killed in December, so anyone would have expected the heating to be on . . . but was it on high? Nothing mentioned in the notes as to the heating, so Christine found the name and number of the first officers on the scene.

"Hi, PC Bates, sorry to bother you on your day off, but can I ask you about your initial visit to the Wentworth house. Can you recall if the heating was on?"

"Yes, ma'am. I remember saying to Jefferies, that's PC Jefferies ma'am, how hot it felt, but assumed the guy liked to have the heating turned up, considering the weather we have been having. . . "

"Yes, many thanks, Bates. Enjoy your holiday, and Happy New Year." Christine put down the phone wondering if she could get an answer from the pathologist on New Year's Day.

*

Marcus walked the quiet cobbled streets of Kingshampton learning the geography, places of interest and escape routes. He spent a couple of days wandering the outer landmarks, of which there were few in this old hamlet. One, however, was of significant interest. A 13th-century church stood in its own grounds surrounded by an equally medieval graveyard. Marcus tried the old wooden door at the East porch but found it locked. He thought this strange, but not unheard off due to the rise of stolen church property.

Determined to find answers, he walked through the graveyard to a lane leading to the seafront. If he tried hard enough, Marcus could imagine himself back in the middle ages. Cobbled streets, old taverns and even older churches were ghostly reminders of another time. Inside the Rose & Crown public house, however, the 21st century hit the visitor square in the eye, and ears. Popular music rang out from multiple wall speakers and arcade video games machines were being played by, what looked like to Marcus, under-aged customers. He ordered a pint of beer and asked the barman about the old church. "Ah, you mean All Saint's. It's not used now as a regular church, just for weddings. It's more a tourist attraction on account of the one-hundred and twenty carved angels adorning the arches. We keep the key here if you want to visit, but only between midday and six o'clock."

Marcus smiled and said he would think about it, not committing himself, but in truth would return for the key very soon.

*

By the following day, Christine Ling had put together a plan of action to sell to her boss, and was determined she would not be sidetracked.

"OK, say I agree, what do you expect to achieve?" DCI Crane asked with more interest than she had expected.

"The answer has to be with the Mace family, somewhere, sir. Daniel Mace did not have a criminal record like all the others. I think he is *'Ground Zero'*, and someone in that family knows the truth."

DCI Crane frowned. He liked her tenacity; he liked her, but would never admit it. He was going to retire in a few years, and already a shortlist was being drawn up by his boss for a replacement DCI, but her name was not on it, not yet. "OK, go," he said, adding. "Take that profiler chap with you, make him earn his keep." Christine smiled. "Yes, sir, I will."

Mr & Mrs Michael Mace still lived in the house they had bought back in 1960. Although both retired, Michael is a keen gardener, and his wife, Sylvia, gives piano lessons two days a week. Their three children have all left the family home; Rachel, the eldest is single and is a school teacher in Poole.

Claire is married and lives in Derby, and their youngest, Frank, is in the Army, currently in the Gulf. Christine Ling and Clive Moran sat and took notes, and sipped tea. "I don't understand why, after all these years you want to talk to us about Daniel's suicide." Michael Mace asked grimly.

Christine had been prepared to ask some awkward questions, but now, face to face with the relatives she was not sure if this was a good idea. The family knew nothing about Daniel's mutilation only that they had been told he took his own life; guilty at what he was and what he had done. His brother, to this day, rejected the accusation he was a pedophile, and that the evidence was circumstantial, claiming the photos could belong to anyone. Christine was inclined to agree, but she had to focus on the family connection. "Mr Mace, did your children get on well with their Uncle?"

It took a few moments for the question to absorb his still active legal mind. His eyes opened wide. "What are you suggesting? Get out!" he shouted, standing and pointing to the door. His wife seemed confused and kept asking, *'what was the matter, Michael?'*

Ling and Moran stayed seated. "Mr Mace, please sit down. We are not suggesting anything. I know this is hard, but we need to know if any of your children argued with your brother, just before he died." Moran asked, his voice calm and controlled. Mrs Mace was blinking, a sign to Moran she was remembering something. "Mrs Mace, do you remember something?"

"Of course she does not." Michael Mace shouted. "There is nothing to remember, is there, Sylvia?" His wife looked drained and sheepish, compared to the confident younger woman she once was when bringing up three children. Frank was eight years younger than the girls, and although he had not been planned, was loved just as much. The girls doted on him, but when they were at boarding school, and Sylvia was working part-time, Uncle Daniel would babysit.

"Mrs Mace," Christine said softly, "is there anything you want to tell me that was not mentioned before?"

Michael Mace was about to explode again when his wife held up her hand. "Michael, it's OK," she said calmly. Turning to the two visitors Sylvia Mace tried to smile, but there was nothing there but painful memories. "Frank was nine. He asked me one day if it was OK for Uncle Daniel to take photographs of him." Mr Mace's face drained of colour but said nothing. "Of course, I said, why not?"

"It's fine, Sylvia. What else was said?" Christine asked.

Mrs Mace avoided her husband's eyes and stared into her lap. "He asked if it was OK to photograph him in his swimming trunks."

Michael Mace exploded. "Rubbish, woman. Do you know what you are implying?"

"Sylvia. This is very important. Did you tell anyone else about this conversation with Frank?"

Mrs Mace nodded, weeping into her handkerchief. "Yes, our Claire."

"What!" Michael Mace asked, his tone still abrasive, and Clive Moran was ready to restrain him if he lost it. "She was just back from her gap-year and you were always busy, Michael. I had to talk to someone." Sylvia explained, now more rationally. "Anyway, Claire said not to worry and she would look into it."

"And how long was that before Daniel committed suicide?" Clive Moran asked. "About six months," Sylvia replied, standing up. "Excuse me. I need to go upstairs." And she left the room, leaving her husband to answer any further questions, unable to face the obvious truth. There was just one more question - Claire's address in Derbyshire.

Claire Baldwin was in her late forty's and married to a landscape gardener, Josh. They had two children and lived a perfectly happy and content life in the wilds of Matlock. Claire's foray into lesbianism had been just that, a foray. She had not regretted it, and had enjoyed the inclusion and secrecy of it all, and had fond memories of the experience, especially with Barbara Star. But that was then, light years ago as far as she was concerned, and rarely thinks back to those days.

"I've informed the local DCI that we are on his patch," Christine acknowledged to Clive Moran. "Don't' want to upset anyone do we," she finished, sarcastically, bringing the car to a halt outside an impressive large country house. "OK," she said, "she knows we are coming, and it's a sure bet she has spoken to her father, who was a barrister after all, and been given advice about not saying anything incriminating, etc. But we must push her; see if there is a spark of guilt in her somewhere that she now regrets." Moran nodded. "I agree, but she is likely to be over-protective towards her brother, so let's be careful. We don't want her to clam up and have had a wasted journey"

Claire greeted the two investigators warmly, offering tea and coffee. "How can I help you, officer?" Claire asked, with confidence.

"I assume you know why we are here. We interviewed your parents a few days ago."

"Yes," Claire said, slightly surprised. "They were quite upset after your visit, father tells me."

Clive Moran took up the questioning. "Claire, your mother, as you probably know, suggested a conversation she had with you on your return to England after your gap-year, about Frank and his Uncle Daniel." He let her absorb the statement before continuing. "Do you remember that conversation, Claire?" Claire was confident by nature and smiled outwardly. "Yes, of course I do."

Christine and Clive looked at each other momentarily, surprised at the frankness of this woman, which was not entirely expected. "Can you tell me what was said, Claire?" Christine asked.

"Mother told me that Uncle Daniel had been taking photos of Frank. She did not want to tell father as he and uncle were very close and he could well have punished Frank for saying such things. That evening I had cancelled a party, a reunion actually, I was going to, so Frank and I could be alone in the house. I asked him if Uncle Daniel was being improper in any way."

"Did he understand that?" Moran asked.

"Not at first. I was trying to be discreet but realised there was no easy way to ask, so I just asked, *'does uncle Daniel touch you anywhere'*, and he nodded yes. I told him not to be ashamed and to stay away from him in future." Claire's smile dwindled at the memory and the three were silent for a moment. Christine picked up the thread again before she shut down completely. "So, what did you do, Claire? Confront your uncle."

"No . . . well, yes . . . at least not straight away," she said, fidgeting with her hair. "I wanted to sleep on it . . . see how it sounded the next day, but before I had time to make any decisions a friend called me whom I was supposed to have met at the reunion I mentioned." Christine was taking notes whilst listening. "Go on Claire, you are doing fine."

"She called to see how I was as she missed me. I said it wasn't me but my brother, and told her what had happened." Clive and Christine looked surprised at this admission. "You told a friend about Frank and Daniel Mace. They must have been a special friend, Claire. Who was it?" Claire sighed and looked ahead at no one in particular. "She and I were very close friends at boarding school, and we shared a lot of secrets . . . girls do, you know, when at that age," she said, in a matter-of-fact way. Clive looked at his partner but Christine pushed on. "Claire, I need to know what happened after you told your friend about Frank."

"She called back a couple of days later and said she had a friend who would like to meet Frank."

"And did they?" Clive asked.

"Yes. The next day. I had to make sure mother and father were not at home. They arrived about four in the afternoon."

"What were their names, Claire? Christine asked again, trying to be patient with the woman. Claire looked as if remembering. "I think she said Mark, I can't remember for sure."

"That's OK, Claire. What is her name?

"Barbara . . . Barbara Star," she said, her lips curling onto a tight smile. "The man, what did he say to Frank?" Christine asked.

"I am not sure . . . I was not in the room. He wanted to be alone with my brother." Christine could not hide her surprise. "You allowed a stranger to be alone with your brother after what he said."

"Yes, but he looked very kind and soft-spoken. Anyway, Barbara said he was a good man . . . and she should know."

"Why is that, Claire?" Clive asked. "Because they lived together." Christine had to stand, her back was aching, and she needed the toilet. Clive studied Claire while they were alone, and he realized she had not once asked why they were there asking about her uncle after all those years. "Claire, are you not curious as to why we are asking about your brother and his uncle, after all these years?"

Claire slowly shook her head as if thinking for an answer. "No, not really. Mother didn't say." Christine reappeared and was ready to leave. Clive Moran stood and shook hands with Claire. "Barbara's friend . . . could it have been Marcus?" Moran asked. Claire thought a moment. "Yes . . . now you mention it, it was. Silly me."

"One last thing please, Claire. The last address you have for your friend."

"Of course . . . but you will probably be better off contacting her at work. She owns Star Galleries in London - you must have heard of them!"

Christine was glad she was not driving. She leant back in the passenger seat and closed her eyes, recalling their recent conversation with Claire. "Are you asleep?" Clive asked. "No, just thinking," Christine answered, stretching. "We now have a connection between the first *Rope Murder* and the visit to Gateshead of Marcus Hartstein. All we have to do is find him." She sounded more positive about this case than he had ever heard her, and it was good to see her smile again. Clive put his thoughts in check. "Agreed, but let's get back. It's a long drive so get some sleep."

*

The next day at just after 1.00pm, Marcus revisited the Rose & Crown and asked for the key to All Saints Church. The friendly barmaid handed it over saying. "Have a good day."

The old church was a curious building, and Marcus was not sure why it was not used anymore. Structurally it must be sound to let tourists enter and explore without risk, otherwise there would be warnings everywhere.

Although not in the slightest bit religious, Marcus always showed respect for places of worship, be they Mosques, Temples, Churches or Synagogues. He unlatched the heavy wooden black doors and entered via the south porch, one of two entrances, and was immediately impressed with the length and width of the Nave. In keeping with the period, the floor was laid with large faded grey flagstones, and the high wooden vaulted ceiling looked impressive. This ceiling, although high, was a gift to Marcus, and he soon started to form a plan.

He spent the next two hours familiarizing the layout of the church and left to return the key as promised.

The problem with a small village like Kingshampton, everyone was a snoop. Marcus stood out a mile as a stranger and the more he visited pubs and restaurants, the more the locals wanted to know about him. This socializing also had a positive side to it. Marcus was able to ask casually about the two churches and gather information on the local Priest. Within three evenings he had a working knowledge of Father Dunfold's routine without even meeting the man, and knew that the following day, Saturday, would be the ideal day to corner his prey.

As arranged he called Barbara at the gallery each evening to keep her up-to-date, but that evening she sounded very agitated. "Marcus," she almost whispered, "the police came to the gallery yesterday. A DS Christine Ling and two others wanting to know if I knew a Marcus Hartstein. Obviously I told them no, but they questioned me for hours. It seems they traced you back to the meeting with young Frank Mace all those years ago, and Claire must have given them my name." Marcus was calculating his options all the time Barbara was relating the events, but he knew this day would probably come, although the timing could be useful if he acted quickly. "Barbara, did DS Ling leave a number?"

*

Christine Ling, DC Taylor and Clive Moran sat around a table in a Chinese restaurant in Croydon stabbing various pieces of fish, chicken and bamboo with chopsticks. "I hate these things," Taylor said, looking around for a waiter to ask for a knife and fork. Christine laughed at her subordinate. "It's easy once you get the hang of it. You must have patience, Taylor. You are a policeman after all."

Taylor smiled sarcastically, and Clive Moran shrugged, not sure who to agree with, so sat on the fence. "I always use a spoon for the rice and stab the meat with the chopstick, that way I don't go hungry."

Christine smiled, looking at him longer than she should have. They ate in silence for a while, and she recalled how impressed she had been with him whilst interviewing Claire Baldwin and Barbara Star.

When they eventually tracked down Ms Star it was agreed Ling would travel to Surrey to interview her with Clive Moran and her DC. Having made contact with the local DCI at Croydon, the three travelled by train to central London, then by taxi to Barbara Star's gallery in Docklands. Christine and her colleagues had rehearsed their interview on the train, and all agreed on the questioning technique they would adopt. They were at a disadvantage to start with; she had no record on file, no photo and no apparent income. The Gallery was listed in Company House, but the tax returns for the past ten years showed little or no profit, and no salary paid to Ms Star. Christine Ling had asked Claire Baldwin not to contact her friend before they had had a chance to interview her, but Christine was not hopeful she would conform. The Gallery looked almost derelict from the outside; a dark brick building dating back over a hundred years, covering three floors. The interior, however, was all 20th century. Bright lights filled the reception area, captivating the visitor's attention to four giant abstract paintings mounted on the longest wall, leading to the reception desk. A well-dressed man, around thirty, Christine guessed, escorted the three visitors through a smoked glass door then along a narrow passage painted red and grey, leading to Barbara's office. To everyone's surprise this was small by comparison to the size of the building. "I am sorry for the lack of space, but I am seldom here these days, so they don't let me have the posh offices anymore," Barbara quipped, offering her guests a seat. "I thought you were the boss," Christine asked, wondering if Ms Star was being totally honest.

"Yes, but I have a wonderful team here now, so *they* boss me around," Barbara said, laughing off the uncomfortable question. Christine finished the introductions and quickly started the interview. She was also initially distracted my Barbara's appearance. According to her notes she was around fifty, but anyone under oath would have said she was not a day over forty. "Ms Star, I believe you know, or knew, a Claire Mace back when you were both boarding at Chaucer's School for Girls." Barbara smiled remembering her old friend. "Yes, of course. We boarded for seven years."

"Do you remember a specific conversation you had with Ms Mace back in 1969 regarding her brother, Frank Mace?" Christine asked, keeping her tone even. Barbara faked a thoughtful look. "If you are referring to Frank and that ghastly uncle of theirs, then yes, she did tell me what happened. He hung himself I believe, and good riddance."

Clive Moran and DC Taylor were taking notes, but Moran took the next question, as arranged. "Yes, Ms Star, but that was six months later. You spoke to her when she did not turn up at a school reunion, I believe." Barbara tried to stifle a laugh. *School Reunion!* "Did I say something . .?"

"No, No. It was not a school reunion as you imaged, it was just a few of us and our house-teacher getting together for drinks." And continued to replay those evenings' events as if it was yesterday. "So, you were good friends, you and Claire - shared everything?" Christine asked, hoping for something of interest.

"By the time of the 'reunion'," she said, making 'speech' signs in the air, "we were all around twenty-three or twenty-four, and had not seen each other since we left for University. I called her to see if she was OK, having not turned-up the previous evening as arranged." Barbara stated, a shade too defiant, which Clive picked up on.

"So, Ms Star, are you married?" he asked with a smile.

"No, never have been, never will be," Barbara answered confidently.

Christine took up the thread. "You knew a Marcus Hartstein. Can you tell me of his whereabouts now, Ms Star?" Barbara didn't flinch, which surprised Clive Moran, indicating she had been warned of their pending arrival. "Marcus, God no. He was someone I met years ago, why?" She asked, turning the question around.

"Because you and he visited Claire Mace to talk about her brother's problem with their uncle, Daniel Mace."

Barbara shrugged. "Yes. I told him I was going and he asked to come along. He was studying psychology at the time and wanted some practical experience. As it turns out he got nothing from the boy. Says he made it all up."

"Really, but you knew Daniel Mace committed suicide six months later?" Clive asked.

"Ha, yes. I guess he was wrong that time." Barbara said, solemnly, causing a pause in the conversation.

"Ms Star," Christine wanted to know, "are you sure you don't know where Marcus Hartstein is. It is really *important* we speak to him." Barbara was intrigued, but she kept her cool. She shook her head. "No, I told you it was years ago. Why now anyway. Why so important you want to find him?" she asked with more than a passing interest.

DS Ling looked at her colleagues for an answer but decided to tell her the official version of events. "We are looking into a series of attacks in the Gateshead area and Marcus Hartstein's name has come to our attention."

Barbara looked genuinely confused. "What has that to do with Daniel Mace or his nephew?"

Christine sighed and forced a smile. "I cannot say, Ms Star. Except that there is a connection and we need to eliminate him from our enquiries as soon as possible."

DC Taylor made an excuse and slipped out of the restaurant to buy some cigarettes. "So, we are back to square one," Christine said, stating the obvious. Clive smiled some encouragement but knew it was not all genuine. "Well, maybe we will get lucky with the CCTV or DNA from around the Dean's house," he said hopefully.

Christine smiled. "Thanks for the support, but we both know he is too good to leave anything behind." And finished the last of the wine. "I have a bottle in my room," Clive said, unexpectedly, causing Christine to nearly choke. "Sorry, I didn't mean to alarm you," he said quickly, trying to reassess the situation. They both laughed, but before Christine could tell him she would love to have a drink, and anything else he was offering, Taylor re-appeared smirking.

"What are you grinning at, Sergeant?" Christine asked.

"Just got chatted up, gov. Good down here, isn't it?"

Chapter Ten

The next day they checked in at Croydon police station to thank DCI Coombes for allowing them to visit his patch. "Sorry you didn't get a result. Anything we can do in the meantime." Coombes offered, hoping to impress his colleagues from *'up North'*. "Not really, sir . . . unless that is, the local beat boys could make a few enquiries with the neighbors at this address in Shirley Heights. See what they know of Ms Star etc. and if they have seen this man. Christine handed Coombes a photo-fit sketch."

"No problem. I'll pass it on. Please make use of a meeting room this morning. What time is your train?" Coombes asked out of interest.

"Not until five, so if we could do some catch-up that would be good, thank you, sir." DCI Coombes showed them to a meeting room on the second floor and introduced them to DS Barber who would see to their every need. Just as they had settled in with coffee and biscuits', a call was put through to Christine from her station. "That was DC Evan's. He's been doing some homework on the heating of each of the houses and has found that the heating was deliberately turned to maximum, accelerating the *rigor mortis*, so he could perform his amputation and be gone before daybreak."

"That's good news, but nothing that leads us to Hartstein. Any news on a wider computer search, or Interpol?" Moran asked, wondering if she would have accepted an invite to his room if Taylor had not returned so soon. "No," she said, "still waiting on that, but I will chase them before we leave." For the next hour the three, or rather Ling and Moran discussed scenarios and counter-measures that may be helpful, but realistically they were stymied. Just as they were preparing to leave, a young female constable put her head around the door. "Ma'am, a caller asking for you. Transferred from your office. Line five."

Christine picked up the phone and pressed button five. "DS Ling."

"Ms Ling. I believe you are looking for me." Christine froze and her eyes opened wide, frantically indicating to Moran to get the call traced. "Who are you?" she asked, stalling.

"You know the answer to that. Be at Cromer police station by six o'clock and I will call you there. That's in Norfolk by the way, and Christine, tell no one. You must come alone." And the line went dead. "Shit," Christine shouted as Moran came in the room followed by DS Barber and DC Taylor. Taylor shook his head indicating he had no luck with the trace. "What the hell is he playing at?" Moran asked, perplexed.

Christine stood while thinking out loud. "Why Cromer? If he wants to talk why not come to us?" she asked, rhetorically, adding "Is it possible to get to Cromer by six in a car? Three hours. Is that possible on a Saturday?"

DS Barber nodded. "Yes, it's possible, but an even quicker way would be by plane." He certainly had everyone's attention.

"We have access to some light aircraft from Biggin Hill Airport, so you could be there in about an hour, or just over, giving you plenty of time to check out local hotels etc., but the downside is they can only take two people besides the pilot." Christine was impressed. "That sounds like a good plan. Clive and I can fly, if you or someone can take my sergeant by car, and rendezvous at Cromer."

"I'll drive us there myself." DS Barber volunteered, and picked up the phone to make the arrangements with Biggin Hill. Christine caught Clive's eye and nodded him to meet her in the corridor. "What is it?" Clive asked when they were alone. "He told me to come alone and not tell anyone."

"He can't possibly think you would drop everything and drive all that way without backup," Clive said, thinking of an explanation himself. Then a light went on.

"He knew you were here, in Croydon. He also knew you couldn't possibly get to Cromer by car from Gateshead in three hours. Barbara Star must have told him." Christine looked annoyed. "We can deal with her later. Let's get there, but Clive, I am not running this past management, is that understood?" Clive Moran smiled and nodded once, which was enough for her to have his full support.

*

Timing was going to be everything if Marcus was to get it right, and not be caught. Mass finished around six-thirty - allow time to clear up and lock up - allow time to get over to All Saints - say seven o'clock. Marcus wrote a note to Father Dunfold and left it on the Alter of his own church, St Clair's, without being seen.

'Be at All Saints at seven sharp if you want your past to stay a secret from your good parishioners'

Dunfold had seen the envelope and thought it a donation from a parishioner, so put it in his jacket pocket to open later as he was running late. Father Dunfold went through Mass almost robotically, trying desperately to keep awake. After Mass, he went as usual to change his robes and noticed the envelope tucked in his jacket pocket. He read it twice, then again, then suddenly felt unstable and sat down on a bench in the changing room. He checked his watch, six-forty seven. With his mind racing, he grabbed his jacket and overcoat and left by the rear door, not wanting to be delayed by the church chaplain or chatty parishioners. He had only visited All Saints once, on a suggestion from the chair-lady of the parish council. *"It's our jewel in the crown, Father. I am sure you will find it inspiring."* Father Dunfold had not been overly inspired by the rather dull and cold interior he recalled, but what was more important now was to remember the quickest way there.

He parked at the end of old rectory lane, about eighty yards from the South entrance, and checked his watch; six-fifty-eight.

The surrounding area was in darkness; the one and only streetlamp was not working, and the church looked deserted, as did the street.

'If this is a practical joke by the choir boys there will be hell to pay', he cursed, heading cautiously towards the medieval church. Within a few yards of the porch door he saw it was slightly ajar, and a soft flickering of candlelight beckoned. "Hello. Anyone there?" he called out. No answer. "If this is a joke I am not amused," he added with a little more confidence. The candlelight became brighter as he stepped further into

the ancient Nave and then suddenly stopped; frozen, at first with disbelieve, and then with fear. The few seconds he had taken to register the scene before him had shut down all his senses and consequently did not hear the footsteps behind him; but he felt the sting of the Taser that awoke those senses and put him in a catatonic stupor, before collapsing helplessly on the cold flagstones.

*

They had been in the air for only fifteen minutes, but Christine was wishing she had taken the car, and hoped they would have made the journey in time, and in one piece. "Not keen on flying?" Clive Moran asked, raising his voice to be heard. "Yes, but prefer to be in something a bit larger, preferably with in-flight service." Clive smiled and hoped he would have the chance to get to know the lovely Ms Ling better after this case had ended, one way or another. Moran had played out several scenarios of how and why Marcus Hartstein had come to murder five Pedophiles over thirty years without being identified and had always returned to the same two conclusions; it wasn't him, or, his name is not Marcus Hartstein. The flight had been worthwhile. They arrived at the old Victorian police station at five o'clock, having been met at the airfield by the local constable. "Who is the senior officer here, constable?" Christine asked, on entering the old building, reminiscent of a rather sad boarding house. "DCI Baldwin, ma'am, but he's based at North Walsham, about ten miles away."

"OK, please call him and tell him who I am, and ask him to come over as soon as possible. And constable, it is most urgent, do you understand?" The seasoned police officer had seen the likes of city CIDs before and was not impressed even now with this young woman, but nodded politely. "Yes, ma'am, urgent. I will tell him." And he left to make the call.

"What do we do now, Christine?" Moran asked, "Wait for DC Taylor or what? We don't even have a real description of this Marcus Hartstein, if that's his real name, only an artist's sketch."

Christine turned suddenly, realizing what Morgan was suggesting. "*If that's his real name*. And when were you going to share your thoughts on that with me, Clive? We need to pool ideas. If you suspect something it's your duty to share it," she sounded cross, but was more angry that she was being led by a suspect instead of pursuing *him*.

Now they had to wait another hour to hear from him again. Christine prayed he would call, because if this was a wide-goose-chase, she would be back on the beat very soon. "Sorry," Clive said, seeing his friend and colleague was on edge. "I only considered the possibility on the plane. You have searched every database for Hartstein without any results. That alone should give cause for concern."

Christine nodded. She was mellower now. This was the most frustrating case she had ever been on for a hundred reasons, but especially as she had no idea of whom she was chasing. She was about to discuss other possibilities when the door opened and a young man in casual clothes joined them. "Hello. DCI Baldwin. What brings you to my patch on a Saturday evening that is so important I have to miss the end of my football."

*

Father Peter Dunfold, like several of his predecessors, stirred from his induced sleep with a throbbing pain in his neck. Like them he was gagged and wrists tied. The sight that had led him to his current predicament was still in front of him and the horror returned on seeing it again; a step ladder and a hangman's noose. The rope was suspended from the wooden rafters, twenty feet above; the noose swinging gently over the top of the ladder. "Hello, Peter. We meet at last." Dunfold heard a man say in a measured tone. He was sitting crossed legged on the cold stone floor and turned sharply to the left and right to get a look at his abductor. "Don't struggle, Peter. You will have your chance to talk very soon, to confess in fact, to your vile crimes towards those children that looked to you, and your fellow *fiends* for protection." As Marcus spoke, he walked slowly around his captive until he stood between him and the ladder. The priest had stopped struggling when Marcus started to speak and followed him hypnotically until he came into full view, and looked up into Marcus's eyes and saw hate and death piercing his very soul. "So, Peter, let's hear what you have to say." Marcus leant down and removed the Duct tape and was prepared for the torrent of abuse and vilification. "Who the hell are you?" Peter shouted predictably. "What is going on?"

*

At six-ten, DC Taylor and DS Barber had arrived by car and they joined their colleagues, together with DCI Baldwin, in a cramped interview room, in fact, the only interview room. "So," DCI Baldwin asked, "if I have this right, you were told to be here in Cromer at six o'clock and wait for further instructions."

"Yes," Christine confirmed, annoyed that her word was being questioned. They sat in near silence for twenty minutes until a phone rang at the outside desk. A constable waved across to his boss and everyone moved into the narrow corridor in front of the enquiry desk. "It's for DS Ling," he said, handing the receiver to her.

"DS Ling here. Who is this . . ." But she was interrupted.

"Ms Ling. The time is six-forty-five. You alone must be at All Saints Church in Kingshampton by seven-fifteen. Do you understand?"

"Yes, but it may take longer. I don't know the area . . ."

"If you leave now you can make it. Take one local driver only." And the line went dead.

"Where is Kingshampton, and can we be there in thirty minutes?"

*

Marcus stepped towards the startled priest and raised him to his feet. "We don't have long, Peter, so you can talk as I prepare you."

"What are you talking about? Who are you? I am Father Dunfold, I . . ." But Marcus interrupted.

"You are nothing. The title *Father* is an abomination. You used your status and title to befriend innocent children. The only father we have is the one who conceived us, not a man pretending to be a father; filling children's minds with lies and confusion." Marcus was holding Dunfold by the shoulders, his rage now unchecked, and shaking with anger.

Dunfold was astonished by this stranger's outburst, but standing face to face with him he could now see real emotion in Marcus's eyes, and Dunfold felt lost and abandoned for the first time since being sent to this wilderness by the Dean. "I do not know what you are talking about," Dunfold pleaded, his expression transfixed on his accuser. "Your sins have found you out, Dunfold. You and your sick associates will perish in Hell for what you have done, and all the angels above will not save you." Dunfold shook his head and then narrowed his eyes, looking above to the old wooden arches along the entire length of the Nave. On each column support, there were three carved angels with wings extended, over one hundred in total, and they all seemed to be staring at Dunfold, judging him for the sinner he was. Dunfold shook his head faster, moaning uncontrollably. "What do you want? Tell me what I can do."

Marcus dragged the pathetic man by the arm, turning him to face the first run of the wooden steps. "You can go to Hell, that's what you can do." And Marcus manhandled him onto each step of the ladder until he was in line with the noose. Marcus quickly took hold of the rope and swiftly placed it around Dunfold's neck, ensuring he would now keep his balance, at least for a while longer. Dunfold steadied himself, knowing he could easily fall from the unsteady ladder and prayed for the first time that evening with conviction. Marcus, now disinterested with the man's ramblings, walked back to the side south entrance which was now locked, and tied the rope securely through the large iron ring handles on the inside of the doors. Another thinner line of rope was attached to the base of the ladder, ensuring its easy removal when stretched, allowing the occupant to swing freely, and die.

"Who are my accusers? What evidence do you have? This is all a mistake. Please let me talk to you." Dunfold called out to the darkness that was before him, as he was now facing northwards along the dark Nave, with Marcus somewhere behind him.

Dunfold didn't get a reply. He turned his neck cautiously, perspiring freely, although the temperature in the medieval church was around four degrees. All was quiet behind him. "Hello. Are you still there? Answer me," he stammered, closing his eyes in frustration and despair. When he opened them he reeled backwards, checking his footing as he balanced on the top run of the ladder. Marcus was looking up at him. His steel-blue eyes were narrowed as if in thought. "Tell me, Dunfold, what makes men like you do what you do?"

"You have it all wrong . . ." Dunfold repeated fervently, but Marcus raised his hand. "Slowly, Peter. Be calm and tell me what I want to know."

Marcus allowed him to slow his breathing and compose himself, but he also knew time was running out. He cocked his head, waiting.

Dunfold spoke more clearly, but all the time fear gripped his throat, and he felt his eyes swelling with salted tears. "I don't know what you want me to say. I don't know you, and I certainly don't know anything about what you are accusing me of." Marcus looked up at the pitiful man begging for his life but felt no compassion, only anger.

"I was hoping you would confess; being a man of the Church." Marcus raised an arm, indicating to their surroundings. "But you remain the sanctimonious predator you are." Marcus slowly circled his captive. "Tell me, Peter, did you really think Wentworth would not try and save his own life if he could?"

Dunfold turned his neck to see where Marcus was, but his white plastic priest collar was stiff and chafed his neck.

"What do you mean; *tried to save his life*? He committed suicide . . ." Dunfold stopped mid-sentence. "You killed him, didn't you?" He called out, seeing a shadowy figure over this left shoulder, and fear returning to his trembling voice.

"*You* are in the confession box, Peter, not me," Marcus replied softly, but Dunfold was shaking his head again and muttering. "No, no, no. He promised me I would be safe here."

Marcus was back in front of the ladder looking up. "Who was that, Peter?" Marcus could almost taste the words he so much wanted to hear. "Who was it, Peter. Tell me." Marcus shouted at the quivering priest. Anticipation was fueling his adrenaline, and he had lost sight of his time-line.

The voice he expected to hear - wanted to hear - was not from the pathetic man standing above him who was about to plead guilty in front of his God and go to Hell for his sins.

"Marcus!" His name resonated through the church, bouncing off the stone walls like an echo; cold and hollow. For a split second he thought it was Barbara calling out his name as he blinked to focus. "Marcus!" There it was again.

"Let him go. We can talk this through." The woman's voice was controlled but stern. The next two minutes would be crucial if Marcus wanted to carry out his planned reprisal. He had come too far and was too angry to give up now. *His* method of justice, no matter how others judged *him*, was the only answer.

Marcus moved so fast to the church's south entrance it surprised even DS Ling. Everything happened as if slow motion; Ling ran the fifty yards towards Dunfold, perched on the top of the wooden step ladder. Marcus, in the shadow of the door, unlocked it and pushed forward, pulling on the thinner rope at the same time, causing the ladder to collapse, and Dunfold to meet his maker.

Earlier, Ling and Moran had tried the south door, and on finding it locked crept in from the east entrance, which is what Marcus wanted her to do. Ling's only hope was to rescue the priest as she saw the ladder slip away from under his feet, leaving, she prayed, her colleagues to apprehend Marcus. Dunfold felt the rope on his neck tighten as the steps disappeared from under him.

His last glimpse of memory was the Dean stroking his head, and of how good life had been back then. Instead of the rope tightening his neck muscles, constricting his breathing, and suffering untold discomfort until he died, Dunfold felt delusional.

Arms of angles had wrapped themselves around his legs to save him. He felt the rope slacken and heard shouting. *'Angles don't shout'* he told himself before fainting.

Clive Moran had been a few paces behind Ling as she grabbed the priest's legs, and he continued running to the south entrance, where the rope was attached. "Hurry, Clive. I can't hold him for much longer, he's too heavy, hurry." Christine shouted in desperation, her arms wrapped around Dunfold's thighs, her head skewered sideways onto his genitals. Moran grappled with the rope and pulled to untie it but noticed something odd. "Christine, it's OK. Let him down." Christine felt the dead weight push her downwards, like quicksand, and her legs give way as she slumped to the stone floor, the priest's body falling over the top of her to lie prostrate and silent. Christine pushed herself on to her hands and knees, and Moran helped her to stand. "I'm sorry, I'm so sorry," she repeated, looking over to where Dunfold was lying.

"Christine, it's OK, he is not dead," Moran said as he leant over the unconscious body of Father Dunfold.

"The rope was purposely left slack - he couldn't have hung even if you hadn't been there. He would have just dropped to the floor and have a twisted ankle, at worst." It took a few moments for what Moran had said to register, and then her frustration turned to anger. "The bastard," her voice echoed around the church once again. Christine was suddenly alert again. "Is he OK?" she asked, nodding to Dunfold. "Yes," Moran answered, "Just fainted. The medics will be here shortly."

"What about Hartstein? Did we get him?" she asked earnestly, but she already knew the answer. Taylor had arrived at her side looking concerned for his boss. "No, ma'am. No sign of him. We think he ran through the graveyard to an ally where he may have had a car waiting."

"OK, I want door-to-door, *now* Taylor. Someone must have heard a car drive off in a hurry."

"Yes, ma'am," Taylor said, hesitating long enough for Christine to notice. "What is it, Taylor."

We found something in one of the isles I think you need to see." And turned to walk back twenty feet along the Nave. Christine and Clive followed. Taylor stopped and pointed to a prayer stool. On top of the faded embroidery sat a brown manila envelope and two black video cases. "Has anyone touched them?" Christine asked, hypnotized by what she was looking at. "No, ma'am."

"OK, bag them and get them to forensics at Croydon . . . no, wait, we will have to go to Norwich I guess. Shit. This is a mess. Give me some gloves."

Christine slowly opened the manila envelope and removed one A4 sheet of typed notepaper.

Dear Ms Ling

I have followed your recent career with interest, and under any other circumstances would have been pleased to make your acquaintance. With this letter you will find two disturbing videos which will help you make the right decisions. I apologize for asking you to witness the content, but it is vital that you do, to ensure there are no loop-holes in the prosecutions.

Warmest regards MH

"Plural. He wrote *prosecutions*, plural. We need to get to Norwich, fast."

*

Marcus arrived back at his cottage at just past midnight, and fell asleep in his favorite armchair; his large shot of Dalwhinnie untouched.

*

Christine had ordered roadblocks around the Norfolk village as far as Norwich, but the Norfolk constabulary was stretched, both in men and budget. Airports and ferry terminals were also alerted, but without a positive description, it was going to be hard to find her man. Mandy Silver had given the police artist the best description she could, but in truth was not a good likeness.

Christine and her team, along with Father Dunfold, arrived at Norwich police station at eight-forty-five, where they met DCI Crampton. "Sounds like you had an exciting evening, detective. Been seeing a lot of our lovely county, I believe." Crampton said, smirking unnecessarily.

Christine ignored the quip. "Yes, sir, but a possible result none-the-less."

"But your man escaped, I hear," Crampton said, his tone more measured.

"Yes, but if I have here what I think it is, the evening will not have been a total waste of time, sir," Christine said, raising the evidence bag to reveal the two video cases. "I would like a private room where I can view these with my DC as well as my profiler, Mr Moran. I would also ask if you would sit in, as senior officer, to ensure we have covered all bases." DCI Crampton nodded, thoughtfully. "What about forensics. It goes against procedure, but you know that."

She was tired and her knees still hurt from the fall, but she was not going to let anything delay this investigation further. "We know he is good, sir. He has not left any DNA or scene traces in all the other cases we believe he is associated with, so, with respect, sir, I do not believe has left any traces on these video boxes either."

"OK, DS Ling, but handle with gloves and get them to forensics as soon as you can. I'll arrange a room in say, thirty-minutes."

"Thank you, sir."

Clive Moran and DC Taylor entered the room as DCI Crampton left. "We will see what all this was about very soon, gentleman. How's our priest?" Christine asked, stretching her legs.

"He wants' a phone call."

"No! Not yet." Christine said forcefully. "Not until we have seen these videos." Taylor and Moran looked at her, taken aback by her sudden outburst. "I think you need to see a doctor," Moran suggested casually, knowing the answer. Christine smiled, "Sorry, it's been a long day." And forced a smile. Then her face changed again on the thought of watching the video. What were they going to witness? Could she handle watching what she thought was on them? Would Marcus Hartstein have gone to all that trouble if they were not incriminating; he could, after all, have posted them - why risk being caught, but the one common denominator was Father Dunfold, and Marcus Hartstein had seemed very preoccupied with the clergy over the past few days.

*

Marcus woke at sunrise, showered and dressed and called Rosa. "Marcus, what time is it?" Rosa asked, wondering if she were dreaming.

Marcus smiled. "Nine twenty. Sorry my love, but can you come down to the cottage tonight. I'm missing you."

"Sure, of course," Rosa confirmed. "Are you OK, Marcus?"

"I am fine . . . now. See you soon, my love."

*

Christine and her colleagues sat in silence at the end of the video screenings. Tears ran down her cheeks, and she made no attempt to conceal them.

Taylor and Moran had also felt the emotional strain on them, with Taylor wiping his eyes several times during the forty-five minutes they had to endure, watching the grotesque scenes unfold in front of them. DCI Crampton was the first to speak. "I have never seen anything like that in all my time as a copper," he said, staring at the now blank TV screen, shaking his head, hypnotically.

"We need to interview Father Dunfold. I need to get him back to Gateshead, sir." Christine said, her voice quiet and respectful as if mourning the dead. But these boys aren't dead, she told herself, and if they can be found they can be helped.

Back on her home-turf in Gateshead it seemed the whole station had heard about her 'knee-dropping' incident, trying to save someone who was not going to die from hanging. *'Morons'*, she told herself, wondering who had elaborated on the church incident and made her out to look foolish in the eyes of her *mentally challenged* colleagues. "Has he been charged, DS Ling?" was the greeting she got from her DCI.

"Yes, sir. Having had Dunfold examined by the medical officer at Norwich to confirm he has a large mole on his left thigh matching the one seen on the video, I formally cautioned Father Peter Dunfold at 10.25pm last night on suspicion of child abuse, imprisonment and buggery of minors under the Child Prevention & Cruelty Act 1956."

DCI Crane sighed behind his desk, wondering if this was the biggest catch of the century or the biggest cock-up ever. "Sir," DS Ling started to say, but hesitated.

"What is it, Ling?" Crane asked gently.

"We now know Wentworth was involved as these videos were taken from his garage, from a locked safe. Dunfold and Wentworth could be part of a much larger pedophile ring. Someone tried to get to the videos before I scared them off, although they didn't know they had already been removed . . . and someone was tipped off that it would be safe to enter the garage as the police protecting the premises had been removed . . . on your orders, sir."

Crane was impressed with his star officer. She had found a connection between all of the rope murders, starting with Daniel Mace, and now she had a name and had witnessed, first hand, the attempted murder of his current victim. "If what you are suggesting DS Ling is true, then that puts me in a very awkward position." Christine stared at her boss not believing he could do those awful things she had witnessed, but she had to follow her line of enquiry, wherever it lead her. "Let's you and I see the videos alone, then we can move forward, agreed."

"Agreed, sir. I'll let you know when I get them back from forensics. I don't hold out much hope but you never know."

*

Christine laid on her bed, in the dark, listing to a Madonna track on the radio. The opening line seemed so ironic, *'Things haven't been the same since you came into my life'.* She turned onto her front, burying her head into the soft pillow. "Shit," she said out loud, "am I attracted to him? He is clever, charming and good looking," she conceded, making a mental list of pros and cons, as any girl does - *don't they?* Christine had had several boyfriends since arriving in the UK, but no one seemed . . . *right.* By that, she knew she meant her father would not have approved of them. Thousands of miles away and she is still as close to her old man as ever. She promised herself she would stop asking for approval, from anyone. It's time she had a break - let her own decisions shape her destiny. Suddenly she opened her eyes and turned over onto her back again, staring at the ceiling. The twenty-tog duvet was warm as a summer's day, but Christine shivered and crossed her arms, rubbing her shoulders and feeling the Goosebumps as she did so. *'Things haven't been the same since you came into my life'.* What if she wasn't thinking of Clive Moran? What if she was thinking of Marcus Hartstein? *'Get out of my head!'* she shouted to the ceiling, but it just stared back at her, smiling faintly.

*

DCI Crane was reading the forensic report as Christine arrived. He looked up as she entered his office, and she could see there had been a development. "Is that forensics?" she asked calmly. "Yes," Crane confirmed, sighing heavily. "It came in just now. Clean except for one partial, not in the CRO. So we have a third person in the circle."

Ninety minutes later DS Ling and DCI Crane had watched the video evidence - the second time around for Ling and she was no better prepared for it than the first time, and again openly wiped away a tear with her handkerchief and couldn't care less what her boss thought of her.

DCI Crane, like many long-serving hardliners at his rank, had a human side which very rarely arose during the course of the working day, but this had been the most brutal, horrifying and saddest evidence he had ever witnessed in his career. He wiped an eye with his jacket sleeve and, like Ling, didn't care. They sat in silence for a moment in the viewing room. Christine turned off the video player and TV screen and repacked the videos into their black boxes. "So, we have Wentworth, we think, filming, with one guy in a monk's robe wearing a mask, and possibly our Father Dunfold from the neck down, seeing his mole matches the one in the video. I think it's time we interviewed your suspect, Christine."

*

Father Peter Dunfold looked drawn and tired. His thick black hair was ruffled and he was unshaved. A night in the cells had not agreed with him. He had been deprived of his Rosary and he was feeling frightened and betrayed.

"Father Peter Dunfold," DS Ling opened the questioning,

"Do you understand the charges I have read out to you?"

"I want a solicitor."

"All in good time. I need to establish some facts first." DS Ling placed the clear evidence wallet on the table containing the two video cases, in front of Dunfold. "Do you recognize these two video boxes, Father?"

Dunfold shook his head. "No. That's all I am saying."

"Really, because I, DCI Crane and three other officers have viewed the sick material in these videos, and we can clearly see you in them, performing heinous acts of indecency with young boys."

Christine's voice had risen throughout her statement, and she felt a hand on her arm. DCI Crane said nothing, but he had had the calming effect he hoped for, and took up the questioning. "We know Wentworth was behind the camera, and you are clearly in at least one of the videos. We just need the name of the other person in the mask, Father, and then it will all be over." Crane's tone was conciliatory but firm. Dunfold looked straight ahead weighing up his options. If he was to go down, why go alone? Wentworth must have sold him out before that madman hung him, and he could do the same to him if he had a chance, but how much did they really know? Suddenly Dunfold smiled, which made Christine Ling want to reach over and hit him. "He was supposed to protect me," he whispered, staring with a glazed expression at the two-way mirror on the opposite wall, whilst he polished his reading glasses. Ling and Crane looked at each other, then back at Dunfold. "Who, Father. Who was to protect you?"

Dunfold moved his stare back towards Christine and replaced his glasses.

"God, of course. Who else?"

*

"If he's going to play the crazy card, sir, we have to confront the Super," Ling said, sitting opposite her boss again in his office. Crane nodded. "Yes, I agree. His brief will certainly tell him to keep a lid on it as soon as it's out we have another suspect."

Crane rubbed his eyes, feeling weary and frustrated. Sex crimes, of any sort, were the hardest to deal with, and the seasoned detective had seen almost everything in his thirty years on the force, yet when it came to involving children he felt he had had enough, and prayed for retirement if these were the cases facing him in the future.

He, like many of his colleagues, were family men; they had kids of all ages, and yet they, and he, did not voice one syllable of personal revulsion while on duty. He knew it must have been hard to ask long-serving colleagues to investigate aspects of this case, knowing what it entailed, but was proud that they all did it without acrimony, and did it with professionalism.

That afternoon Christine received six boxes of evidence into the secure and sanitized evidence room taken from Father Dunfold's home, together with any other DNA and print results that weren't his.

One piece of evidence had been placed on top of the first box with a note from the head of SOCO. *'You will find this of interest'*. Christine was wearing a white plastic protective bodysuit and blue latex gloves. She opened the clear plastic wallet and slid out a black A5 Filofax. Turing the cover she noticed on the first page a list of jumbled words. She then turned the index tab for A and saw two initials, DA. Then a thought struck her and she skipped to D. There were two entries: PD and GD. She wondered if PD was Peter Dunfold. Her heart pounding, she turned the plastic page tabs to W. One entry; HW. Harry Wentworth? There were over forty initials. How was she supposed to identify the real names? Did Dunfold have a photographic memory, or was there another book; maybe with names and phone numbers. They had to contact each other, somehow.

*

DCI Crane was meeting with Chief Superintendent in twenty minutes, and they still hadn't made a match on the partial fingerprint. It would have been good to have everything at the meeting and confirm, *'case closed, sir'.* Crane was also determined to ensure DS Ling took the merit for her part in perusing Hartstein. "But you still haven't caught him, have you?" Jarvis shot back, clearly frustrated, not acknowledging the positive aspects of their achievements.

Crane clenched his fist under his boss's desk. "Sir, we have proof positive on Wentworth and Father Dunfold, and a high probability of a match on the video case, and when we get the names from this book, we will have the largest paedophile ring ever known in the UK." Crane's temper was obvious, and Jarvis leant back in his high-backed leather chair, watching his DCI let off steam, and considering his response. "Mike, of course, you and your team . ."

"DS Ling, sir. *Her* team worked the case and got these results." Crane interrupted without thought.

"Of course, Mike, DS Ling. She has done well. A good story for the PR people. We need more women in the force." Jarvis half-smiled, tapping a finger on his desk. "About this book here," he said, pointing to the evidence bag DCI Crane had laid on the desk. "You say it's in code."

"No, sir. The initials in the address book need a code to identify the names, and, we think, places where they met."

Jarvis nodded. "I know someone in Scotland Yard who could fast-track this for us. I am in London tomorrow as it happens. Let me see what I can do." And before Crane could answer, or protest, Jarvis was on his feet showing Crane the door. "I'll call you from London if I have any news."

Back in his office, Crane sat assessing his options when Christine Ling put her head around the door. "How did it go with Jarvis, sir?"

"He has taken the notebook with him to London. Says he knows someone at Scotland Yard who could figure out the code . . . perhaps." Crane said, unconvincingly. "You did make copies?"

Christine shook her head. "No, not yet. I was going to do it now."

"Shit," Crane said, rubbing his forehead. "If that goes missing we have nothing."

"We have Dunfold, sir. That is a result, surely."

"Yes, of course. But that book contains vital information about his contacts, probably some or all who are pedophiles." Crane looked at DS Ling for a glimmer of hope. "Can you remember any of the entries?" he asked, hopefully.

"I looked under W and found HW, and assumed it is Harry Wentworth, and D, and found PD, and again assumed it was Peter Dunfold. I didn't have time to look further, but there was a list of something on the first page, not initials, just jumbled words."

"And," Crane asked, hoping for something.

"Well I can't remember all of them except the first one, *'Seek vital demon'*, whatever that means." Then Christine had a thought. "Can I ask a friend of mine? She works on the local Guardian paper. They may have a crossword genius there who could look at this. It's a long shot, but . . ."

"Yes, that's good. Long shots are fine." Crane smiled, looking at his watch. "Must go. Family dinner with in-laws tonight. Call me as soon as you have anything."

Christine called Mandy Silver and arranged to meet for a drink, promising her a longer evening than the previously aborted one.

*

Before Christine left for the weekend, she had to type up her report. It took longer than she had hoped and called Mandy to say she would be half-an-hour late. Satisfied, but exhausted, she re-read the ten-page report and put it in a buff folder, planning to put it on Crane's desk on the way out. "Ma'am," she heard Taylor enter her office. "Sorry, but the fingerprint search came back negative. No one we know on record," he confirmed, hating being the bearer of bad news. "It could be our man Hartstein," Taylor suggested, grabbing at straws.

"I don't think he is that careless," Christine said in thought. "Assuming we place Dunfold and Wentworth together, let's check out prints from all their known associates.

Wentworth worked at the school, so check all staff there, and as for Dunfold, there was no contact with each other after he fled to Norfolk, so concentrate on his previous associates at the boys home . . . and Taylor, don't forget the Dean's house."

DC Taylor looked perplexed. "He will go berserk."

Christine smiled, guiltily, "Good."

*

Christine reached the wine bar, full of apologies, just as Mandy was pouring her second glass of wine. "It's OK," Mandy said, raising her hand, "I don't want to hear any excuses. Just catch me up and we are quits."

The two friends hugged and Christine sipped from the glass her friend had poured out over twenty minutes ago. "Hell, woman. You could have kept it cool. This is lukewarm." But smiled, seeing the funny side. "Sorry, Man, but I've had a shitty day, again, but I do have something I need to ask you, in total confidence."

"Of course, my angel. How can I help?"

*

DC Taylor had worked overtime many times before, but this weekend he was looking forward to sitting in front of the TV and watching the start of the six-nations Rugby Cup; England v France. Watching the highlights was not the same, especially if he knew the final score. He, and a handpicked team, had tracked down most of the staff at Wentworth's school when he was a caretaker, but getting close to anyone who knew Father Dunfold two years ago was proving difficult.

The Dean, as predicted, shouted his objections loud and clear and informed DC Taylor his job was on the line, but the stone-faced DC stood his ground. "We can do this here, sir, or at the station." He thought the Dean was going to burst a blood vessel. His neck inflated even wider than his twenty-inch collar, and his face reddened with rage. Taylor eventually got all his prints, and left the Dean's residence knowing that was worth missing the Rugby for.

*

Come Monday morning, Christine Ling was at her desk at seven-fifteen. Her weekend had been a mixture of ups and downs. On the down-side, she wanted to go to the cinema with Mandy to see the new Tom Cruise film, *Jerry Maguire*, but Mandy was babysitting her ten-year-old niece and suggested seeing *James and the Giant Peach*. Christine could hardly refuse, so they went and saw *James and the Giant Peach*. Afterwards, over a Big Mac and milkshake, Mandy whispered in Christine's ear. "Well, has he asked you out yet?" she asked, desperate to hear any gossip. "Why are you whispering auntie Mandy?" The ten-year-old asked between mouthfuls of burger.

"Yes, auntie Mandy, why are you whispering?" Christine mocked, and they all laughed. "OK, OK," Mandy said curtly. "I was trying to be discreet, but obviously that didn't work. So has he called you, your civilian helper . . ?"

"Clive Moran," Christine helped her with the name. "No, he has not, and it would not be ethical to see someone I work with. We have strict rules about that." They parted outside Macdonald's, and Christine promised to phone her friend the next day.

On the upside, Sunday afternoon around six p.m, her dad called for a catch-up.

They touched on every subject possible, but skirted around the one her dad really wanted to ask, *Are you seeing anyone?*

At eight o'clock Taylor put his head around her office door. "Morning' gov. How was your weekend?" Taylor asked, not usually one for small talk.

"Up and down. How did the fingerprinting go?" Christine wanted to know. "When do we get some results back?"

Taylor knew she was impatient for a result so had asked the lab to speed things up. "Hopefully by lunchtime, gov. The Dean was not impressed by the way. You may get a call from upstairs," he said, pointing upwards. She knew what he meant. "I'll worry about that when it comes, Taylor. Now, anything back on our man Hartstein from the Home Office?"

DC Taylor shook his head. "Nothing, which makes me think they don't have anything, or don't want us to know anything. Either way, we still don't know a damn thing about the man."

Christine Ling was looking thoughtful and agreed on what she was hearing. She was about to suggest another meeting with Barbara Star when her phone rang. She replaced the receiver and frowned. "News, Ma'am?" Taylor asked, seeing her boss's expression. "Could be, Taylor. The lab has a match on our partial print, and it's from the Dean's residence."

By eight-forty-five Christine had briefed DCI Crane and had assembled her team. "Should we wait for the Super to get in, sir?" Christine asked, hoping there would not be a delay. DCI Crane shook his head. "Sod it. No.

"Let's go." And Christine Ling led her ten-strong team across town to the Dean's residence. The door was answered by the Dean's valet. "I have a warrant to search this residence. Take me to the Dean please." Ling said to the man standing in front of her wearing a shocked expression. "He . . . he's busy."

Christine pushed pass the valet, and she and DCI Crane made their way to the Dean's office and entered without knocking. The Dean looked up from his writing with profound disgust at the interruption. "What is the meaning of this?" he insisted. Christine took no time in explaining. "Dean, we have a warrant for the arrest of Martin Christie. Where is he, Dean?"

The Dean sat back down in his chair, his face confused at what he had just heard. "Martin? Are you sure? On what charge?"

"The same as Father Dunfold. Indecent assault, buggery and false imprisonment to a minor or minors, for starters. Seems you made another bad choice in staff, Dean." Christine's face was expressionless. This was her second arrest of a pedophile, and she was angry.

Angry, that such crimes could be made against innocent children; angry that she had to watch the vile actions of these wicked men, and angry that they could be hidden and protected by others in positions of power.

"We will need to search your residence, Dean, as Christie works here and of course his home. What is his address, Dean?"

Martin Christie had not turned up for work that Monday morning; in fact he had left the Dean's house Friday evening, just after the Dean had received a phone call. The police searched his home and found many articles on children, as well as photographs and more videotapes, all of which showed him and other unidentified men in the act of gross indecency towards young boys. Martin Christie was eventually arrested in Amsterdam four months later and extradited to the UK, where he stood trial with Peter Dunfold. With such overwhelming evidence, they were each given a life sentence, and to serve a minimum of fifteen years before parole was even considered. During the trial, Christine Ling was disappointed that neither of the two defendants gave up any other names of the other men in the videos, or of anyone else they were in close contact with. The Filofax Chief Superintendent took with him to London was never seen again on the grounds that it had been *lost in transit* after leaving it with Scotland Yard.

Two years later DCI Crane retired and fought hard for Christine Ling to be appointed as the new DCI. Her application was turned down by Chief Superintendent Jarvis. Ten months later Christine accepted a DCI post in Slough which she successfully carried out until her retirement in 2004.

*

It gave Marcus no real pleasure in reading about the trial. It did give him some satisfaction that justice was about to be done, and he would no longer have to resort to other judiciary measures; *Nothing, or in this case, no one, is sacrosanct.* He remembered Dyke telling him that many years ago, and if he had learnt anything, it was just that; *nothing is forever; no one is untouchable; there is nothing that cannot be changed if the will is there.*

The past four years had turned him into a virtual recluse in his country cottage, although that was manageable. Barbara visited as often as she could, without being followed by the police, but they had given up, unofficially, on trying to trace the *'rope killer'*. Christine Ling had visited Barbara one day after her retirement, on a social level, to see if she could, or would, depart any further information on Marcus Hartstein. Needless to say, her visit was a wasted one.

Marcus had always been comfortable with his own company, even as a boy he had had no choice but to play alone for years on end. Then, when in England after the war, he was alone for many years while Barbara spent her time at boarding school and then university. Lonely years. Time to think. Now at nearly sixty-six it was time to act. Thinking about the past was over. He needed answers.

Chapter Eleven

2000

He hadn't planned any of it . . . fate had dealt his hand, but on reflection, fate could have been far crueller than she had been. What kind of life would he have had in Austria, even if he hadn't been taken away? What were the chances of his survival? He had no close relatives, and the ones he had were all Nazis. Marcus stirred and turned on his side. He was lying in bed, alone. The warm spring weather had created a storm, and Marcus was feeling it in his bones. Especially his knee where he had injured it when he was very young by falling out of a tree. He bent his left knee several times then stretched it out to make it 'click'. It worked for a while, but the irritation was always there.

Rosa had gone to stay with Charlie and Isabel in London for the weekend. Barbara was at an art exhibition in Chicago, so Marcus was alone. Alone to dream. Alone to think. Alone to find the truth, if it wanted to be found. A week ago he had gone to London and walked into MI5 hopeful for answers. The receptionist called through for someone to come and see Marcus. Soon, a young man in his early thirties, smartly dressed in a suit and tie approached him. "How can I help you?" he asked, getting straight to the point, and not offering his name.

"I am trying to contact my old handler, Richard Dyke," Marcus informed him. "It is important and personal," he added, passing the young man a folded piece of paper.

"Please ask him to call me." The young man opened the note. *'Unicorn 01 686 7712'* "I can't promise, you understand, but I will see what I can do," he said, pocketing the note and offering his hand, indicating the meeting was over. Marcus breathed in the early spring air and walked the length of the Southbank to Tower Bridge.

London looked wonderful on a bright spring day, and he allowed himself a rare respite from his torment, and mingled with tourists and day-trippers for a few hours pretending he was just another visitor without a care in the world.

*

Pedophilia is not limited to any one country. It is a disease that has spread the world over centuries; silently for most of the time. The occasional alert to those who should have helped was usually ignored and dismissed as fanciful or dangerously liable. Only in the late 20th century, and early 21st century did the public and media show their united disgust and revulsion at these despicable acts of cruelty to children of either sex. Of course, those affected in such a way during earlier times when it was not possible to find comfort in a concerned relative, or figure of authority had to suffer in silence; sometimes for years.

Most abuse is carried out by a relative, or someone close to the victim, in an authoritarian way. Escape was uncommon, and assistance by even those who suspected something wrong was rare for fear of retaliation, or even worse, cohesion.

Marcus's exploitation would have ended either way on that fateful day back in late 1945. He was not to know the Allies were only miles away. Just a few hours and his ordeal would have been over. His mother may have been arrested, but he would have been free of her.

"Marcus, stay in your room and hide until I come to get you . . . do you understand? Do not move from here." Liza whispered through the bedroom door.

"Ok," he whispered back, fighting back tears and the cold. He had heard Liza arrive earlier and almost immediately heard his mother's raised voice. *"What are you doing here? Where have you been? Answer me . . ."* But then silence.

Liza tiptoed down the stairs to see Marius standing in the kitchen doorway holding a knife, dripping with blood. She slowly walked past him into the kitchen. "WHAT HAVE YOU DONE?" she cried out. "WHAT HAVE YOU DONE?"

"Nothing," Marcus whispered from his hiding place. *"Nothing."* And moved even further back into the darkness of the room, now feeling very frightened and confused. *What did she mean?* He asked himself - his mind racing for answers.

"Keep your voice down," Marius said, reaching out for Liza's hand, but she recoiled and sat on the bottom of the stairs, her arms folded, shaking her head. "That was not right," she said, keeping her voice low. "What will Marcus think? How will he see you now, Marius, his brother, having killed his mother?"

Marius dropped the knife and wiped his hands on the tablecloth, unconcerned about anything to do with his former home. "He will come to thank me, Liza, for saving him from the abuse he has suffered all those years." Marius stood, hands-on-hips, looking frustrated at his lover, questioning his actions. "He is safe now, Liza. You must realise that. We can take him with us and be safe in Switzerland, and start a new life, the three of us." He moved to touch Liza but she was still reeling from the sight she had witnessed. Her employer hanging from the airing rail, hoisted eight feet high, but what had turned Liza's stomach was the sight of blood oozing, like waves of red lava from her wrists, where Marius had removed her hands.

"Why, Marius, why the hands?" she asked forcefully, trying to keep her voice under control.

Marius squatted to face his distraught girlfriend and brushed a tear away with his finger. "It seemed . . . a form of justice, I suppose. She can't touch anyone else again, and they will blame the Russians."

"The war is over Marius . . . she would have been arrested . . ."

"Enough!" Marius exclaimed, standing. "We must go. Russian troops are in the area, and if they find us we are dead, all of us." Liza nodded, but refused the offer from Marius to help her stand. "Don't . . . not yet," she said, waving her arms so she did not come into contact with him. "I will fetch Marcus." And turned to go back upstairs when Marius called over to her. "Liza, freeze," he whispered, his face taut, his eyes piercing, head cocked, listening.

"What is it?"

Marius bounded up the stairs two at the time. Liza followed. They stood at the front landing window and gingerly parted the curtains.

"Shit." Marius spat. "Russians. One personnel carrier. Not many but they will be here any minute. No time to spare, we must leave now." Marius almost cleared the stairs in one bound. "Come, quick," he called, seeing Liza was halfway down the staircase. "But what of Marcus?" she said, fear triggering her thoughts and causing her body to tremble.

Marius turned back to the bottom of the stairs. "We must go. There is no time. We can travel faster. He will be OK and I promise we will come back for him when it is safe."

"But you said they will kill us, all of us, including Marcus."

"No, they will not harm a boy, trust me, Liza. We must go now." Marius reached Liza and took her hand, pulling her with him. They reached the French-windows just as they heard the vehicle pull-up outside the front door. "Run, Liza. We must follow the hedgerow along the perimeter to the brook, and then make for the thicket, and the forest beyond." Liza nodded without speaking, but just as Marius was about to start the *'dash'*, Liza touched his shoulder. "Promise me you will come back for him, otherwise I stay here."

Even before Marius had been a soldier, he had assessed situations and tactical advantages, which was one of the reasons his father had managed to secure him a job at regional command, analyzing intelligence and assessing its authenticity. The immediate situation was real and dangerous, and there was no advantage in staying. "I promise," he replied, managing a faint reassuring smile. They silently made their way across the patio to the edge of the lawn and followed the Leylandii as far as the stream. They crossed the water and reached the thicket just as the patio was illuminated by the lounge lights. Looking back from their concealed vantage point they saw a large uniformed man standing on the patio, lighting a cigarette. Marius assumed he was a Major or Colonel, but could not see the uniform insignia. "Let's wait a little longer, please Marius. I want to see Marcus is safe." Liza pleaded. Marius nodded his approval but wished they were moving.

Major Alexis Davidovich was pleased with his find. "What an opulent house, eh, Corporal. What do you think? Will you be comfortable here tonight?" And let out a raucous laugh. "Yes, sir, most comfortable."

Just then another soldier came to the patio doors, leaning on them for support, his face ashen, his eyes frozen with fear. "Sir . . . you must . . ." But nausea got the better of him and puked within a foot of his superior.

"What the fuck . . . Private Sokol, pull yourself together. What's happened?"

The soldier was unable to speak but pointed behind him in the direction of the kitchen. Indicating to the others to follow, the Major headed back inside, walking slowly with side-arm at the ready. The Major then noticed the blood on the floor and nodded to the Corporal to enter the kitchen. Corporal Dimitriev was apprehensive entering a room not knowing what was waiting for him, but remembering his colleague had not fired his gun it was safe to assume the room was not a threat.

He gingerly opened the kitchen door and taking a crouching position crept into the room. Within three feet of entering he had slipped on the congealed blood and landed on his back, staring at Frau von Hartstein, with decapitated hands, hanging from a laundry airier.

On hearing the commotion, Major Davidovich entered briskly, his pistol poised to shoot. "Shit," he exclaimed and left the room immediately, seeking out the bottle of brandy he had seen in the living room.

"We must leave, Liza. It will be too dark to travel soon. Please come." Liza sighed and nodded, knowing it was sensible, but saying a silent prayer for Marcus, and promising him they will return.

The Major sank two straight shots of brandy and shook his head trying to remember what he thought he just saw in the kitchen. "Dimitriev, Sokol!" He shouted. "Here, now!"

The Corporal entered the lounge, wiping the blood off his trousers. "Get Sadowski in here, I need this house searched top to bottom."

"Yes, sir." Sokol nodded and left to fetch their driver, but before he could get to the front door, Private Sadowski came barging into the house. "Sir, more soldiers coming. I think they are British."

The Major had heard the news as he met his men in the hall. "OK. Show their senior officer into the lounge and guard the kitchen and stairs. No one is to go into the kitchen, do you understand?"

"Yes, sir," his men replied in unison.

*

It was mid-May before Marcus received a call from his former employer. "Dyke, here. Who's that?"

"Unicorn," Marcus said, half-smiling on hearing Dyke's voice.

"I am surprised to hear from you, Marcus. Thought you would be somewhere exotic by now. What can I possibly do for you?"

"We need to meet. I want to know everything you know about my brother, Marius von Hartstein." There was the expected silence the other end of the line. Marcus had caught him off guard after all.

"What makes you think I know him, or anything about him?"

"You had a file on me from British Intelligence over forty years ago stating I had killed my mother. Ferris thought the Russians wanted me, seeing they had shot my father, but they also wanted Marius, my brother, who was in the German Army - am I refreshing your memory now, Richard."

"If you know all that what else do you want?" Dyke asked, fearing the worse.

"I want to know where my brother is, and if he is with Liza, the woman who looked after me, and I believe fled with Marius."

Silence again. "Marcus, it's been a long time. What good would it do you now? They may not even be alive; he was ten years older than you after all." Dyke knew immediately he had made a mistake.

"So, you know a little detail like that do you. And where did that come from if not British Intelligence? I want the address, Richard." Marcus's voice now more resolute than ever, knowing he had the upper hand. He could hear Dyke breathing down the phone. He would give him thirty seconds then he would turn up the threats.

"Winterthur." Dyke finally said after twenty seconds. "It's. . ."

"I know where it is. Thank you. Do you have a name?"

"Kasper. It was her name, but I don't know if they used it for long."

Funny, Marcus thought. How did he not know that? "Thank you, Richard. Enjoy retirement."

*

Colonel John Myers entered the Schloss flanked by his Major and was shown into the lounge as instructed. Major Davidovich was standing, and on recognizing a senior officer, saluted. Colonel Myers returned the salute. "Do you speak English?" Myers asked.

"Vy govorite po-russki?" Davidovich replied, with a grin.

Major Myers turned to his aid. "Major Ferris, I think we need an interpreter, as this overweight fat bastard does not speak English."

Davidovich laughed. "I resent that, Colonel. I am not overweight," he said, patting his stomach. "Major Davidovich, commanding the 3rd brigade out of Vienna, what's left of it." He finished sourly.

"Colonel Myers," Myers said, introducing himself. "This is Major Ferris, and if I may say Major you are a long way from Vienna."

"Yes, and I wish I was there." Davidovich sat on the comfortable sofa, indicating Myers to sit opposite. "I prefer to stand thank you, Major. Why are you here?" Myers added, becoming impatient.

"We had intelligence this is the home of a very prominent Nazi Colonel, Herbert von Hartstein. He has, or had, connections to Goring." Davidovich lit a cigarette and breathed the fumes in heavily. "Russian," he indicated, waving the cigarette in the air.

"I tried some American ones and they are weak as piss," he laughed out loud.

He needed to know if von Hartstein was still in the house, dead or alive, and knew he had to pacify this British Colonel to help assist him. He also knew the reputation his fellow comrades had made for themselves on entering Vienna, a reputation he was not personally proud of. "Von Hartstein may have been here recently. We were about to search the house when you arrived."

"What makes you think he was here?" Myers asked.

Davidovich trod out his cigarette on the rug. "Follow me, Colonel, and I hope you have not had dinner yet."

He led the two British officers out into the hallway that lead to the kitchen. "OK, Sadowski, let these gentlemen in," he said to the Private. Sadowski slowly stood aside lowering his rifle so the three men could enter the kitchen. Myer's and Ferris's reaction was no different. "Jesus Christ!" Ferris exclaimed. "Why would Hartstein do a thing like this, and who is she?"

"Get her down, man." Myers commanded to Davidovich, and yes, let's search this place."

Major Ferris brought in six of his twelve platoon and gave orders to search all the floors. Myers suggested to the Russian Major his men should search the outer perimeter before it got too dark. "Yes, Colonel, but I would prefer von Hartstein alive if he is here."

Young Marcus had moved deeper and deeper into the corner of his mother's dressing room, hiding under a plethora of long flowing dresses. He could hear muffled voices below, but not Liza's anymore. These voices were not known to him. These voices were not speaking German either. The door to the bedroom was locked but that didn't stop the soldier shooting the lock off. All was quiet for a few minutes when the dressing room door suddenly opened, and he saw the legs of a soldier wearing muddy boots, leaving marks on the clean polished floor. Satisfied no one was there the soldier left, and Marcus exhaled, hanging his head wondering how long he should stay hidden. He did not have to wait long. The swish of the clothes being pulled across the rail startled Marcus just as it was supposed to. The soldier leant down and pulled Marcus out of his hiding place by the arm. Marcus didn't utter a sound. He just looked frightened and confused. Downstairs the officers were gathered in the lounge discussing the split-up of Austria when the soldier burst into the room, holding Marcus by the collar. "Found him hiding upstairs, sir. Hasn't said a word yet."

All eyes turned to Marcus, standing alone, frightened, cold and hungry. No mother, father, or brother to help him. Here he stood, abandoned, not knowing anything about the liberation of his country, or the four allied countries that would be controlling it for the next ten years. He knew nothing about his mother, only a few feet away, now lying on the kitchen floor, minus her hands.

The Russian was the first to speak. "Come with us," he said in perfect German. And the officers ushered the boy out of the room into the kitchen. Marcus's eyes widened, his breathing became rapid as he shook his head from side to side. "No, no, no," he kept repeating. "No, no, no . . ."

"Get him out of here," Myers shouted, "and someone cover her body."

Marcus was ushered back to the lounge and pushed on to an armchair. One his father always used. No one was allowed to sit there, ever. He heard the last words Liza had said through that closed bedroom door; 'WHAT HAVE YOU DONE?'

* * *

June was approaching fast, nearly half a year gone already, Marcus thought. The years seem to be rolling by faster than ever, making him feel older than sixty-five. Generally, he never worried about his age or health. Both had been kind to him and allowed him infinite pleasures which other men could only dream of.

It was dreams however, that had been causing Marcus to consider the future. *Put your house in order,* as he had heard it once described; *tie up loose ends . . . keep promises.* That last one he knew he could not keep; *promising to always be there for Barbara and Rosa - promising to find Rosa's brother* - letting people down was not easy for him to admit, but he had, or would, fail, on both accounts.

"A toast," Marcus said, raising a glass of champagne, "to the two most beautiful women a man could be so fortunate to know and to have."

Barbara and Rosa looked at each other. "I am not sure we can toast ourselves," Barbara suggested with a curious grin, "but the champagne is welcome none-the-less."

Rosa touched her friend's hand, seeing she was thinking aloud; her forehead wrinkled with curiosity, her eyes narrowed. "What is it, Barbara?"

Barbara looked up at Marcus, head cocked waiting for him to answer the question. Marcus always knew she was clever at any level, and she was the one person he could keep no secrets from. "You're going away, aren't you, Marcus?" she said calmly, smiling to ease the tension.

Marcus nodded slowly. "Yes, tomorrow. I am going to Switzerland to find the truth about my past."

"But you are coming back, aren't you?" Rosa said, with loving concern in her voice.

"Yes, of course. Don't worry, I will be around for a long time, I promise . ."

"DON'T do that, Marcus!" Barbara snapped, standing to face him. Her eyes piercing him. "Don't' make promises you won't keep."

A tear formed and trickled down one cheek. "I . . . we . . . know you will not be around forever, but don't insult us by saying you will, Marcus. We both love you and just want you here . . . not chasing a nightmare from over forty years ago. Please,

Marcus, leave it." Barbara's face was awash with tears, and she was trembling. Rosa took her in her arms, looking at a bewildered Marcus over Barbara's shoulder.

Marcus put down his glass and hugged Barbara from behind and Rosa slowly pulled away and sat back on the sofa. Marcus turned her around to face her, kissing her forehead and letting his arms encircle her, gentling rocking from side to side, calming the moment. Barbara lifted her face to his and smiled. "I must look a mess. I'll go and do my face again."

"Rubbish, you look fine," Marcus said, reaching for his handkerchief and wiping away residue tear lines from her cheeks. "There, good as new." Barbara smiled again. "I am sorry, I . . . don't usually get that emotional," she said, reaching out for Rosa's hand. Rosa stood and the two women embraced once more, each feeling the binding attachment they have for each other.

"So," Rosa asked, "where are you going, and how will you find the answers you are looking for?"

Marcus nodded silently. "I know it seems foolish, even foolhardy to chase these memories, but wouldn't you want to know the truth if it was out there. Wouldn't you, Rosa, go to any lengths to find your brother if you knew you had the *faintest* hope of success? Well, I have that faint hope, and it lies in Switzerland. If I return as I leave, in ignorance, then I can come to terms with that, and I will have closure."

The two women nodded. They knew nothing was going to change his mind now. All they could do was support him, and pray he found what he was looking for.

That night, all three made love together. It was gentle and caring as always, but the intensity was almost unbearable to Barbara as she clawed his back from under him, and pounded her fists on his broad shoulders as he entered her. Rosa was lying next to them, stroking Barbara's arm, and when Barbara reached out for her Rosa gripped her hand just as she felt Marcus's release, and her body quivered and arched with the ecstasy she felt from her own *liberate elation*.

Marcus reluctantly slipped out of bed at four in the morning, leaving the two women secure in each other's arms. He blew each of them a kiss and left for Heathrow, and a flight he hoped that would release him from his *dunkle Traum* forever.

*

"What have you done young man? Answer me" The Russian Major barked at the frightened and bewildered boy in German.

Colonel Myers turned to Major Ferris and asked, "Do we have any speaking German personnel here, Major?"

"I'll check, sir. I'm a little rusty myself."

"Major," Myers intervened, "as this property is in the British sector I must insist you allow us to take the boy and interrogate him."

Davidovich stopped shouting at the boy. "Colonel, if the boy is related to von Hartstein then he is our prisoner, by association."

Myers tapped his baton thoughtfully on his left hand, like a teacher taunting a naughty pupil. "Major, I would strongly suggest you reassess your position here. Firstly, if the boy is a suspect in a crime then it may be considered a civil case, and the local police can handle it. If we decide to interrogate him ourselves, it will be because he is in our sector, and thirdly," Myers turned and pointed to the window with his baton, "I think we have considerably more men than you."

Just then Major Ferris returned. "Corporal Morris speaks German, sir," he whispered to his boss.

Myers nodded. "Have the men secure the premises and escort our Russian friends back to their vehicle," he ordered clearly, for Davidovich to hear.

Marcus was listening, but not understanding a word these men were saying, but realized they were holding his fate in their hands. He had heard snippets of conversation about Russians raping and pillaging since they overran his country, but he had no idea if other soldiers from other counties were any better. He waited and prayed Liza would come back and sort this out, or even Marius, wherever he was.

"OK, Colonel, you can take the boy, but I will put in a formal request for his transfer if he is associated with von Hartstein." Davidovich saluted Myers and took his leave.

Myers, Ferris and Corporal Morris stood staring at Marcus. "Ask him his name, Corporal."

"Wie heißen Sie?" Marcus just stared at the three men, shaking his head.

"Perhaps he can't speak, or is traumatized by what he just saw out there," Ferris suggested. "Ask him if that is his mother in the kitchen."

"Ist, dass Ihre Mutter in der Küche?" Marcus nodded yes.

"Good. He understands you. Now ask him if he killed her."

"Did you kill your mother?" Marcus frowned at the question.

"Liza said I did. I don't remember. . ."

Morris repeated the question. Marcus looked at him blankly. "Ich glaube nicht, dass so." He whispered.

"Well, what did he say, Corporal?"

"He said he don't remember, sir." Morris lied. Saying he didn't think so would suggest possible guilt, and Morris thought the boy looked too frightened and incapable to be a killer; and who kills their own mother, anyway?

*

Marcus took the six a.m. Swiss Air flight to Zurich then booked a hire car to drive to Winterthur. He arrived just after midday. The popular Swiss town was bustling with commuters and tourists exploring its lattice-work of old streets and historical buildings. After parking up he headed for the nearest Tourist Information office. There he purchased a street map and asked the helpful receptionist if she could recommend a good hotel.

The Hotel Krone was centrally situated in Marketgasse, and ideal for commuting either by foot or by car, depending on where Marcus's enquiries took him. After checking in he immediately grabbed the hotel telephone books and looked for the name Dyke had given him; Kasper. Marcus found just five Kasper's listed, none with the name Marius or Liza, but he would have expected that. He was not sure how old Liza had been back in 1945 but guessed she was around twenty-five, which would make her seventy-six - ten years older than himself. He called each of the numbers asking for a Liza or Marius around those ages. The first four drew blanks. Only one left. "Hello, I am trying to contact some old friends of mine, a Liza and Marius Kasper; they would be in their sixties and seventies by now."

"Who is this?" A woman's voice asked.

"My name is Marcus . . . Marcus von Hartstein. Does the name von Hartstein mean anything to you?" Silence.

He could hear the woman breathing and thinking. "Please, if you know them, please tell me. I am in Winterthur for a few days at the Hotel Krone." The line went dead. Marcus redialed but it just rang and rang. Had he found a link or was this woman just afraid of speaking to strangers, or confused or . . . or what . . . Marcus was back at square one. He walked through the old town center stopping for a coffee and pastry at a street cafe in the bright June sunshine wishing the girls were with him. He and Barbara had had many good holidays together, but just a couple with Rosa. He decided they would all go away together after this was over to somewhere exotic and beautiful. Bali or Sri Lanka, perhaps. After a stroll around town he headed back to the hotel. "Herr Hartmann, there is a message for you." And the receptionist handed him a note.

It was handwritten neatly, in German; *Meet me at Cafe Alltag at seven tonight.*

There was no name or any way to identify the writer, but Marcus had to assume it was the woman he had spoken to earlier that day . . . no one else knew he was there. Marcus arrived at six-thirty to survey the cafe and surrounding area. Cafe Alltag was small, with just a few tables and chairs outside, but had more seating inside on two floors. He took a seat outside and ordered a coffee. After two coffees' it was approaching seven-thirty and no one remotely interesting had passed by or entered the cafe. He was about to leave when a tall attractive woman in jeans and a black T-Shirt, wearing sunglasses, stood over him. "Did you call me this morning asking for Kasper?"

Marcus looked up at the woman trying to assess him. She was in her mid-thirties he guessed, and that was about all he had time to register. She sat down opposite him. "You are the only single man here, and you have been looking up and down the street for over thirty minutes. Are you Marcus von Hartstein?" Marcus grinned and nodded. "And you are?"

She removed her sunglasses, tossing her long auburn hair back over her shoulders revealing a heavily studied ear. "My name is Anna. But I am not sure I know the people you are looking for, she said too casually." Within a matter of a couple of minutes she had filled Marcus with hope, only to burst the bubble in one breath.

"Then why all this 'cloak and dagger' stuff?" Marcus asked, annoyed his time had been wasted. Anna took out a packet of cigarettes, and lit one. "I'll have a glass of white wine, please."

Marcus ordered a bottle of local white wine and waited for Anna to talk. "What are you to these people you are looking for?" She asked, sipping the chilled wine.

Marcus wasn't sure if he needed to tell her anything, but he had no other leads, *so what the hell*, he thought. "The lady I am looking for would be around seventy-five. She was my nanny back in 1944, and I heard she retired here, and, as I was in the area thought I would say hello."

Anna looked at him over the rim of her sunglass. "You had a nanny?"

"Yes, and a housekeeper."

"And where was this. In Switzerland?"

Marcus hesitated. Had he said too much without getting anything back? He poured another glass for each of them, then, leaning forward so no one else could hear, whispered, "Mariahof."

If he could have seen Anna's eyes behind her sunglasses he would have seen they were wide open in shock. She took a sip of wine to calm herself. *It was true then mother; someone did come asking for you after all those years*. Anna thought it was just a story from her mother's wild imagination . . . saying one day someone called Marcus will come asking for her, but unless they say where they lived in Austria, have nothing to do with them. Anna would pacify her by occasionally saying someone asked about her today, but they didn't say the *secret word*. But now . . . Jesus . . . she was right . . . *I'm so sorry mother not to have believed in you.* "Are you OK, Anna?" Marcus asked as she had not spoken for a few minutes. He noticed her arm tattoo and thought of Rosa.

Anna removed her sunglasses, and Marcus saw the tears in her eyes and her quivering lips. "Tell me, Anna. Who are you, please" Marcus begged.

*

When Colonel Myers was satisfied the house was secure, he ordered all papers, photographs and personal belongings to be boxed and taken with them back to camp. Photographs were also taken of the corpse.

Marcus was escorted out into a waiting personal carrier to be taken to the camp, and perhaps never return to his home which held many good, as well as bad, memories for him in the ten years he had lived there. Driving through the countryside, he saw people waving at the soldiers, and shouting, *'Hello'* and *'Thank You'*. Marcus closed his eyes and imagined himself cuddling up next to his mother, smelling her soft woolen jumper and feeling the warmth of it on his face, and her arms around him, keeping him safe.

*

"My name is Anna Kasper. . ," she hesitated, composing herself, "and my mother knew a Marcus von Hartstein, from Mariahof."

Marcus closed his eyes and leant back, absorbing the words he had longed to hear. He almost not dares to ask the next question. "Is she . . . alive still?"

Anna nodded. "Yes. She is seventy-four and in poor health. She is in a nursing home on the outskirts of Graz. I called her this morning, which I never do usually, but I had to know if she wanted to meet you, if you were who you said you were."

Marcus didn't hide his anticipation. "And does she?"

"Yes, she will see you, but she cannot talk for long. She has respiratory problems."

Marcus could hardly have hoped for a better answer and outcome. Now, Liza can answer his questions and put his mind at rest that he did not kill his mother. "And what of your father? What was his name?" Marcus had to know.

"Mother was with someone she never really talked about, or wouldn't talk about. He left her one day, but she won't say why. She met my father a few years later in Geneva and they were married six weeks later. She never thought she would have children - she was thirty-six when she had me - it was a difficult birth and it left her scarred, physically and mentally." Anna drank some more and lit another cigarette to calm her nerves.

"Father left us when I was ten. You see, she couldn't make love, ever again." Anna dipped her head, in thought. "Plus her health deteriorated, caused they say by anemia from when she was younger. Probably from during the war."

Marcus listened with empathy wishing things had turned out better for her, and she and Marius had had a wonderful long life together. As Anna did not seem to know much about Marius he did not press the matter but hoped Liza could fill in the blanks soon.

They agreed to meet the next day and drive together to Graz. The nursing home was a large modern building, nothing like Marcus expected. It was set in five acres of managed gardens with a three-tier fountain in the center, surrounded with benches and occasional tables, overlooking the beautiful river Mur.

The interior was impressive, and the bright reception area was welcoming. Anna spoke to the receptionist and was told her mother was in her room but could be taken by wheelchair into the garden if she wanted to.

Liza was sitting in a comfortable high back chair by a window, with a stunning view of the river Mur. Marcus froze momentarily on seeing her, frail and elderly, but still recognized her as the beautiful Liza he once knew.

She smiled on seeing him, and slowly raised her hand. Marcus held the fragile fingers and kissed her forehead, lingering over her a moment longer. "Anna," she gasped in short breaths, "I would like to speak to Marcus alone, my dear." Anna nodded and left the two to their memories. "I will be in the garden when you are ready to leave." Knowing she would not be saying goodbye to her mother.

Marcus pulled up a chair and sat square, facing Liza. "You took your time," she said hoarsely, trying not to laugh. The chest pain was worse when she was excited or laughed, which was a rare occasion nowadays. Marcus took her hand again, caressing the bony fingers, noticing the deep blue veins running up her arm. "How did this happen?" He asked solemnly.

"It crept up on me as so many bad things do. Not eating properly during the war didn't help, but other factors compounded the symptoms . . . but I want to know about you, Marcus. You survived. You did well, I see," she said, turning around the conversation.

"I . . . I was lucky, I suppose. Things could have turned out very different for me." And began to relate, slowly, the events that led to his arrival in Britain and subsequent life, although omitting certain chapters that would have been too upsetting for her. There was a lull in the conversation when a career brought in tea and cakes. Liza stared at the ever-flowing river Mur, the clear aquamarine shimmering against the sun's rays. "I do like it here, Marcus," she finally said. Then, looking at her once lovely charge, she saw the boy she once knew, the boy she and Marius had left to the mercy of his captors.

The only sound was the gentle humming of the cooling fan, which was set on low, but gave a most welcome respite to the soaring midday temperature. Marcus wanted to ask but kept biting his tongue. He looked around her bedroom to curb his anxiety. *This is what it comes down to* he thought; a twenty by twenty-foot room - a self-contained box storing the minimum of personal effects each patient is allowed to keep. He turned suddenly. "Liza, whatever it takes, I can pay for any treatment you need, anything, anywhere. Just tell me what to do."

Liza bit her lower lip, trying to smile at the same time. Tears formed again, and Marcus found a tissue to wipe them away.

"It's too late, Marcus. They are good here and I haven't got long - a few months at most. My only wish is that Anna would forgive me . . ."

"Forgive you . . . for what?"

"She has been distant to me for some years now, more so since I came here three years ago. She had to fend for herself growing up - I was too ill to care for her most of the time, and her father was not around; out getting drunk every night, and sometimes not coming home at all." She said with bitterness in her voice.

Liza was staring out of the window again, not able to make eye contact. "I told her a stranger may come asking for me one day, but she thought I was going crazy."

She turned to meet Marcus's stare. "But I'm not, am I, Marcus."

"No. You are not crazy. Never have been," he said with affection.

Liza looked away again, her fingers wrapped around a button on her cardigan. Marcus could see she was looking agitated again.

"Do you want to tell me anything about what happened, Liza? You are the only one who knows the truth. If you don't, then I will respect that, and leave you to take it with you."

The frail woman sighed heavily, the chest pain barely sufferable, but she had to let Marcus have some closure. Have some peace of mind - he deserved that. "He had come back to the house to collect me, and you, to take us away to safety. He assumed your father and mother had fled to Italy or Switzerland. We could travel quite easily with the papers we had, you see, we had both been working for the Resistance since 1943." Marcus's eyes widened. "Good God. Did my father know this?"

"I don't know. He may have suspected as Marius deserted his job in late 1944 and joined the French Resistance based in Switzerland, under the leadership of the German commander Otto Kühne. Marius had vital information on troop movements, and became a crucial member of the movement, albeit for only the last year of war, but he helped save lives." Liza sipped some water. She closed her eyes and replayed the final scene in her mind. "Well, your father had not returned and was never found. Marius came back just as your mother was preparing to leave, and was going to take you with her. They had an argument; Marius saying he would never let you go with her, and accused her of the evil things she had done to you and other children." Marcus listened, trying to match his recall with Liza's.

"In the argument, Marius picked up a kitchen knife and stabbed her in the ribs. She died instantly." Liza wiped away another tear.

"But why do what he did . . . the other thing?"

Liza blinked and squeezed her eyes shut, wishing this day had not arrived, although she had wished it for many years. "Marius wanted to make it look like the Russians had done it . . . they had been responsible for many atrocities, and one more would not be questioned if she was a Nazi."

She opened her eyes to see Marcus's eyes swelling. They gripped each other's hands and cried for each other. "Thank you, Liza. I know that was difficult, but I now know the truth, and I can rest in peace." Marcus stood and stretched. Looking out he could see Anna smoking and talking to an orderly.

"What happened to Marius, Liza? Is he alive?"

Liza shook her head slowly. "No. Marius took his own life in 1969. He and I had parted by then and I had married a man from Geneva. I don't know why he did it, Marcus. Perhaps the guilt was too much to bear. We will never know."

Marcus felt numb. He closed his eyes and remembered the last time he saw him at his own birthday party. That was a good memory he will always have of his brother.

"So, when you called out, *'What have you done'* you were talking to Marius?" He smiled to relax her, or so he thought.

Liza looked away too quickly. She too saw her daughter talking and laughing, wishing they could have done more of that, as mothers and daughters should do. "Of course, Marcus. You don't think you killed your mother, do you? You were only ten years old. It is as I have told you." Liza said, turning to look Marcus in the face with an air of finality.

Liza tapped on the bedroom window to attract her daughter's attention. She waved her over and mouthed, *'Come here'*. Anna nodded and dropped her cigarette before walking back into the main building. "Are you ready to leave?" Anna asked Marcus, standing at her mother's door.

"Yes, I think so. We are finished here, aren't we?" He leant over and kissed his old friend on the cheek.

"It was good to see you, Marcus. I am glad it turned out OK for you, and enjoy the future. It's worth enjoying."

Marcus waited outside for Anna to say goodbye, but she reappeared within a minute. "What is it between you two? She has suffered enough you know, through no fault of her own." Marcus's tone was bordering on frustration, but he controlled his voice just so Anna could hear him. "Please, go back and tell her you love her, and you will see her soon."

"It's not that easy . . . she . . ." Anna was lost for words, and excuses, and for the second time in twenty-four hours Marcus had seen through that armor she thinks protects her feelings.

Marcus put his hands on her shoulders. "She needs you. Talk to her. Read to her. Tell her about your life, warts and all, or lie if you must - sometimes a white lie is a good thing. She hasn't got long - you will only regret it if you don't."

Anna swallowed the lump in her throat, as well as her pride in that moment. She kissed Marcus and returned to her mother's room. Marcus waited for an hour before she emerged again, smiling coyly. On the drive back to Winterthur, Marcus had one further question unanswered. "How did Marius die, Anna? Did she ever tell you?"

"Yes, she did. He jumped from the island at the Rheinfall, the largest, fastest flowing waterfall in Europe. His body was never found, but no one survives those currents."

Marcus thought a fit forty-two-year old could easily survive if they were well prepared. But Anna was right; the currents would have been too strong in those waters, even for Marius.

On the flight back, Marcus kept replaying their conversation over in his mind, but *'You don't think you killed your mother, do you?'* was the part he remembered most.

2002

The realization of knowing he had not killed his mother did nothing to relieve the years of self-analysis and torment he had endured. His own brother, and Liza, had planted the suggestion in his mind without giving a thought to the consequences of how he would handle the accusation of *murderer*. Had he committed all those reprisals out of ignorance and hate, and not due process? The weight of guilt can be a heavy burden to carry for most men, but Marcus had to believe he had taken the right action; otherwise his life would have been worthless. He also consoled himself with the fact he had had a wonderful parallel life, thanks to Barbara and all the *friends* they had acquired over the years. His life had not been totally in vain in that respect, but now he wanted to, no, needed to, slip quietly away from that world he had created, and move on, albeit for a short time maybe, into a world of reality and normality.

Writing to Barbara and Rosa was the hardest thing, but they would know for sure he had found peace, and they could mourn him openly one day. He took a flight to Lyon where he hired a car and drove fifty miles north to a little village called Fleurie. Just outside the village he stopped for a coffee and opened his black leather A5 portfolio. He read the entry for 1985: Simone. "£2,500. 45 Rue Des Vendanges, Fleurie.

The mid-afternoon sun was hot, and few people were out and about in this small but productive vine producing area. Having asked for directions in the village centre, he slowly approached the small café and home of his old friend and lover, Simone, but faltered as he walked closer to the alfresco table and chairs. He guessed his heart rate was higher than normal, although after years of jogging he was quickly able to control it. A young man walked out of the open-fronted cafe on seeing him.

"Bonjour, monsieur." He said with a smile. Marcus studied him for a moment and smiled, nodding. "Monsieur. Are you Ok?" The young man asked with concern on seeing the elderly man's complexion.

"I am fine, thank you," Marcus replied, taking a seat at one of the tables, catching his breath, but also looking closely at the young man in front of him. "Tell me. What is your name?"

"Henri, monsieur."

"Henri . . . a good name. Is this your cafe, Henri?"

"Yes, monsieur. Since my mother died, four years ago."

Marcus felt lightheaded for the second time that morning.

'I have a son.'

"I am so sorry to hear that. Was she ill?" Marcus asked, trying to control his breathing.

"The doctors could not explain it, but they thought she actually wanted to die . . . a broken heart they said, but we don't understand that. She had everything to live for, especially her two grandchildren."

As if on cue, a woman in her mid-thirties came out of the cafe carrying a young girl. A slightly older boy was holding her free hand. "Ahh, here is my wife, Sofia, with the children." The woman handed the young girl to her father and shook hands with Marcus.

Marcus stood to greet them. "Have we met, monsieur? You look familiar," the wife asked, shading her eyes from the sun.

Marcus shook his head. "No, madam, I would have remembered, I assure you." She blushed and smiled. "You have the same charm as my husband, monsieur. I wonder where you men learn such things." And laughed embarrassingly.

Henri introduced his children. "This is Hanna, she is five next week, and this young man is Marcus. He is seven. Say hello children."

As far as he could recall Marcus could not remember ever showing emotion in public, but now, his eyes swelled with tears. He sat down and wiped his face. If only she were here now - the two of them fulfilling a dream he never thought would be possible . . . here with his son and grandchildren. Marcus had a family. His life was complete, at last.

2003

It was several years after Mandy Silver had asked a favor of her work colleague, Graham King, to see if he could decipher some jumbled words that Christine Ling had given her. King was a crossword compiler and loved to solve puzzles, but this one had eluded him for a long time. He kept returning to the letters on his computer screen *'Seek vital demon',* but whenever he rearranged them, nothing made sense, except one possibility.

"Hi, Mandy, Graham here. That word puzzle you gave me some time ago, could your friend have miss-spelt one of the words because if I change the first word to *Sleek*, I get *Stoke Mandeville*."

THE END

Some History

Sacrosanct: respected, inviolate, unimpeachable, unchallengeable, and invulnerable.

Also: protected, defended, secure, safe.

There are those, who, throughout history have used the definition of Sacrosanct to stand for; sacred, holy, untouchable - unchangeable.

Nothing is Sacrosanct. *Anything can be changed. Anyone can be bought to account.* It takes courage to act - it is cowardice to do nothing - our children are relying on you.

All characters and events in this book are of course fictitious, but the subject matter of child abuse is very real. I must also state, categorically, I do not condone vigilante action against anyone, under any circumstances. If you suspect a crime is being committed, please contact the police.

My use of the title represents, I hope, a society where those responsible for vile crimes against children, *no matter who there are,* will be brought to justice - they MUST be made to know this. They MUST be made aware that they are NOT *untouchable, protected, secure or safe.*

There are many organizations, in every country, that offer support to all who have been abused, no matter how many years have passed, who want to talk to someone.

The reference in the last paragraph to Stoke Mandeville, refers to the UK hospital where the celebrity DJ Jimmy Savile abused twenty-two patients between 1965 and 1988.

After his death, hundreds of allegations of sexual abuse were made against him, leading the police to believe that Savile was a predatory sex offender, and that he may have been one of Britain's most prolific sexual offenders. There had been allegations during his lifetime, *but they were dismissed and accusers ignored or disbelieve.*

In June 2014, investigations into Savile's activities in 28 NHS hospitals, including Leeds General Infirmary and Broadmoor psychiatric hospital, concluded that he had sexually assaulted staff and patients aged between 5 and 75 over several decades.

Such were the allegations, in October 2012 the Metropolitan Police commenced Operation Yewtree, an investigation into sexual abuse allegations, predominantly the abuse of children by Savile and other high profile personalities.

Child sex abusers are not confined to 'personalities'. Sadly, the majority of these assaults are carried out by relatives or friends of the family.

In recent years a shocking culture of 'grooming' has developed in many large cities in the UK, with what was thought to be the worst-case ever recorded on a Council in Rotherham. According to an estimate from the Children's Commissioner for England in 2011, 2,409 children were identified as victims of exploitation by gangs over a 14-month period from 2010-11, while at least 16,500 were said to be at high risk over the course of a year   (Source: BBC news)

* * *

Even as this manuscript is being written, British newspapers are reporting daily on the biggest cover-ups in political history.

Cyril Smith (1928 - 2010) MP of Rochdale. Following his death there had been 144 complaints by 2014. All previous attempts to bring him to justice by his accusers, while he was alive, were dismissed, *and his accusers ignored or disbelieve.* It emerged that Smith had been arrested in the early 1980s in relation to these offences, but a high-level cover-up reportedly led to him being released within hours, the evidence destroyed and the investigating officers prevented from discussing the matter under the Official Secrets Act. (Source: Wikipedia)

Frank Beck who was a convicted child sex offender in the United Kingdom. He was employed by the Leicestershire County Council as the officer-in-charge of several children's homes in Leicestershire, between 1973 and 1986. He was sentenced to five life sentences of his vile crimes, but died of a heart-attack after only serving two years. During his trial in 1991, he accused a high-profile public figure - Greville Ewan Janner, (Baron Janner) - of abusing a child while in his care. Between then and 2010 the police did not pass any files the Crown Prosecution Services. It is highly regarded that 'high ranking' senior police officers and political pressure was behind the cover-up. Now, in 2015, public outrage is demanding action. (Source: Wikipedia)

Acknowledgements

My personal thanks to the following people who helped me through the rough patches.

My wife, Carol and friend Margaret Andreae - Thank you for your much-needed help and for pointing out the obvious.

Steve Kershaw, CID (Retired)

Mick Payton-Photographer. http://mickpaytonerotic.co.uk/

Andy Guy, Norfolk Constabulary

Other references sourced were stated from Wikipedia and the BBC News on-line

Cover Image: vlue © 123RF.com

www.ingramcontent.com/pod-product-compliance
Lightning Source LLC
Chambersburg PA
CBHW070605300426
44113CB00010B/1415